I0010022

Command Line Fundamentals

Learn to use the Unix command-line tools and
Bash shell scripting

Vivek N

Command Line Fundamentals

Copyright © 2018 Packt Publishing

All rights reserved. No part of this book may be reproduced, stored in a retrieval system, or transmitted in any form or by any means, without the prior written permission of the publisher, except in the case of brief quotations embedded in critical articles or reviews.

Every effort has been made in the preparation of this book to ensure the accuracy of the information presented. However, the information contained in this book is sold without warranty, either express or implied. Neither the author, nor Packt Publishing, and its dealers and distributors will be held liable for any damages caused or alleged to be caused directly or indirectly by this book.

Packt Publishing has endeavored to provide trademark information about all of the companies and products mentioned in this book by the appropriate use of capitals. However, Packt Publishing cannot guarantee the accuracy of this information.

Author: Vivek N

Technical Reviewer: Sundeep Agarwal

Managing Editor: Neha Nair

Acquisitions Editor: Koushik Sen

Production Editor: Samita Warang

Editorial Board: David Barnes, Ewan Buckingham, Simon Cox, Manasa Kumar, Alex Mazonowicz, Douglas Paterson, Dominic Pereira, Shiny Poojary, Saman Siddiqui, Erol Staveley, Ankita Thakur, and Mohita Vyas

First Published: December 2018

Production Reference: 1211218

ISBN: 978-1-78980-776-9

Table of Contents

Command-Line Building Blocks 53

Shell Scripting   165

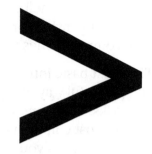

Preface

About

This section briefly introduces the author, the coverage of this book, the technical skills you'll need to get started, and the hardware and software required to complete all of the included activities and exercises.

About the Book

From the Bash shell to traditional UNIX programs, and from redirection and pipes to automating tasks, *Command Line Fundamentals* teaches you all you need to know about how command lines work.

The most basic interface to a computer, the command line, remains the most flexible and powerful way of processing data and performing and automating various day-to-day tasks. *Command Line Fundamentals* begins by exploring the basics and then focuses on the most common tool, the Bash shell (which is standard on all Linux and macOs/iOS systems). As you make your way through the book, you'll explore the traditional UNIX command-line programs implemented by the GNU project. You'll also learn how to use redirection and pipelines to assemble these programs to solve complex problems. Next, you'll learn how to use redirection and pipelines to assemble those programs to solve complex problems.

By the end of this book, you'll have explored the basics of shell scripting, which will allow you to easily and quickly automate tasks.

About the Author

Vivek N is a self-taught programmer who has been programming for almost 30 years now, since the age of 8, with experience in X86 Assembler, C, Delphi, Python, JavaScript, and C++. He has been working with various command-line shells since the days of DOS 4.01, and is keen to introduce the new generation of computer users to the power it holds to make their lives easier. You can reach out to him through his Gmail ID rep.movsd.

Objectives

- Use the Bash shell to run commands
- Utilize basic Unix utilities such as `cat`, `tr`, `sort`, and `uniq`
- Explore shell wildcards to manage groups of files
- Apply useful keyboard shortcuts in shell
- Employ redirection and pipes to process data
- Write both basic and advanced shell scripts to automate tasks

Audience

Command Line Fundamentals is for programmers who use GUIs but want to understand how to use the command line to complete tasks more quickly.

Approach

Command Line Fundamentals takes a hands-on approach to the practical aspects of exploring UNIX command-line tools. It contains multiple activities that use real-life business scenarios for you to practice and apply your new skills in a highly relevant context.

Hardware Requirements

For the optimal student experience, we recommend the following hardware configuration:

- Processor: Any modern processor manufactured after 2010
- Memory: 4 GB RAM
- Storage: 4 GB available hard disk space

Software Requirements

The ideal OS for this book is a modern Linux distribution. However, there are many dozens of flavors of Linux, with different versions, and several other OS platforms, including Windows and macOS/iOS, which are widely used. In order to make the book accessible to students using any OS platform or version, we will use a virtual machine to ensure a uniform isolated environment. If you are not familiar with the term, a virtual machine lets an entire computer be simulated within your existing one; hence, you can use another OS (in this case, a tiny cut-down Linux distribution) as if it were running on actual hardware, completely isolated from your regular OS. The advantage of this approach is a simple, uniform experience for all students, regardless of the system used. Another advantage is that the VM is sandboxed and anything performed within it will not interfere in any way with the existing system. Finally, VMs allow snapshotting, which allows you to undo any serious mistakes you may make with little effort. Once you have completed the exercises and activities in this book in the VM, you can experiment with the command-line support that is available on your individual system. Those who wish to use the commands learned in this book on their systems directly should refer to the documentation for their specific platforms, to ensure that they work as expected. For the most part, the behaviors are standard, but some platforms might only support older versions of some commands, might lack some options for some commands, or completely lack support for certain commands:

- *Linux*: All up-to-date Linux distributions will support all the commands and techniques taught in this book. Some may require the installation of additional packages.

- *Windows*: The Windows Linux Subsystem allows a few Linux distributions, such as Ubuntu and Debian, to run from within Windows. Some packages may require installation to support everything covered in this book.

- *macOS and iOS*: These OSes are based on FreeBSD, which is a variant of UNIX, and they include most of the GNU tools. Some packages may require installation to support everything covered in this book.

> **Note**
>
> If you use the VM, all the sample data required to complete the exercises and activities in this book will automatically be fetched and installed in the correct location, when the VM is started the first time. On the other hand, if you decide to use your native OS install, you will have to download the ZIP files (**Lesson1.zip** to **Lesson4.zip**) present in the code repository on GitHub and extract them into the home directory of your user account. The data consists of four folders, called **Lesson1** to **Lesson4**, and several commands in the exercises rely on the data being in the locations ~**/Lesson1** and so on. It is recommended that you stick to the VM approach unless you know what you are doing.

Installation and Setup

Before you start this book, you need to install the following software. You will find the steps to install these here:

Installing VirtualBox

Download the latest version of VirtualBox from https://www.virtualbox.org/wiki/Downloads and install it.

Setting up the VM

1. Download the VM appliance file, `Packt-CLI.ova`, from the Git repository here: https://github.com/TrainingByPackt/Command-Line-Fundamentals/blob/master/Packt-CLI.ova.

2. Launch VirtualBox and select **File | Import Appliance**:

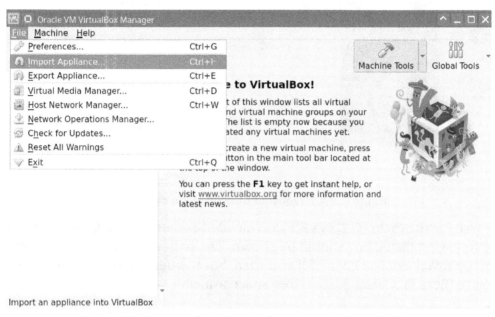

Figure 0.1: A screenshot showing how to make the selection

The following dialog box will appear:

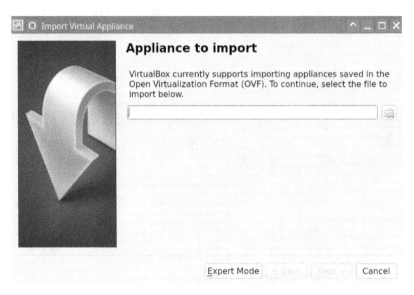

Figure 0.2: A screenshot displaying the dialog box

3. Browse for the **Packt-CLI.ova** file downloaded earlier and click **Next**, after which the following dialog box should be shown. The path where the Virtual Disk Image is to be saved can be changed if you wish, but the default location should be fine. Ensure there is at least 4 GB of free space available:

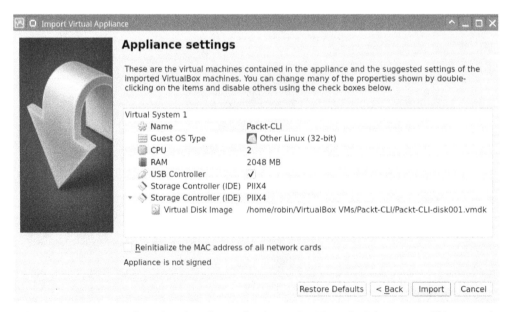

Figure 0.3: A screenshot showing the path where the Virtual Disk Image will be saved

4. Click **Import** to create the virtual machine. After the process completes, the VM name will be visible in the left-hand panel of the VirtualBox window:

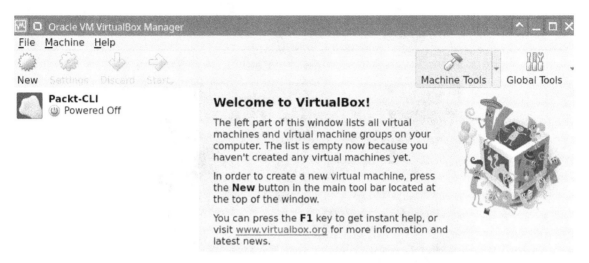

Figure 0.4: A screenshot showing the successful installation of VirtualBox

5. Double-click the VM entry, `Packt-CLI`, to start the VM. You will see a lot of text scroll by as it boots up, and after a few seconds a GUI desktop will show up. The window may maximize to your entire screen; however, you can resize it to what-ever is convenient. The desktop inside will adjust to fit in. Your system is called a *host* and the VM within is called a *guest*. VirtualBox may show a couple of informa-tion popups at the top of the VM. Read the information to understand how the VM mouse and keyboard capture works. You can click the little buttons at the extreme right of the popups that have the message **Do not show this message again** to prevent them from showing up again. More information can be found at https://www.virtualbox.org/manual/ch01.html#keyb_mouse_normal.

> **Note**
>
> In case the VM doesn't start at all, or you see an error message "Kernel Panic" in the VM window, you can usually solve this by enabling the virtualization settings in BIOS. See https://www.howtogeek.com/213795/how-to-enable-intel-vt-x-in-your-computers-bios-or-uefi-firmware/ for an example tutorial.

When the VM starts up for the first time, it will download the sample data and snippets for this book automatically. The following window will appear:

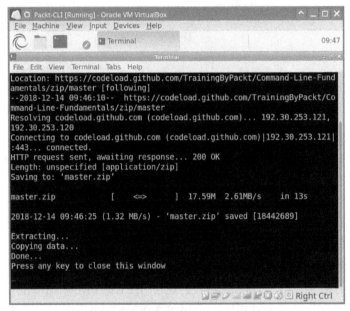

Figure 0.5: A screenshot displaying the first-time setup script progress

There are four launcher icons in the toolbar on top, which are shown here:

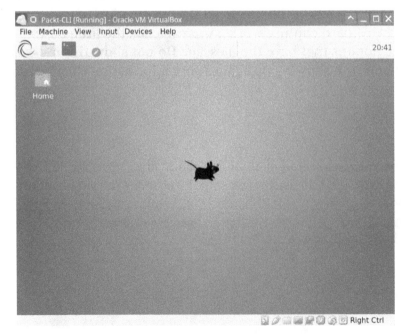

Figure 0.6: A screenshot displaying the launcher icons

- The first launcher is the Root menu, which is like the Start menu of Windows. Since the guest OS is a minimal, stripped-down version, many of the programs shown there will not run. The only entry you will need to use during this book is the **Log Out** option.

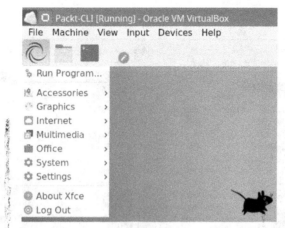

Figure 0.7: A screenshot showing the Root menu

- The second launcher is the **Thunar** file manager. By default, it opens the home directory of the current user, called **guest** (note that the **guest** username has no connection to the term "guest" used in the context of virtual machines). The sample data for the chapters is in the folders **Lesson1** to **Lesson4**. All the snippets and examples in the book material assume this location. The **Snippets** folder contains a subfolder for each chapter with all the exercises and activity solutions as text files.

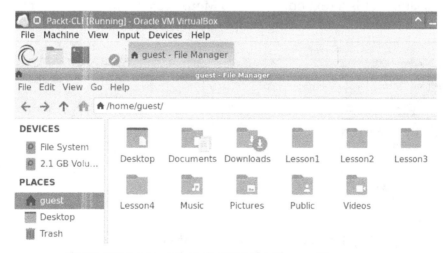

Figure 0.8: A screenshot showing the Thunar file manager

- The third launcher is the command-line terminal application. This is what you will need to use throughout the book. Notice that it starts in the home directory of the logged-in user, **guest**.

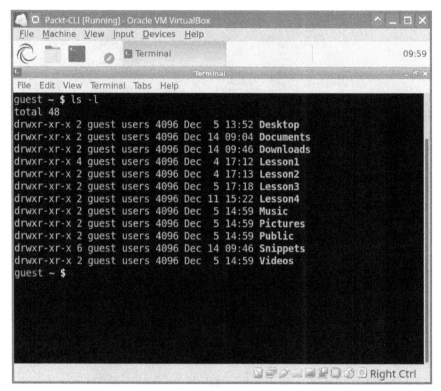

Figure 0.9: A screenshot showing the command-line terminal

- The final launcher is a text editor called **Mousepad**, which will be useful for viewing the snippets and writing scripts during the book:

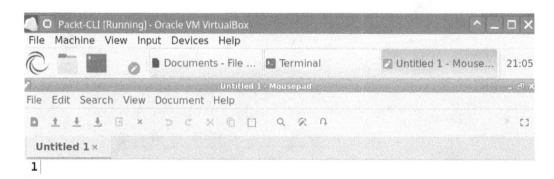

Figure 0.10: A screenshot of the text editor

Guidelines and Tips for using the VM

- The desktop environment in the guest OS is called XFCE and is very similar to *Windows* XP. The top toolbar shows the running tasks. The windows behave just like any other desktop environment.

- Within the console, you can select text with the mouse and paste it onto the command line with the middle mouse button (this is distinct from the clipboard). To copy selected text in the console to the clipboard, press *Ctrl+Shift+C* and to paste from the clipboard into the command line press *Ctrl+Shift+V* (or right-click and choose **Paste)**. This will be useful when you try out the snippets. You can copy from the editor and paste into the command line, although it is recommended that you type them out. Be careful not to paste multiple or incomplete commands into the console, as it could lead to errors.

- To shut down the guest OS, click **Log Out** from the Root menu to get the following dialog:

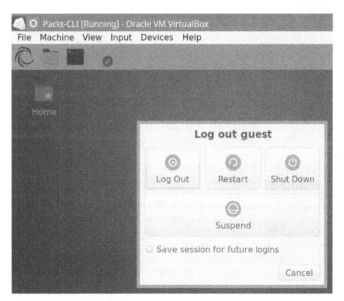

Figure 0.11: A screenshot showing the dialogue box that appears on shut down

- To close the VM (preserving its state) and resume later, close the VM window and choose **Save the machine state**. Next time the VM is started, it resumes from where it was. Usually, it would be preferable to use this option than choosing **Shut down**, as shown earlier.

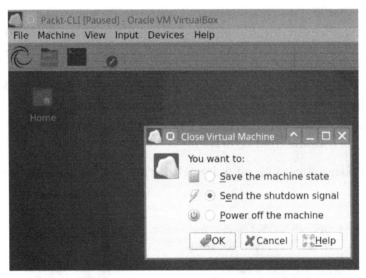

Figure 0.12: A screenshot showing how to save your work before closing the VM

- The VM allows the guest and host OS to share the clipboard, so that text that you copy to the clipboard in the host, can be pasted into applications in the guest VM and vice versa. This is useful if you prefer to use your own editor rather than the one included in the VM.

- It is strongly recommended that you close the shell window after completion of each exercise or activity, and open a fresh instance for the next.

- During the book, it is possible that you, by mistake, will end up changing the sample data (or the guest OS itself) in such a way that you cannot complete the exercises. To avoid starting from scratch, you are advised to create a *snapshot* of the VM after each exercise or activity is performed. This can be done by clicking **Snapshots** in the VirtualBox window:

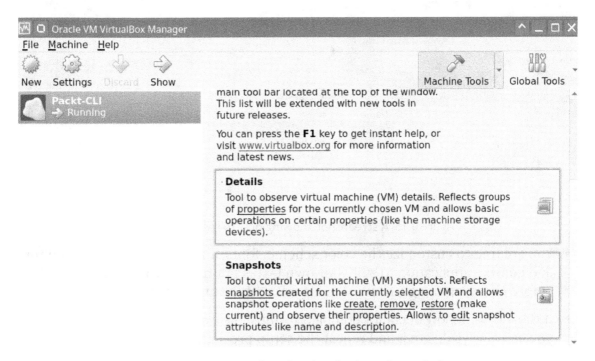

Figure 0.13: A screenshot showing the Snapshots window

- Click **Take** to save the current state of the VM as a snapshot:

Figure 0.14: A screenshot showing how to take a snapshot

You can take any number of snapshots and restore them, taking the guest OS back to the exact state as when you saved it. Note that snapshots can only be restored when the guest has been shut down. Snapshots will take up some disk space. Deleting a snapshot does not affect the current state:

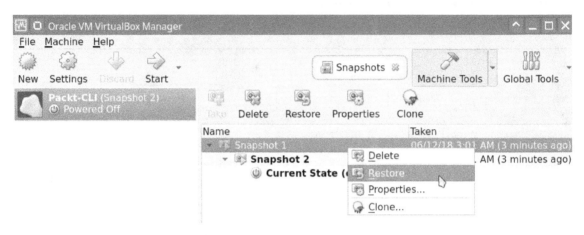

Figure 0.15: A screenshot showing how to restore the OS

- You are free to customize the color scheme, fonts, and preferences of the editor and console application to suit your own tastes but be sure to take a snapshot before changing things, to avoid being left with an unusable guest OS.

- If the VM somehow becomes completely unusable (which is quite unlikely), you can always delete it and repeat the setup process.

- If you get logged out by mistake, log in as **guest** with the password **packt**.

Installing the Code Bundle

Copy the code bundle for the class to the **C:/Code** folder.

Conventions

Code words in text, folder names, filenames, file extensions, pathnames, user input, and example strings are shown as follows: "Navigate to the **data** folder inside the `Lesson2` folder."

A block of code is set as follows: The text typed by the user is in bold and the output printed by the system is in regular font:

```
$ echo 'Hello World'
Hello World
```

New terms and important words are shown in bold. Words that you see on the screen, for example, in menus or dialog boxes, appear in the text like this: "Click **Log Out** from the Root menu."

Additional Resources

The code bundle for this book is also hosted on GitHub at https://github.com/TrainingByPackt/Command-Line-Fundamentals.

We also have other code bundles from our rich catalog of books and videos available at https://github.com/PacktPublishing/. Check them out!

You can also find links to the Official GNU Bash Manual and Linux man pages at https://www.gnu.org/software/bash/manual/html_node/index.html and https://linux.die.net/man/, respectively.

1

Introduction to the Command Line

Learning Objectives

By the end of this chapter, you will be able to:

- Describe the basics of a filesystem
- Navigate a filesystem with command-line tools
- Perform file management tasks using the command line
- Utilize shell history and tab completion to efficiently compose commands
- Utilize shell-editing shortcuts to efficiently work with the command line
- Write and use wildcard expressions to manage groups of files and folders

This chapter gives a brief history of the command line, explains filesystems, and describes how to get into and out of the command line.

Introduction

Today, with the widespread use of computing devices, **graphical user interfaces** (**GUIs**) are all-pervasive and easily learned by almost anyone. However, we should not ignore one of the most powerful tools from a bygone era, which is the **command-line interface** (**CLI**).

GUIs and CLIs approach user interaction from different angles. While GUIs emphasize user-friendliness, instant feedback, and visual aesthetics, CLIs target automation and repeatability of tasks, and composition of complicated task workflows that can be executed in one shot. These features result in the command line having widespread utility even today, nearly half a century since its invention. For instance, it is useful for web administrators to administer a web server via a shell command-line interface: instead of running a local CLI on your machine, you remotely control one that is running thousands of miles away, as if it were right in front of you. Similarly, it is useful for developers who create the backends of websites. This role requires them to learn how to use a command line, since they often need to replicate the web server environment on their local machine for development.

Even outside the purely tech-oriented professions, almost everyone works with computers, and automation is a very helpful tool that can save a lot of time and drudgery. The CLI is specifically built to help automate things. Consider the task of a graphic designer, who downloads a hundred images from a website and resizes all of them into a standard size and creates thumbnails; a personnel manager, who takes 20 spreadsheet files with personnel data and converts all names to upper case, checking for duplicates; or a web content creator, who quickly replaces a person's name with another across an entire website's content.

Using a GUI for these tasks would usually be tedious, considering that these tasks may need to be performed on a regular basis. Hence, rather than repeating these manually using specific applications, such as a download manager, photo editor, spreadsheet, and so on, or getting a custom application written, the professional in each case can use the command line to automate these jobs, consequently reducing drudgery, avoiding errors, and freeing the person to engage in the more important aspects of their job. Besides this, every new version of a GUI invalidates a lot of what you learned earlier. Menus change, toolbars look different, things move around, and features get removed or changed. It is often a re-learning exercise filled with frustration. On the other hand, much of what we learn about the command line is almost 100% compatible with the command line of 30 years ago, and will remain so for the foreseeable future. Rarely is a feature added that will invalidate what was valid before.

Everyone should use the command line because it can make life so much easier, but there is an aura of mystery surrounding the command line. Popular depictions of command-line users are stereotypical asocial geniuses. This skewed perception makes people feel it is very arcane, complex, and difficult to learn—as if it were magic and out of the reach of mere mortals. However, just like any other thing in the world, it can be learned incrementally step-by-step, and unlike learning GUI programs, which have no connection to one another, each concept or tool you learn in the command line adds up.

Command Line: History, Shells, and Terminology

It is necessary for us to explore a little bit of computing history to fully comprehend the rationale behind why CLIs came into being.

History of the Command Line

At the dawn of the computing age, computers were massive electro-mechanical calculators, with little or no interactivity. Stacks of data and program code in the form of punched cards would be loaded into a system, and after a lengthy execution, punched cards containing the results of the computation would be spit out by the machines.

This was called **batch processing** (this paradigm is still used in many fields of computing even today). The essence of batch processing is to prepare the complete input dataset and the program code by hand and feed it to the machine in a batch. The computation is queued up for execution, and as soon as it finishes, the output is delivered, following which the next computation in the queue is processed.

As the field progressed, the age of the **teletypewriter** (**TTY**) arrived. Computers would take input and produce human—readable output interactively through a typewriter-like device. This was the first time that people sat at a terminal and interacted continuously with the system, looking at results of their computations live.

Eventually, TTYs with paper and mechanical keyboards were replaced by TTYs with text display screens and electronic keyboards. This method of interaction with a computer via a keyboard and text display device is called a **command-line interface** (**CLI**), and works as follows:

1. The system prompts the user to type a sentence (a command line).

2. The system executes the command, if valid, and prints out the results.

3. This sequence repeats indefinitely, and the user conducts their work step by step.

In a more generic sense, a CLI is also called a **REPL**, which stands for **Read**, **Evaluate**, **Print**, **Loop**, and is defined as follows:

1. Read an input command from the user.

2. Evaluate the command.

3. Print the result.

4. Loop back to the first step.

The concept of a REPL is seen in many places—even the flight control computer on NASA's 1998 Deep Space 1 mission spacecraft had a REPL controlled from Earth, which allowed scientists to troubleshoot a failure in real-time and prevent the mission from failing.

Command-Line Shells

CLIs that interface with the operating system are called **shells**. As shells evolved, they went from being able to execute just one command at a time, to multiple commands in sequence, repeat commands multiple times, re-invoke commands from the past, and so on. Most of this evolution happened in the UNIX world, and the UNIX CLI remains up to date the de facto standard.

There are many different CLIs in UNIX itself, which are analogous to different dialects of a language—in other words, the way they interpret commands from the user varies. These CLIs are called shells because they form a shell between the internals of the operating system and the user.

There are several shells that are widely used, such as the **Bourne shell**, **Korn shell**, and **C shell**, to name a few. Shells for other operating systems such as Windows exist too (**PowerShell** and **DOS**). In this book, we will learn a modern reincarnation of the Bourne shell, called **Bash** (**Bourne Again Shell**), which is the most widely used, and considered the most standard. The Bash shell is part of the GNU project from the Free Software Foundation that was founded by Richard Stallman, which provides free and open source software.

During this book, we will sometimes introduce common abbreviations for lengthy terms, which the students should get accustomed to.

Command-Line Terminology

Before we can delve into the chapters, we will learn some introductory command-line terms that will come handy throughout the book.

- **Commands**: They refer to the names that are typed to execute some function. They can be built into the shell or be external programs. Any program that's available on the system is a command.

- **Arguments**: The strings typed after a command are called its arguments. They tell the command how to operate or what to operate on. They are typically options or names of some data resource such as a file, URL, and so on.

- **Switches/Options/Flags**: These are arguments that typically start with a single or double hyphen and request a certain optional behavior from a command. Usually, an option has a short form, which is a hyphen followed by a single character, and a longer version of the same option, as a double hyphen followed by an entire word. The long option is easier to remember and often makes the command easier to read. Note that options are always case-sensitive.

The following are some examples of switches and arguments in commands:

```
ls -l --color --classify
grep -n --ignore-case 'needle' haystack.txt 'my data.txt'
```

In the preceding snippet, `ls` and **grep** are commands, `-l`, `--color`, `-classify`, `-n`, and `--ignore-case` are flags, and `'needle'`, `haystack.txt` and `'my data.txt'` are arguments.

Exploring the Filesystem

The space in which a command line operates is called a **filesystem** (**FS**). A lot of shell activity revolves around manipulating and organizing files; thus, learning the basics of filesystems is imperative to learning the command line. In this topic, we will learn about filesystems, and how to navigate, examine, and modify them via the shell. For regular users of computers, some of these ideas may seem familiar, but it is necessary to revisit them to have a clear and unambiguous understanding.

Filesystems

The UNIX design philosophy is to represent every object on a computer as a file; thus, the main objects that we manipulate with a command line are files. There are many different types of file-like objects under UNIX, but for our purposes, we will deal with simple data files, typically ASCII text files, that are human readable.

From this UNIX perspective, the system is accessible under what is termed a filesystem (FS). An FS is a representation of the system that's analogous to a series of nested boxes, each of which is called a **directory** or **folder**. Most of us are familiar with this folder structure, which we would have encountered when using a GUI file manager.

A directory that contains another directory is called the *parent* of the latter. The latter is called a *sub-directory* of the former. On UNIX-like systems, the outermost directory is called the **root directory**, and each directory can contain either files or other directories in turn. Some files are not data, but rather represent devices or other resources on the system. To be concise, we will refer to folders, regular files, and special files as **FS objects**.

Typically, every user of a system has their own distinct **home directory**, named after the user's name, where they store their own data. Various other directories used by the operating system, called **system directories**, exist on the filesystem, but we need not concern ourselves with them for the purposes of this book. For the sake of simplicity, we will assume that our entire filesystem resides on only a single disk or partition (although this is not true in general):

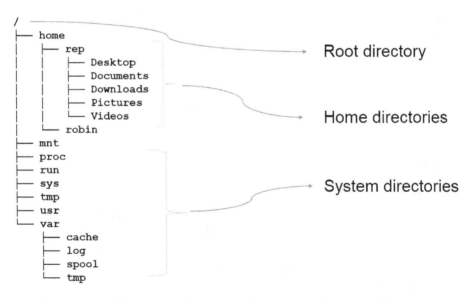

Figure 1.1: An illustration of an example structure of a typical filesystem

The notation used to refer to a location in a filesystem is called a **path**. A path consists of the list of directories that need to be navigated to reach some FS object. The list is separated by a forward slash, which is called a **path separator**. The complete location of an FS object, including its path from the root directory onward, is called a **fully qualified pathname**.

Paths can be absolute or relative. An **absolute path** starts at the root directory, whereas a **relative path** starts at what is called the **current working directory** (**CWD**). Every process that runs on a system is started with its CWD set to some location. This includes the command-line process itself. When an FS object is accessed within the CWD, the name of the object alone is enough to refer to it.

The root directory itself is represented by a single forward slash; thus, any absolute path starts with a single forward slash. The following is an example of an absolute path relative to the root directory:

```
/home/robin/Lesson1/data/cupressaceae/juniperus/indica
```

Special syntax is used to refer to the current, parent, and user's home directories:

- **./** refers to the current directory explicitly. The CWD is implicit in many cases, but is useful when the current directory needs to be explicitly specified as an argument to some commands. For instance, the same directory that we've just seen can be expressed relative to the CWD (**/home/robin**, in this case) as follows: one pathname specifying **./** explicitly and one without:

  ```
  ./Lesson1/data/cupressaceae/juniperus/indica
  Lesson1/data/cupressaceae/juniperus/indica
  ```

- **../** refers to the parent directory. This can be extended further, such as **../../../**, and so on. For instance, the preceding directory can be expressed relative to the parent of the CWD, as follows:

  ```
  ../robin/Lesson1/data/cupressaceae/juniperus/indica
  ```

  The **../** takes us to one level up to the parent of all the user home directories, and then we go back down to **robin** and the rest of the path.

- **~/** refers to the home directory of the current user.

~robin/ refers to the home directory of a user called "robin". This is a useful shorthand, because the home directory of a user could be configured to be anywhere in the filesystem. For example, macOS keeps the users' home directories in **/Users**, whereas Linux systems keep it in **/home**.

> **Note**
>
> The trailing slash symbol at the end of a directory pathname is optional. The shell does not mandate this. It is usually typed only to make it obvious that it is the name of a directory rather than a file.

Navigating Filesystems

We will now look briefly at the most common commands for moving around the filesystem and examining its contents:

- The **cd (change directory)** command changes the CWD to the path specified as its argument—if the path is non-existent, it prints an error message. Specifying just a single hyphen as the argument to **cd** changes the CWD to the last directory that was navigated from.

- The **pwd (print working directory)** command simply displays the absolute path of the CWD.

- The **pushd** and **popd (push directory and pop directory)** commands are used to bookmark the CWD and return to it later, respectively. They work by pushing and popping entries on to an internal **directory stack**, hence the names **pushd** and **popd**. Since they use a stack, you can push multiple values and pop them later in reverse order.

- The **tree** command displays the hierarchical structure of a directory as a text-based diagram.

- The **ls (list)** command displays the contents of one or more specified directories (by default, the CWD) in various formats.

- The **cat** (**concatenate**) command outputs the concatenation of the contents of the files specified to it. If only one file is specified, it simply displays the file. This is a quick way to look at a file's content, if the files are small. **cat** can also apply some transformations on its output, such as numbering the lines or suppressing multiple blank lines.

- The **less** command can be used to interactively scroll through one or more files easily, search for a string, and so on. This command is called a **pager** (it lets text content be viewed page by page). On most systems, **less** is configured to be the default pager. Other commands that require a pager interface will request the default pager from the system for this purpose. Here are some of the most useful keyboard shortcuts for **less**:

  (a) The *up* or *down* and *Page Up* or *Page Down* keys scroll vertically.

  (b) The *Enter* and spacebar keys scroll down by one line and one screenful, respectively.

  (c) < and > or *g* and G characters will scroll to the beginning and end of the file, respectively.

  (d) / followed by a string and then *Enter* searches for the specified string. The occurrences are also highlighted.

  (e) *n* and N jump to the next or previous match, respectively.

  (f) *Esc* followed by *u* turns off the highlights.

  (g) *h* shows a help screen, with the list of shortcuts and commands that are supported.

  (h) *q* exits the application or exits the help screen if it is being shown.

  There are many more features for navigating, searching, and editing that **less** provides, which we will not cover in this basic introduction.

Commonly Used Options for the Commands

The following options are used with the **ls** command:

- The **-l** option (which stands for long list) shows the contents with one entry per line—each column in the listing shows some specific information, namely permissions, link count, owner, group, size, and modification time, followed by the name, respectively. For the purposes of this book, we will only consider the size and the name. Information about the type of each FS object is indicated in the first character of the permissions field. For example, - for a file, and **d** for a directory.

- The --**reverse** option sorts the entries in reverse order. This is an example of a long option, where the option is a complete word, which is easy to remember. Long options are usually aliases for short options–in this case, the corresponding short option is -**r**.

- The --**color** option is used to make different kinds of FS objects display in different colors–there is no corresponding short option for this.

The following options are used with the **tree** command:

- The -**d** option prints only directories and skips files

- The -**o** option writes the output to a file rather than the display

- The -**H** option generates a formatted HTML output, and typically would be used along with -**o** to generate an HTML listing to serve on a website

Before going ahead with the exercises, let's establish some conventions for the rest of this book. Each chapter of this book includes some test data to practice on. Throughout this book, we will assume that each chapter's data is in its own folder called **Lesson1**, **Lesson2**, and so on.

In all of the exercises that follow, it is assumed that the work is in the home directory of the logged-in user (here, the user is called **robin**).

Exercise 1: Exploring Filesystem Contents

In this exercise, we will navigate through a complex directory structure and view files using the commands learned so far. The sample data used here is a dataset of conifer trees, hierarchically structured as per botanic classification, which will be used in future activities and exercises too.

1. Open the command-line shell.

2. Navigate to the **Lesson1** directory and examine the contents of the folder with the **ls** command:

```
robin ~ $ cd Lesson1
robin ~/Lesson1 $ ls
data data1
```

In the preceding code snippet, the part of the first line up to the $ symbol is called a **prompt**. The system is prompting for a command to be typed. The prompt shows the current user, in this case robin, followed by the CWD **~/Lesson1**. The text shown after the command is what the command itself prints as output.

> **Note**
>
> Recall that ~ means the home directory of the current user.

3. Use the **cd** command to navigate to the **data** directory and examine its contents with **ls**:

```
robin ~/Lesson1 $ cd data
robin ~/Lesson1/data $ ls
cupressaceae  pinaceae  podocarpaceae  taxaceae
```

> **Note**
>
> Notice that the prompt shown afterward displays the new CWD. This is not always true. Depending on the configuration of the system, the prompt may vary, and may even be a simple $ symbol with no other information shown.

4. The **ls** command can be provided with one or more arguments, which are the names of files and folders to list. By default, it lists only the CWD. The following snippet can be used to view the subdirectories within the **taxaceae** and **podocarpaceae** directories:

```
robin ~/Lesson1/data $ ls taxaceae podocarpaceae
podocarpaceae/:
acmopyle     dacrydium      lagarostrobos  margbensonia  parasitaxus
podocarpus   saxegothaea
afrocarpus   falcatifolium  lepidothamnus  microcachrys  pherosphaera
prumnopitys  stachycarpus
dacrycarpus  halocarpus     manoao         nageia        phyllocladus
retrophyllum sundacarpus

taxaceae/:
amentotaxus  austrotaxus  cephalotaxus  pseudotaxus  taxus  torreya
```

The dataset contains a directory for every member of the botanical families of coniferous trees. Here, we can see the top-level directories for each botanical family. Each of these has subdirectories for the genii, and those in turn for the species.

5. You can also use **ls** to request a long output in color, as follows:

```
robin ~/Lesson1/data $ ls -l --color
total 16
drwxr-xr-x 36 robin robin 4096 Aug 20 14:01 cupressaceae
drwxr-xr-x 15 robin robin 4096 Aug 20 14:01 pinaceae
drwxr-xr-x 23 robin robin 4096 Aug 20 14:01 podocarpaceae
drwxr-xr-x  8 robin robin 4096 Aug 20 14:01 taxaceae
```

6. Navigate into the **taxaceae** folder, and then use the **tree** command to visualize the directory structure at this point. For clarity, specify the **-d** option, which instructs it to display only directories and exclude files:

```
robin ~/Lesson1/data $ cd taxaceae
robin ~/Lesson1/data/taxaceae $ tree -d
```

You should get the following output on running the preceding command:

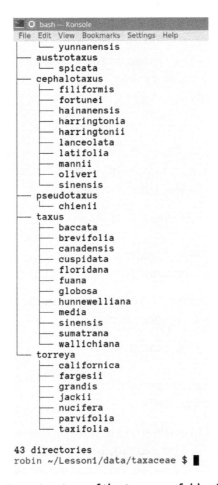

bash — Konsole
File Edit View Bookmarks Settings Help

```
                    └─ yunnanensis
          ├─ austrotaxus
          │   └─ spicata
          ├─ cephalotaxus
          │   ├─ filiformis
          │   ├─ fortunei
          │   ├─ hainanensis
          │   ├─ harringtonia
          │   ├─ harringtonii
          │   ├─ lanceolata
          │   ├─ latifolia
          │   ├─ mannii
          │   ├─ oliveri
          │   └─ sinensis
          ├─ pseudotaxus
          │   └─ chienii
          ├─ taxus
          │   ├─ baccata
          │   ├─ brevifolia
          │   ├─ canadensis
          │   ├─ cuspidata
          │   ├─ floridana
          │   ├─ fuana
          │   ├─ globosa
          │   ├─ hunnewelliana
          │   ├─ media
          │   ├─ sinensis
          │   ├─ sumatrana
          │   └─ wallichiana
          └─ torreya
              ├─ californica
              ├─ fargesii
              ├─ grandis
              ├─ jackii
              ├─ nucifera
              ├─ parvifolia
              └─ taxifolia

43 directories
robin ~/Lesson1/data/taxaceae $ ▮
```

Figure 1.2: The directory structure of the taxaceae folder (not shown entirely)

7. **cd** can be given a single hyphen as an argument to jump back to the last directory that was navigated from:

```
robin ~/Lesson1/data/taxaceae $ cd taxus
robin ~/Lesson1/data/taxaceae/taxus $ cd -
/home/robin/Lesson1/data/taxaceae
```

Observe that it prints out the absolute path of the directory it is changing to.

> **Note**
>
> The home directory is stored in **/home** on UNIX-based systems. Other operating systems such as Mac OS may place them in other locations, so the output of some of the following commands may slightly differ from that shown here.

8. We can move upwards in the hierarchy by using .. any number of times. Type the first command that follows to reach the home directory, which is three levels up. Then, use **cd** - to return to the previous location:

```
robin ~/Lesson1/data/taxaceae $ cd ../../..
robin ~ $ cd -
/home/robin/Lesson1/data/taxaceae
robin ~/Lesson1/data/taxaceae $
```

9. Use **cd** without any arguments to go to the home directory. Then, once again, use **cd** - to return to the previous location:

```
robin ~/Lesson1/data/taxaceae $ cd
robin ~ $ cd -
/home/robin/Lesson1/data/taxaceae
robin ~/Lesson1/data/taxaceae $
```

10. Now, we will explore commands that help us navigate the folder structure, such as **pwd**, **pushd**, and **popd**. Use the **pwd** command to display the path of the CWD, as follows:

```
robin ~/Lesson1/data/taxaceae $ pwd
/home/robin/Lesson1/data/taxaceae
```

The **pwd** command may not seem very useful when the CWD is being displayed in the prompt, but it is useful in some situations, for example, to copy the path to the clipboard for use in another command, or to share it with someone.

11. Use the **pushd** command to navigate into a folder, while remembering the CWD:

```
robin ~/Lesson1/data/taxaceae $ pushd taxus/baccata/
~/Lesson1/data/taxaceae/taxus/baccata ~/Lesson1/data/taxaceae
```

Use it once again, saving this location to the stack too:

```
robin ~/Lesson1/data/taxaceae/taxus/baccata $ pushd ../sumatrana/
~/Lesson1/data/taxaceae/taxus/sumatrana ~/Lesson1/data/taxaceae/taxus/
baccata ~/Lesson1/data/taxaceae
```

Using it yet again, now we have three folders on the stack:

```
robin ~/Lesson1/data/taxaceae/taxus/sumatrana $  pushd ../../../pinaceae/
cedrus/deodara/
~/Lesson1/data/pinaceae/cedrus/deodara ~/Lesson1/data/taxaceae/taxus/
sumatrana ~/Lesson1/data/taxaceae/taxus/baccata ~/Lesson1/data/taxaceae
robin ~/Lesson1/data/pinaceae/cedrus/deodara $
```

Notice that it prints out the list of directories that have been saved so far. Since it is a stack, the list is ordered according to recency, with the first entry being the one we just changed into.

12. Use **popd** to walk back down the directory stack, successively visiting the folders we saved earlier. Notice the error message when the stack is empty:

```
robin ~/Lesson1/data/pinaceae/cedrus/deodara $ popd
~/Lesson1/data/taxaceae/taxus/sumatrana ~/Lesson1/data/taxaceae/taxus/
baccata ~/Lesson1/data/taxaceae
robin ~/Lesson1/data/taxaceae/taxus/sumatrana $ popd
~/Lesson1/data/taxaceae/taxus/baccata ~/Lesson1/data/taxaceae
robin ~/Lesson1/data/taxaceae/taxus/baccata $ popd
~/Lesson1/data/taxaceae
robin ~/Lesson1/data/taxaceae $ popd
bash: popd: directory stack empty
```

The entries on the directory stack are added and removed from the top of the stack as **pushd** and **popd** are used, respectively.

13. Each of the folders for a species has a text file called **data.txt** that contains data about that tree from Wikipedia, which we can view with **cat**. Use the **cat** command to view the file's content, after navigating into the **taxus/baccata** directory:

    robin ~/Lesson1/data/taxaceae $ **cd taxus/baccata**
    robin ~/Lesson1/data/taxaceae/taxus/baccata $ **cat data.txt**

The output will look as follows:

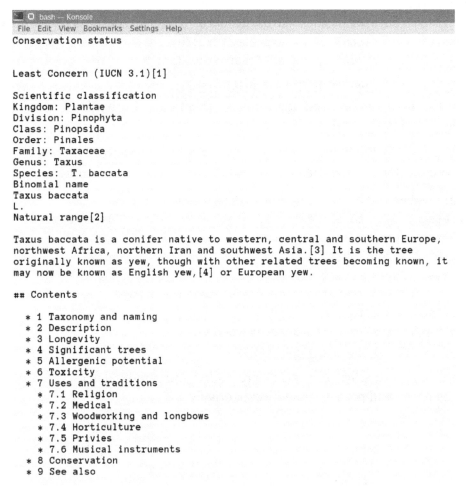

```
bash -- Konsole
File  Edit  View  Bookmarks  Settings  Help
Conservation status


Least Concern (IUCN 3.1)[1]

Scientific classification
Kingdom: Plantae
Division: Pinophyta
Class: Pinopsida
Order: Pinales
Family: Taxaceae
Genus: Taxus
Species:  T. baccata
Binomial name
Taxus baccata
L.
Natural range[2]

Taxus baccata is a conifer native to western, central and southern Europe,
northwest Africa, northern Iran and southwest Asia.[3] It is the tree
originally known as yew, though with other related trees becoming known, it
may now be known as English yew,[4] or European yew.

## Contents

   * 1 Taxonomy and naming
   * 2 Description
   * 3 Longevity
   * 4 Significant trees
   * 5 Allergenic potential
   * 6 Toxicity
   * 7 Uses and traditions
     * 7.1 Religion
     * 7.2 Medical
     * 7.3 Woodworking and longbows
     * 7.4 Horticulture
     * 7.5 Privies
     * 7.6 Musical instruments
   * 8 Conservation
   * 9 See also
```

Figure 1.3: A screenshot showing a partial output of the data.txt file

Notice that the output from the last command scrolled outside the view rapidly. **cat** is not ideal for viewing large files. You can scroll through the window manually to see the contents, but this may not extend to the whole output. To view files in a more user-friendly, interactive fashion, we can use the **less** command.

14. Use **ls** to see that there is a file called **data.txt**, and then use the **less** command to view it:

```
robin ~/Lesson1/data/taxaceae/taxus/baccata $ ls -l
total 40
-rw-r--r-- 1 robin robin 38260 Aug 16 01:08 data.txt
robin ~/Lesson1/data/taxaceae/taxus/baccata $ less data.txt
```

The output is shown here:

```
Conservation status


Least Concern (IUCN 3.1)[1]

Scientific classification
Kingdom: Plantae
Division: Pinophyta
Class: Pinopsida
Order: Pinales
Family: Taxaceae
Genus: Taxus
Species:  T. baccata
Binomial name
Taxus baccata
L.
Natural range[2]
```

Figure 1.4: A screenshot showing the output of the less command

In this exercise, we have practiced the basic commands used to view directories and files. We have not covered all of the options available with these commands in detail, but what we have learned so far will serve for most of our needs.

Given this basic knowledge, we should be able to find our way around the entire filesystem and examine any file that we wish.

Manipulating a Filesystem

So far, we have looked at commands that only examine directories and files. Now we will learn how to manipulate filesystem objects. We will not be manipulating the contents of files yet, but only their location in the filesystem.

Here are the most common commands that are used to modify a filesystem. The commonly used options for some of these commands are also mentioned:

- **mkdir (make directory)** creates the directory specified as its argument. It can also create a hierarchy of directories in one shot.

  The **-p** or **--parents** flag can be used to tell **mkdir** to create all the parent directories for the path if they do not exist. This is useful when creating a nested path in one shot.

- **rmdir (remove directory)** is used to remove a directory. It only works if the directory is empty.

  The **-p** or **--parents** flag works similarly to how it does in **mkdir**. All the directories along the path that's specified are deleted if they are empty.

- **touch** is used to create an empty file or update an existing file's timestamp.

- **cp (copy)** is used to copy files or folders between directories. When copying directories, it can recursively copy all subdirectories, too. The syntax for this command is as follows:

  ```
  cp <sources> <dest>
  ```

  Here, **<sources>** is the paths of one or more files and folders to be copied, and **<dest>** is the path of the folder where **<sources>** are copied. This can be a filename, if **<sources>** is a single filename. The following options can be used with this command:

  The **-r** or **--recursive** flag is necessary when copying folders. It recursively copies all of the folder's contents to the destination.

  The **-v** or **--verbose** flag makes **cp** print out the source and destination pathname of every file it copies.

- **mv (move)** can be used to rename an object and/or move it to another directory.

> **Note**
>
> The **mv** command performs both renaming and moving. However, these are not two distinct functions. If you think about it, renaming a file and moving it to a different path on the same disk are the same thing. Inherently, a file's content is not related to its name. A change to its name is not going to affect its contents. In a sense, a pathname is also a part of a file's name.

- **rm (remove)** deletes a file permanently, and can also be used to delete a directory, recursively deleting all the subdirectories. Unlike sending files to the *Trashcan* or *Recycle Bin* in a GUI interface, files deleted with **rm** cannot be recovered. This command has the following options:

  The **-r** or **--recursive** flag deletes folders recursively.

  The **-v** or **--verbose** flag makes **rm** print out the pathname of every file it deletes.

  The **-i** or **--interactive=always** options allows review and confirmation before each entry being deleted. Answering **n** rather than **y** to the prompts (*Enter* must be pressed after *y* or *n*) will either skip deleting some files or skip entire directories.

  -I or **--interactive=once** prompts only once before removing more than three files, or when removing recursively, whereas **-i** prompts for each and every file or directory.

Exercise 2: Manipulating the Filesystem

In this exercise, we will learn how to manipulate the FS and files within it. We will modify the directories in the **Lesson1** folder by creating, copying, and deleting files/folders using the commands that we learned about previously:

1. Open a command-line shell and navigate to the directory for this lesson:

   ```
   robin ~ $ cd Lesson1/
   robin ~/Lesson1 $
   ```

2. Create some directories, using **mkdir**, that classify animals zoologically. Type the commands shown in the following snippet:

   ```
   robin ~/Lesson1 $ mkdir animals
   robin ~/Lesson1 $ cd animals
   robin ~/Lesson1/animals $ mkdir canis
   robin ~/Lesson1/animals $ mkdir canis/familiaris
   robin ~/Lesson1/animals $ mkdir canis/lupus
   robin ~/Lesson1/animals $ mkdir canis/lupus/lupus
   robin ~/Lesson1/animals $ mkdir leopardus/colocolo/pajeros
   mkdir: cannot create directory 'leopardus/colocolo/pajeros': No such file
   or directory
   ```

3. Notice that **mkdir** normally creates subdirectories that are only in already-existing directories, so it raises an error when we try to make **leopardus/ colocolo/pajeros**. Use the **--parents** or **-p** switch to overcome this error:

```
robin ~/Lesson1/animals $ mkdir -p leopardus/colocolo/pajeros
robin ~/Lesson1/animals $ mkdir --parents panthera/tigris
robin ~/Lesson1/animals $ mkdir panthera/leo
```

4. Now, use **tree** to view and verify the directory structure we created:

```
robin ~/Lesson1/animals $ tree
```

The directory structure is shown here:

```
├── canis
│   ├── familiaris
│   └── lupus
│       └── lupus
├── leopardus
│   └── colocolo
│       └── pajeros
└── panthera
    ├── leo
    └── tigris

10 directories, 0 files
```

Figure 1.5: The directory structure of the animals folder

5. Now use the **rmdir** command to delete the directories. Try the following code snippets:

```
robin ~/Lesson1/animals $ rmdir canis/familiaris/
robin ~/Lesson1/animals $ rmdir canis
rmdir: failed to remove 'canis': Directory not empty
robin ~/Lesson1/animals $ rmdir canis/lupus
rmdir: failed to remove 'canis/lupus': Directory not empty
```

6. Notice that it raises an error when trying to remove a directory that is not empty. You need to empty the directory first, removing **canis/lupus/lupus**, and then use the **-p** option to remove both **canis/lupus** and its parent, **canis**:

```
robin ~/Lesson1/animals $ rmdir canis/lupus/lupus
robin ~/Lesson1/animals $ rmdir -p canis/lupus
```

7. Now, use **tree** to view the modified directory structure, as follows:

```
robin ~/Lesson1/animals $ tree
```

The directory structure is shown here:

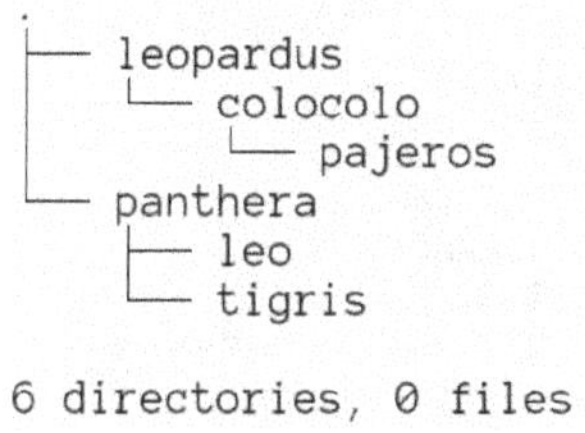

```
.
├── leopardus
│   └── colocolo
│       └── pajeros
└── panthera
    ├── leo
    └── tigris

6 directories, 0 files
```

Figure 1.6: A screenshot of the output displaying the modified folder structure of the animals folder

8. Create some directories with the following commands:

```
robin ~/Lesson1/animals $ mkdir -p canis/lupus/lupus
robin ~/Lesson1/animals $ mkdir -p canis/lupus/familiaris
robin ~/Lesson1/animals $ ls
canis   leopardus   panthera
```

9. Create some dummy files with the **touch** command, and then view the entire tree again:

```
robin ~/Lesson1/animals $ touch canis/lupus/familiaris/dog.txt
robin ~/Lesson1/animals $ touch panthera/leo/lion.txt
robin ~/Lesson1/animals $ touch canis/lupus/lupus/wolf.txt
robin ~/Lesson1/animals $ touch panthera/tigris/tiger.txt
robin ~/Lesson1/animals $ touch leopardus/colocolo/pajeros/colocolo.txt
robin ~/Lesson1/animals $ tree
```

The output will look as follows:

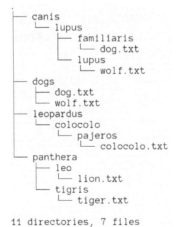

```
       ── canis
       │   └─ lupus
       │       ├─ familiaris
       │       │   └─ dog.txt
       │       └─ lupus
       │           └─ wolf.txt
       ├─ leopardus
       │   └─ colocolo
       │       └─ pajeros
       │           └─ colocolo.txt
       └─ panthera
           ├─ leo
           │   └─ lion.txt
           └─ tigris
               └─ tiger.txt

10 directories, 5 files
```

Figure 1.7: A screenshot of the output displaying the revised folder structure
of the animals folder

10. Use **cp** to copy the **dog.txt** and **wolf.txt** files from the **familiaris** and **lupus** directories into a new directory called **dogs**, as follows:

```
robin ~/Lesson1/animals $ mkdir dogs
robin ~/Lesson1/animals $ cp canis/lupus/familiaris/dog.txt dogs/
robin ~/Lesson1/animals $ cp canis/lupus/lupus/wolf.txt dogs/
robin ~/Lesson1/animals $ tree
```

The output will look as follows:

```
       ── canis
       │   └─ lupus
       │       ├─ familiaris
       │       │   └─ dog.txt
       │       └─ lupus
       │           └─ wolf.txt
       ├─ dogs
       │   ├─ dog.txt
       │   └─ wolf.txt
       ├─ leopardus
       │   └─ colocolo
       │       └─ pajeros
       │           └─ colocolo.txt
       └─ panthera
           ├─ leo
           │   └─ lion.txt
           └─ tigris
               └─ tiger.txt

11 directories, 7 files
```

Figure 1.8: A screenshot of the output displaying the revised folder structure of the animals folder,
along with the newly copied files

11. Now clone the entire **panthera** directory into a new directory called **cats** using **cp**:

```
robin ~/Lesson1/animals $ mkdir cats
robin ~/Lesson1/animals $ cp -r panthera cats
robin ~/Lesson1/animals $ tree
```

The output will look as follows:

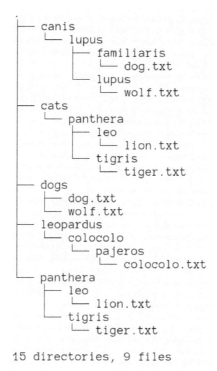

```
    ├── canis
    │   └── lupus
    │       ├── familiaris
    │       │   └── dog.txt
    │       └── lupus
    │           └── wolf.txt
    ├── cats
    │   └── panthera
    │       ├── leo
    │       │   └── lion.txt
    │       └── tigris
    │           └── tiger.txt
    ├── dogs
    │   ├── dog.txt
    │   └── wolf.txt
    ├── leopardus
    │   └── colocolo
    │       └── pajeros
    │           └── colocolo.txt
    └── panthera
        ├── leo
        │   └── lion.txt
        └── tigris
            └── tiger.txt

15 directories, 9 files
```

Figure 1.9: A screenshot of the output displaying the revised folder structure of the animals folder

12. Now use the **--verbose** option with **cp** to copy the files with verbose progress displayed and print the output using the **tree** command:

```
robin ~/Lesson1/animals $ mkdir bigcats
robin ~/Lesson1/animals $ cp -r --verbose leopardus/ panthera/ bigcats
'leopardus/' -> 'bigcats/leopardus'
'leopardus/colocolo' -> 'bigcats/leopardus/colocolo'
'leopardus/colocolo/pajeros' -> 'bigcats/leopardus/colocolo/pajeros'
'leopardus/colocolo/pajeros/colocolo.txt' -> 'bigcats/leopardus/colocolo/
pajeros/colocolo.txt'
'panthera/' -> 'bigcats/panthera'
'panthera/tigris' -> 'bigcats/panthera/tigris'
'panthera/tigris/tiger.txt' -> 'bigcats/panthera/tigris/tiger.txt'
'panthera/leo' -> 'bigcats/panthera/leo'
'panthera/leo/lion.txt' -> 'bigcats/panthera/leo/lion.txt'

robin ~/Lesson1/animals $ tree bigcats
```

The output of the **tree** command is shown here:

```
bigcats
├── leopardus
│   └── colocolo
│       └── pajeros
│           └── colocolo.txt
└── panthera
    ├── leo
    │   └── lion.txt
    └── tigris
        └── tiger.txt

6 directories, 3 files
```

Figure 1.10: A screenshot of the output displaying the folder structure of the animals folder after a recursive directory copy

13. Now use **mv** to rename the **animals** folder to **beasts**:

```
robin ~/Lesson1/animals $ cd ..
robin ~/Lesson1 $ mv animals beasts
robin ~/Lesson1 $ cd beasts
robin ~/Lesson1/beasts $ ls
bigcats  canis  cats  dogs  leopardus  panthera
```

14. Use **mv** to move an individual file to a different path. We move **dogs/dog.txt** to the CWD as **fido.txt** and move it back again:

```
robin ~/Lesson1/beasts $ mv dogs/dog.txt fido.txt
robin ~/Lesson1/beasts $ ls
bigcats  canis  cats  dogs  fido.txt  leopardus  panthera
robin ~/Lesson1/beasts $ mv fido.txt dogs/
```

15. Use **mv** to relocate an entire folder. Move the whole **canis** folder into **dogs**:

```
robin ~/Lesson1/beasts $ mv canis dogs
robin ~/Lesson1/beasts $ tree dogs
```

The revised folder structure is shown here:

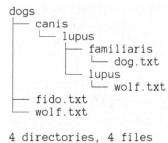

```
dogs
├── canis
│   └── lupus
│       ├── familiaris
│       │   └── dog.txt
│       └── lupus
│           └── wolf.txt
├── fido.txt
└── wolf.txt

4 directories, 4 files
```

Figure 1.11: A screenshot of the output displaying the folder structure of the animals folder after relocating a folder

16. Use the **-v** or **--verbose** option with **mv** to make it report each item being moved. In this case, there was only one file being moved, but this can be a long list:

```
robin ~/Lesson1/beasts $ mkdir panthers
robin ~/Lesson1/beasts $ mv --verbose panthera panthers
renamed 'panthera' -> 'panthers/panthera'
robin ~/Lesson1/beasts $ tree panthers
```

The output is shown here:

```
panthers
└── panthera
    ├── leo
    │   └── lion.txt
    └── tigris
        └── tiger.txt

3 directories, 2 files
```

Figure 1.12: A screenshot of the output displaying the folder structure of the animals folder after moving a folder

17. Use **tree** to view the dogs folder (before we use **rm** to delete it):

    ```
    robin ~/Lesson1/beasts $ tree dogs
    ```

    The output is shown here:

    ```
    dogs
    ├── canis
    │   └── lupus
    │       ├── familiaris
    │       │   └── dog.txt
    │       └── lupus
    │           └── wolf.txt
    ├── fido.txt
    └── wolf.txt

    4 directories, 4 files
    ```

    Figure 1.13: A screenshot of the output displaying the folder structure of the animals folder before the deletion of files

18. Delete the files one by one with **rm**:

    ```
    robin ~/Lesson1/beasts $ rm dogs/fido.txt
    robin ~/Lesson1/beasts $ rm dogs/wolf.txt
    robin ~/Lesson1/beasts $ rm dogs/canis/lupus/familiaris/dog.txt
    robin ~/Lesson1/beasts $ rm dogs/canis/lupus/lupus/wolf.txt
    robin ~/Lesson1/beasts $ tree dogs
    ```

    The output is shown here:

    ```
    dogs
    └── canis
        └── lupus
            ├── familiaris
            └── lupus

    4 directories, 0 files
    ```

    Figure 1.14: The folder structure of the animals folder after the deletion of files

19. Remove the complete directory structure with the **-r** or **--recursive** switch of **rm**:

    ```
    robin ~/Lesson1/beasts $ ls
    bigcats  cats  dogs  leopardus  panthers
    robin ~/Lesson1/beasts $ rm -r dogs
    robin ~/Lesson1/beasts $ ls
    bigcats  cats  leopardus  panthers
    ```

    As we can see, the entire **dogs** directory was silently removed without warning.

20. Use the **-i** flag to remove items interactively. Each individual operation is prompted for confirmation:

> **Note**
>
> Depending on your system configuration, the prompts you see for the following command and the one in step 21 may be in a different order or worded differently. The system will prompt you for every deletion to be performed, regardless.

```
robin ~/Lesson1/beasts $ rm -r -i panthers
rm: descend into directory 'panthers'? y
rm: descend into directory 'panthers/panthera'? y
rm: descend into directory 'panthers/panthera/leo'? y
rm: remove regular empty file 'panthers/panthera/leo/lion.txt'? n
rm: remove directory 'panthers/panthera/leo'? n
rm: descend into directory 'panthers/panthera/tigris'? n
robin ~/Lesson1/beasts $ ls
bigcats  cats  leopardus  panthers
```

Now use the **-I** flag to remove items interactively. Confirmation is asked only a few times, and not for each file:

```
robin ~/Lesson1/beasts $ rm -r -I bigcats
rm: remove 1 argument recursively? y
robin ~/Lesson1/beasts $ ls
cats  leopardus  panthers
```

21. Use the **-v** or **--verbose** option to make **rm** report each file or directory that's removed:

```
robin ~/Lesson1/beasts $ rm -r -v panthers/
removed 'panthers/panthera/leo/lion.txt'
removed directory 'panthers/panthera/leo'
removed 'panthers/panthera/tigris/tiger.txt'
removed directory 'panthers/panthera/tigris'
removed directory 'panthers/panthera'
removed directory 'panthers/'
```

22. Now clear the entire folder we used for this exercise so that we can move on to the next lesson with a blank slate:

```
robin ~/Lesson1/beasts $ cd ..
robin ~/Lesson1 $ ls
beasts   data   data1
robin ~/Lesson1 $ rm -r beasts
robin ~/Lesson1 $ ls
data   data1
```

In this exercise, we learned how to change or extend the structure of the filesystem tree. We have yet to learn how to create and manipulate the content within files, which will be covered in future chapters.

Activity 1: Navigating the Filesystem and Viewing Files

For this activity, use the conifer tree dataset that has been supplied as a hierarchy of folders representing each tree's Family, Genus, and Species. Every species has an associated text file called **data.txt** containing information about the species, which has been mined from a Wikipedia page. Your aim is to navigate this hierarchy via the command line and answer basic questions about certain species by looking it up the data in those text files. Navigate through the directories within the example dataset provided for this lesson and answer the following questions:

1. Provide two common names for the species *Cedrus Deodara*, which belongs to the *Pinaceae* family.

2. Look up information about *Abies Pindrow* in the *Pinaceae* family and fill in the following blank: "The name pindrow derives from the tree's name in _____".

3. How many species of the *Taxus* genus in the family *Taxaceae* are documented in this dataset?

4. How many species in total are documented in this dataset?

Follow these steps to complete this activity:

1. Use the **cd** command to navigate to the appropriate folder and use **less** to read the relevant information.

2. Use the **cd** command to navigate to the appropriate folder and view the file with **less**. Use the **/** command to search for the phrase "derives from" and read the rest of the sentence to get the answer.

3. Navigate to the right folder and run the **tree** command, which reports the number of directories in it. Each directory is a species.

4. Navigate to the top-level **data** folder and run the **tree** command, which reports the number of files. Each file is associated with one species.

The expected answers for the preceding questions are as follows:

1. Any two of the following: deodar cedar, Himalayan cedar, deodar, devdar, devadar, devadaru

2. Nepali

3. 12

4. 770

> **Note**
>
> The solution for this activity can be found on page 270.

Activity 2: Modifying the Filesystem

For this activity, you will be using the conifer tree sample dataset that is in the ~/ **Lesson1/data** folder. You need to collect the data for all trees from the family *taxaceae* and the genus *torreya* into one folder. Each file should be named **<species>.txt**, where **<species>** is the name of the species/folder. Execute the following steps to complete this objective:

1. Use the **cd** command to go into the **Lesson1** folder and create a new folder called **activity2**.

2. Navigate to the folder for the genus specified and view the subfolders which represent each species.

3. Use the **cp** command to copy a data file from one sub-directory of the **data/ taxaceae/torreya** folder into the output folder.

4. Use the **mv** command to rename the file as per the species name.

5. Repeat steps 3 and 4 for all the species that are requested.

The expected listing of the **activity2** folder is as follows:

```
robin ~/Lesson1/activity2 $ ls -l
total 52
-rw-r--r-- 1 robin robin  5644 Nov 29 15:02 californica.txt
-rw-r--r-- 1 robin robin  4133 Nov 29 15:02 fargesii.txt
-rw-r--r-- 1 robin robin  5462 Nov 29 15:02 grandis.txt
-rw-r--r-- 1 robin robin  3836 Nov 29 15:02 jackii.txt
-rw-r--r-- 1 robin robin  5911 Nov 29 15:02 nucifera.txt
-rw-r--r-- 1 robin robin     2 Nov 29 15:02 parvifolia.txt
-rw-r--r-- 1 robin robin 10552 Nov 29 15:02 taxifolia.txt
```

Figure 1.15: A screenshot of the expected listing of the activity2 folder

> **Note**
>
> The solution for this activity can be found on page 270.

So far, we have explored the space in which a shell command-line operates. In a GUI, we deal with an abstract space of windows, menus, applications, and so on. In contrast, a CLI is based on a lower layer of the operating system, which is the filesystem.

In this topic, we have learned what a filesystem is and how to navigate it, and examined its structure or looked at the contents of files in it using the command line. We also learned how to modify the FS structure and perform simple file management tasks.

We learned how the shell is a way to provide precise, unambiguous, and repeatable instructions to the computer. You may have noticed the fact that most command-line tools perform just one simple function. This stems from one of the UNIX design philosophies: *Do only one thing but, do it well*. These small commands can be combined like the parts of a machine into constructs that can automate tasks and process data in complex ways.

The focus of this topic was mainly to get familiar with the FS, the arena where most of the command-line work happens. In the next topic, we will learn how to reduce effort when composing commands, making use of several convenience features in Bash.

Shell History Recall, Editing, and Autocompletion

In the previous section, we have experienced the fact that we need to repeatedly type some commands, and often type out the pathnames of files and folders. Indeed, it can get quite tedious if we work with long or hard-to-spell pathnames (both of which are present in our tree dataset). To counter this, we can use a few convenient features of modern command-line shells to reduce typing effort. We will explore these useful keyboard shortcuts for the command line in this section.

The GNU Bash shell uses an interface library called **readline**. This same interface is used by several programs (for example, gdb, python, and Node.js); hence, what you learn now applies to the CLIs of all those.

The readline interface supports **emacs** and **vi** modes. The keyboard shortcuts in these modes are derived from the ones in the iconic editors of those names. Since the default is the **emacs** mode, we will study only that.

> **Note**
>
> When indicating shortcuts, the convention is to show a combination of the *Ctrl* key and another key using the caret symbol '^' with the key. For example, *Ctrl + C* is indicated by ^C.

Command History Recall

The Bash shell retains a history of the past commands that were typed. Depending on the system configuration, anywhere from a few hundred to a few thousand commands could be maintained in the history log. Any command from the history can be brought back and re-executed (after optionally modifying it).

Basic History Navigation Shortcuts

History is accessed by using the following shortcuts:

- The up and down arrow keys move through the command history.

- *Esc + <* and *Esc + >* or *Page Up* and *Page Down* or *Alt + <* and *Alt + >* move to the first and last command in the history. The other shortcuts listed may or may not work depending on the system's configuration.

- *Ctrl + S* and *Ctrl + R* let you incrementally search for a command in the history forward and backward, respectively, by typing any substring of the command.

Navigating through the history of past commands with the up and down arrow keys or with *Esc* + < and *Esc* + > is quite straightforward. As you navigate, the command appears on the prompt, and can be executed by pressing *Enter* immediately, or after editing it.

> **Note**
>
> In the aforementioned shortcuts, remember that < and > implies that the *Shift* key is held down, since these are the secondary symbols on the keyboard.

To view the entire history, we can use the **history** command:

```
robin ~ $ history
```

An example output is shown here:

```
 1   cd Lesson1
 2   ls
 3   mkdir animals
 4   cd animals
 5   mkdir canis
 6   mkdir canis/familiaris
 7   mkdir canis/lupus
 8   mkdir canis/lupus/lupus
 9   mkdir --parents panthera/tigris
10   mkdir panthera/leo
11   mkdir leopardus/colocolo/pajeros
12   mkdir -p leopardus/colocolo/pajeros
13   tree
14   rmdir canis/familiaris/
15   rmdir canis
16   rmdir canis/lupus
17   rmdir canis/lupus/lupus
18   rmdir -p canis/lupus
19   tree
20   mkdir -p canis/lupus/lupus
21   mkdir -p canis/lupus/familiaris
22   ls
```

Figure 1.16: A screenshot of the output displaying the shell command history

This command can perform other tasks related to history management as well, but we will not concern ourselves with that for this book.

Incremental Search

This feature lets you find a command in the history that matches a few characters that you type. To perform a forward incremental search, press *Ctrl* + S, upon which the shell prompt changes to something like this:

```
robin ~ $ ^S
(i-search)`':
```

When we press *Ctrl* + R instead, we see the following prompt:

```
robin ~ $ ^R
(reverse-i-search)`':
```

i-search stands for **incremental search**. When these prompts are displayed, the shell expects a few characters that appear within a command to be typed. As they are typed, the command which matches those characters as a substring is displayed. If there is more than one command that matches the input, the list of matches can be iterated with *Ctrl* + R and *Ctrl* + S backward and forward, respectively.

The incremental search happens from the point where you have currently navigated in the history (with arrow keys and so on). If there are no more matches in the given direction, the prompt changes to something similar to what is shown here:

```
(failed reverse-i-search)`john': man join
```

At this point, we can do the following:

- Backspace the search string that was typed, to widen the range of matches and find one.

- Change the search direction. We can press *Ctrl* + S if we were searching backward or press *Ctrl* + R if we were searching forward, to return to any previous match that was crossed over.

- Press *Esc* to exit the search and accept whatever match was shown last.

- Press *Ctrl* + G to exit the search and leave the command line empty.

> **Note**
>
> On some systems, *Ctrl* + S does not activate incremental search. Instead, it performs an unrelated function. To make sure it works as we require it to, type the following command once in the console before the exercises here: **stty -ixon**.

Remember that the search happens relative to the current location in history, so if you start a search without navigating upward in the history, then searching forward would have no effect, since there are no commands after the current history location (that is, the present). This means that searching backward with *Ctrl + R* is generally the more frequently used and useful feature. Most of the time, a history search comes in handy for retyping a long command from the recent past, or for retrieving a complex command typed long ago, whose details have been forgotten.

As you progress in your command-line knowledge and experience, you will find that although it is easy to compose complicated command lines when you have a certain problem to solve, it is not easy to recollect them after a long period of time has passed. Keeping this in mind, it makes sense to conserve your mental energy, and reuse old commands from history, rather than try to remember or recreate them from scratch. Indeed, it is possible to configure Bash to save your entire history infinitely so that you never lose any command that you ever typed on the shell.

Exercise 3: Exploring Shell History

In this exercise, we will use the history search feature to repeat some commands from an earlier exercise. Make sure that you are in the **Lesson1** directory before starting:

1. Create a temporary directory called **data2** to work with:

   ```
   robin ~/Lesson1 $ mkdir data2
   robin ~/Lesson1 $ cd data2
   robin ~/Lesson1/data2 $
   ```

2. Press *Ctrl + R* to start a reverse incremental search, and then type "animals". The most recent command with that string will be shown.

3. Press *Ctrl + R* two times to search backward until we get the command we need, and then press *Enter* to execute it:

   ```
   (reverse-i-search)`animals': mkdir animals
   robin ~/Lesson1/data2 $ mkdir animals
   robin ~/Lesson1/data2 $ cd animals
   ```

4. Find the command that created the directory for the species of the domestic dog **canis/lupus/familiaris**. The string **familiaris** is quite unique, so we can use that as a search pattern. Press *Esc + <* to reach the start of the history and *Ctrl + S* to start searching forward from that point. Type "fa" and press *Ctrl + S* two more times to get the command we are searching for. Finally, press *Enter* to execute it:

   ```
   (i-search)`fa': mkdir -p canis/lupus/familiaris
   robin ~/Lesson1/data2/animals $ mkdir -p canis/lupus/familiaris
   ```

5. Repeat the same command, except change the directory to create **canis/lupus/lupus**. Press the *up* arrow to get the same command again. Change the last word to **lupus** and press *Enter* to create the new directory:

```
robin ~/Lesson1/data2/animals $ mkdir -p canis/lupus/lupus
```

In this brief exercise, we have seen how to retrieve commands that we typed previously. We can move through the history linearly or search for a command, saving ourselves a lot of retyping.

Command-Line Shortcuts

There are many keyboard shortcuts on Bash that let you modify an already typed command. Usually, it is more convenient to take an existing command from the history and edit it to form a new one, rather than retype everything.

Navigation Shortcuts

The following are some navigation shortcuts:

- The left or right arrow keys, as well as *Home* or *End* work as per standard conventions. *Ctrl* + A and *Ctrl* + E are alternatives for *Home* and *End*.

- *Alt* + F and *Alt* + B jump by one word forward and backward, a word being a contiguous string that consists of numbers and letters.

Clipboard Shortcuts

The following are some clipboard shortcuts:

- *Alt* + *Backspace* cuts the word to the left of the cursor

- *Alt* + D cuts the word to the right of the cursor, including the character under the cursor

- *Ctrl* + W cuts everything to the left of the cursor until a whitespace character is encountered

- *Ctrl* + K cuts everything from the cursor to the end of the line

- *Ctrl* + U cuts everything from the cursor to the start of the line, excluding the character under the cursor

- *Ctrl* + Y pastes what was just cut

- *Alt* + Y cycles through the previously cut entries one by one (works only after pasting with *Ctrl* + Y)

Other Shortcuts

The following are some other shortcuts that may come in useful:

- *Alt* + \ deletes all whitespace characters that are at the cursor, that is, it joins two words that are separated by whitespaces.
- *Ctrl* + T swaps the current and previous character. This is useful to correct typos.
- *Alt* + T swaps the current and previous word.
- *Ctrl* + *Shift* + _ undoes the last keypress.
- *Alt* + R reverts all changes to a line. This is useful to revert a command from history back to what it was originally.
- *Alt* + U converts the characters from the cursor position until the next word boundary to uppercase.
- *Alt* + L converts the characters from the cursor position until the next word boundary to lowercase.
- *Alt* + C capitalizes the first letter of the word under the cursor and moves to the next word.

There are several other shortcuts, but these are the most useful. It is not necessary to memorize all of these, but the navigation and cut/paste shortcuts are certainly worth learning by heart.

> **Note**
>
> The clipboard that the readline interface in Bash uses is distinct from the clipboard provided in the GUI. The two are independent mechanisms and should not be confused with each other. When you use any other command-line interface that uses readline, for example, the Python shell, it gets its own independent clipboard.

Exercise 4: Using Shell Keyboard Shortcuts

In this exercise, we will try out some of the command-line shortcuts. For simplicity, we will introduce the **echo** command to help with this exercise. This command merely prints out its arguments without causing any side effects. The examples here are contrived to help illustrate the editing shortcuts:

1. Run the following command:

    ```
    robin ~/Lesson1/data2/animals $ echo one two three four five/six/seven
    one two three four five/six/seven
    ```

2. Press the up arrow key to get the same command again. Press *Alt* + B three times. The cursor ends up at **five**. Type "thousand" followed by a space, and press *Enter* to execute the edited command:

    ```
    robin ~/Lesson1/data2/animals $ echo one two three four thousand five/six/
    seven
    one two three four thousand five/six/seven
    ```

3. Now use the cut and paste shortcuts as follows: press the up arrow key to get the previous command, press *Alt* + *Backspace* to cut the last word **seven** into the clipboard, press *Alt* + B twice (the cursor ends up at **five**), use *Ctrl* + Y to paste the word that we cut, type a forward slash, and finally press *Enter*:

    ```
    robin ~/Lesson1/data2/animals $ echo one two three four thousand seven/
    five/six/
    one two three four thousand seven/five/six/
    ```

4. Press the up arrow key to get the previous command, press *Alt* + B four times (the cursor ends up at **thousand**), press *Alt* + D to cut that word (notice that an extra space was left behind), press *End* to go to the end of the line, use *Ctrl* + Y to paste the word that we cut, and press *Enter* to execute the command:

    ```
    robin ~/Lesson1/data2/animals $ echo one two three four  seven/five/six/
    thousand
    one two three four seven/five/six/thousand
    ```

5. Press the up arrow key to get the previous command again, press *Alt* + *B* three times (the cursor ends up at **five**), press *Ctrl* + *K* to cut to the end of the line, press *Alt* + *B* to go back one word (the cursor ends up at **seven**), use *Ctrl* + *Y* to paste the word that we cut, type a forward slash, and press *Enter* to execute the command:

```
robin ~/Lesson1/data2/animals $ echo one two three four  five/six/thousand/
seven/
one two three four five/six/thousand/seven/
```

6. Press the up arrow key to get the previous command once more, press *Alt* + *B* three times (the cursor ends up at **six**), press *Ctrl* + *U* to cut to the start of the line, press *Alt* + *F* to move forward one word (the cursor ends up at **/thousand**), press *Ctrl* + *Y* to paste the content we cut earlier, press *Home* and type **echo**, and then press the spacebar and then *Enter* to execute the command:

```
robin ~/Lesson1/data2/animals $ echo sixecho one two three four  five//
thousand/seven/
sixecho one two three four five//thousand/seven/
```

In this exercise, we have explored how to use the editing shortcuts to efficiently construct commands. With some practice, it becomes quite unnecessary to compose a command from scratch. Instead, we compose them from older ones.

Command-Line Autocompletion

We all use auto-suggest on our mobile devices, but surprisingly, this feature has existed on Bash for decades. Bash provides the following context-sensitive completion when you type commands:

- File and pathname completion
- Command completion, which suggests the names of programs and commands
- Username completion
- Options completion
- Customized completion for any program (many programs such as Git add their own completion logic)

Completion is invoked on Bash by entering a few characters and pressing the *Tab* key. If there is only one possible completion, it is immediately inserted on to the command line; otherwise, the system beeps. Then, if *Tab* is pressed again, all the possible completions are shown. If the possible completions are too numerous, a confirmation prompt is shown before displaying them.

> **Note**
>
> Depending on the system's configuration, the number of possible command completions seen will vary, since different programs may be installed on different systems.

Exercise 5: Completing a Folder Path

In this exercise, we will explore hands-on how the shell autocompletes folder paths for us:

1. Open a new command shell and return to the directory that we recreated from history in the earlier exercise:

    ```
    robin ~ $ cd Lesson1/data2/animals
    robin ~/Lesson1/data2/animals $
    ```

2. Type **cd canis/** and press *Tab* three times. It completes the command to **cd canis/ lupus/** and shows two possible completions:

    ```
    robin ~/Lesson1/data2/animals $ cd canis/lupus/
    familiaris/ lupus/
    robin ~/Lesson1/data2/animals $ cd canis/lupus/
    ```

3. Type **f** and press *Tab* to choose the completion **familiaris**:

    ```
    robin ~/Lesson1/data2/animals $ cd canis/lupus/familiaris/
    ```

Exercise 6: Completing a Command

In this exercise, we will use command completion to suggest commands (after each sequence here, clear the command line with *Ctrl + U* or *Alt + Backspace*):

1. Type "les" and press *Tab* to produce the completion:

   ```
   robin ~/Lesson1/data2/animals $ less
   ```

2. Type "rmd" and press *Tab* to produce the completion:

   ```
   robin ~/Lesson1/data2/animals $ rmdir
   ```

3. If we do not type enough characters, the number of possible completions may be a large one. For instance, type "g" and press *Tab* twice (it beeps the first time to indicate that there is no single completion). The shell shows a confirmation prompt before showing all possible commands that start with "g", since there are too many:

   ```
   robin ~/Lesson1/data2/animals $ g
   Display all 184 possibilities? (y or n)
   ```

   In such cases, it is more practical to say **n**, because poring over so many possibilities is time-consuming, and defeats the purpose of completion.

Exercise 7: Completing a Command using Options

In this exercise, we will use command completion using options to suggest the long options for commands (after each sequence here, clear the command line with *Ctrl + U*):

1. Type "ls --col" and press *Tab* to produce the completion:

   ```
   robin ~/Lesson1/data2/animals $ ls --color
   ```

2. Type "ls --re" and press *Tab* twice to produce the list of two possible completions:

   ```
   robin ~/Lesson1/data2/animals $ ls --re
   --recursive   --reverse
   ```

3. Then, type "c" and press *Tab* to select **--recursive** as the completion:

   ```
   robin ~/Lesson1/data2/animals $ ls --recursive
   ```

After performing these exercises, we have learned how the shell autocompletes text for us based on the context. The autocompletion is extensible, and many programs such as **docker** and **git** install completions for their commands, too.

Activity 3: Command-Line Editing

You are provided with the following list of tree species' names:

1. *Pinaceae Cedrus Deodara*

2. *Cupressaceae Thuja Aphylla*

3. *Taxaceae Taxus Baccata*

4. *Podocarpaceae Podocarpus Alba*

Each line has the family, genus, and species written like this: *Podocarpaceae Lepidothamnus Intermedius*. You need to type out each of these entries and use command-line shortcuts to convert them into a command that prints out the path of the **data.txt** file associated with the species.

You need to work out the most efficient way to compose a command, reducing typing effort and errors. Use the conifer tree sample data for this chapter that is in the **~/ Lesson1/data** folder and follow these steps to complete this activity:

1. Navigate to the **data** folder.

2. Type out a line from the file manually, for example, **Podocarpaceae Lepidothamnus Intermedius**.

3. Use as few keystrokes as possible to generate a command that prints out the name of the file associated with that species, in this case: **echo podocarpaceae/ lepidothamnus/intermedius/data.txt**.

4. Repeat steps 3 and 4 for all the entries.

You should obtain the following paths for the **data.txt** files for the given species:

```
pinaceae/cedrus/deodara/data.txt

cupressaceae/thuja/aphylla/data.txt

taxaceae/taxus/baccata/data.txt

podocarpaceae/podocarpus/alba/data.txt
```

> **Note**
>
> If you are typing any piece of text multiple times, you can save time by typing that only once and then using the cut and paste functionality. You might want to experiment with the behavior of the two "cut word" shortcuts for this particular case. The solution for this activity can be found on page 272.

In this topic, we have examined the more hands-on interactive facilities that command-line shells provide. Without the time-saving features of history, completion, and editing shortcuts, the command line would be very cumbersome. Indeed, some old primitive command shells from the 1980s such as MS-DOS lacked most, if not all, of these features, making it quite a challenge to use them effectively.

Going forward, we will delve deeper into file management operations by utilizing a powerful concept called wildcard expansion, also known as shell globbing.

Shell Wildcards and Globbing

In the preceding exercises and activities, notice that we often perform the same operation on multiple files or folders. The point of a computer is to never have to manually instruct it to do something more than once. If we perform any repeated action using a computer, there is usually some way that it can be automated to reduce the drudgery. Hence, in the context of the shell too, we need an abstraction that lets us handle a bunch of files together. This abstraction is called a **wildcard**.

The term wildcard originates from card games where a certain card can substitute for whatever card the player wishes. When any command is sent to the shell, before it is executed, the shell performs an operation called **wildcard expansion** or **globbing** on each of the strings that make up the command line. The process of globbing replaces a wildcard expression with all file or pathnames that match it.

> **Note**
>
> This wildcard expansion is not performed on any quoted strings that are quoted with single or double quotes. Quoted arguments will be discussed in detail in a future chapter.

Wildcard Syntax and Semantics

A wildcard is any string that contains any of the following special characters:

- A ? matches one occurrence of any character. For example, `?at` matches *cat*, *bat*, and *rat*, and every other three letter string that ends with "at".

- A * matches zero or more occurrences of any character. For example, `image.*` matches *image.png*, *image.jpg*, *image.bmp.zip*, and so on.

- A ! followed by a pair of parentheses containing another wildcard expands to strings that do not match the contained expression.

> **Note**
>
> The exclamation operator is an "extended glob" syntax and may not be enabled by default on your system. To enable it, the following command needs to be executed: `shopt -s extglob`.

There are a few more advanced shell glob expressions, but we will restrict ourselves to these most commonly used ones for now.

Wildcard Expansion or Globbing

When the shell encounters a wildcard expression on the command line, it is internally expanded to all the files or pathnames that match it. This process is called **globbing**. Even though it looks as though one wildcard argument is present, the shell has converted that into multiple ones before the command runs.

Note that a wildcard can match paths across the whole filesystem:

- `*` matches all the directories and files in the current directory
- `/*` matches everything in the root directory
- `/*/*` matches everything exactly two levels deep from the root directory
- `/home/*/.bashrc` matches a file named `.bashrc` that is in every user's home directory

At this point, a warning is due: this powerful matching mechanism of wildcards can end up matching files that the user never intended if the wildcard was not specified correctly. Hence, you must exercise great care when running commands that use wildcards and modify or delete files. For safety, run **echo** with the glob expression to view what files it gets expanded to. Once we are sure that the wildcard is correct, we can run the actual command that affects the files.

> **Note**
>
> Since the shell expands wildcards as individual arguments, we can run into a situation where the number of arguments exceeds the limit that the system supports. We should be aware of this limitation when using wildcards.

Let's dive into an exercise and see how we can use wildcards.

Exercise 8: Using Wildcards

In this exercise, we will practice the use of wildcards for file management by creating folders and moving files with specific file formats to those folders.

> **Note**
>
> Some of the commands used in this exercise produce many screenfuls of output, so we only show them partially or not at all.

1. Open the command line shell and navigate to the **~/Lesson1/data1** folder:

   ```
   robin ~ $ cd Lesson1/data1
   ```

   There are over 11,000 files in this folder, all of which are empty dummy files, but their names come from a set of real-world files.

2. Use a wildcard to list all the GIF files: ***.gif** matches every file that ends with **.gif**:

   ```
   robin ~/Lesson1/data1 $ ls *.gif
   ```

   The output is shown here:

   ```
   man.gif                      zandance.gif
   margarita_parrot.gif         zoidberg-dance.gif
   mario.gif                    zoidberg.gif
   mario_luigi_dance.gif        zoltar.gif
   matrix.gif                   zombie.gif
   meatwad.gif                  zombocom.gif
   meditating.gif
   ```

   Figure 1.17: A screenshot of the output displaying a list of all GIF files within the folder

3. Create a new folder named **gif**, and use the wildcard representing all GIF files to move all of them into that folder:

   ```
   robin ~/Lesson1/data1 $ mkdir gif
   robin ~/Lesson1/data1 $ mv *.gif gif
   ```

4. Verify that there are no GIF files left in the CWD:

   ```
   robin ~/Lesson1/data1 $ ls *.gif
   ls: cannot access '*.gif': No such file or directory
   ```

5. Verify that all of the GIFs are in the **gif** folder:

   ```
   robin ~/Lesson1/data1 $ ls gif/
   ```

The output is shown here:

```
robin ~/Lesson1/data1 $ ls gif
00fidget.gif                    meeseeks.gif
aaw_yeah.gif                    mega.gif
abe.gif                         megalizard.gif
aeropress.gif                   megaman.gif
agite.gif                       megamanx.gif
air_punch.gif                   merger.gif
akak.gif                        merica.gif
alert.gif                       metaknight.gif
alex_jones_meltdown.gif         metal2.gif
alienprobe.gif                  metroid.gif
allo-crying.gif                 mexa_parrot.gif
allo-drool.gif                  mic_drop_boom.gif
allo-happy.gif                  micdrop.gif
```

Figure 1.18: A screenshot of a partial output of the gif files within the folder

6. Make a new folder called **jpeg** and use multiple wildcard arguments with **mv** to move all JPEG files into that folder:

```
robin ~/Lesson1/data1 $ mkdir jpeg
robin ~/Lesson1/data1 $ mv *.jpeg *.jpg jpeg
```

7. Verify with **ls** that no JPEG files remain in the CWD:

```
robin ~/Lesson1/data1 $ ls *.jpeg *.jpg
ls: cannot access '*.jpeg': No such file or directory
ls: cannot access '*.jpg': No such file or directory
```

8. List the **jpeg** folder to verify that all the JPEGs are in it:

```
robin ~/Lesson1/data1 $ ls jpeg
```

The output is shown here:

```
robin ~/Lesson1/data1 $ ls jpeg
2cents.jpg                      mckayla.jpg
49ers.jpg                       meelo.jpg
4pda.jpg                        messi.jpg
9000.jpg                        mets.jpg
abby.jpg                        mic_drop.jpg
abradolf-lincler.jpg            microsoft.jpg
admiral_akbar.jpeg              milton.jpg
afc.jpg                         minion-fire.jpg
air-guitar_head-bang.jpg        m.jpg
a.jpg                           monopoly.jpg
ak.jpg                          mrhankey.jpeg
aks.jpg                         mr_magoo.jpg
aliensguy.jpg                   mrmeseeks.jpg
```

Figure 1.19: A screenshot of a partial output of the .jpeg files within the folder

9. List all **.so (shared object library)** files that have only a single digit as the trailing version number:

```
robin ~/Lesson1/data1 $ ls *.so.?
```

The output is shown here:

```
robin ~/Lesson1/data1 $ ls *.so.?
ld-linux.so.2                        libkopete_oscar.so.1
ld-linux-x86-64.so.2                 libkopete_otr_shared.so.1
ld-lsb.so.2                          libkopeteprivacy.so.1
ld-lsb.so.3                          libkopete.so.1
ld-lsb-x86-64.so.2                   libkopetestatusmenu.so.1
ld-lsb-x86-64.so.3                   libkopete_videodevice.so.1
liba52.so.0                          libkparts.so.4
libaa.so.1                           libkpimidentities.so.4
libabw-0.1.so.1                      libkpimtextedit.so.4
libaccounts-glib.so.0                libkpimutils.so.4
libaccounts-qt5.so.1                 libkprintutils.so.4
libaccountsservice.so.0              libkpty.so.4
libacl.so.1                          libkrad.so.0
```

Figure 1.20: A screenshot of a partial output of the .so files ending with a dot, followed by a one-character version number

10. List all files that start with "google" and have an extension;

```
robin ~/Lesson1/data1 $ ls google*.*
google_analytics.png  google_cloud_dataflow.png  google_drive.png  google_
fusion_tables.png google_maps.png  google.png
```

11. List all files that start with "a", have the third character "c", and have an extension:

```
robin ~/Lesson1/data1 $ ls a?c*.*
archer.png  archive_entry.h  archive.h  archlinux.png  avcart.png
```

12. List all of the files that do not have the **.jpg** extension:

```
robin ~/Lesson1/data1 $ ls !(*.jpg)
```

The output is shown here:

```
0.png
1000.png
10-4.png
1down.png
1password.png
1.png
1train.png
1up.png
2train.png
33.png
3train.png
42.png
4ball.png
4d.png
4train.png
5train.png
6train.png
76ers.png
```

Figure 1.21: A screenshot of a partial output of the non-.jpeg files in the folder

13. Before we conclude this exercise, get the sample data back to how it was before in preparation for the next activity. First, move the files within the **jpeg** and **gif** folders back to the current directory:

```
robin ~/Lesson1/data1 $ mv gif/* .
robin ~/Lesson1/data1 $ mv jpeg/* .
```

Then, delete the empty folders:

```
robin ~/Lesson1/data1 $ rm -r gif jpeg
```

Now, having learned the basic syntax, we can write wildcards to match almost any group of files and paths, so we rarely ever need to specify filenames individually.

Even in a GUI, it takes more effort than this to select groups of files in a file manager (for example, all .gifs) and this can be error-prone or frustrating when hundreds or thousands of files are involved.

Activity 4: Using Simple Wildcards

The supplied sample data in the **Lesson1/data1** folder has about 11,000 empty files of various types. Use wildcards to copy each file to a directory representing its category, namely *images*, *binaries*, and *misc.*, and count how many of each category exist. Through this activity, you will get familiar with using simple wildcards for file management. Follow these steps to complete this activity:

1. Create the three directories representing the categories specified.

2. Move all of the files with the extensions .**jpg**, .**jpeg**, .**gif**, and .**png** to the **images** folder.

3. Move all of the files with the extensions .**a**, .**so**, and .**so**, followed by a period and a version number, into the **binaries** folder.

4. Move the remaining files with any extension into the **misc** folder.

5. Count the files in each folder using a shell command.

You should get the following answers: 3,674 images, 5,368 binaries, and 1,665 misc.

> **Note**
>
> The solution for this activity can be found on page 273.

Activity 5: Using Directory Wildcards

The supplied sample data inside the **Lesson1/data** folder has a taxonomy of tree species. Use wildcards to get the count of the following:

1. The species whose family starts with the character **p**, and the genus has **a** as the second character.

2. The species whose family starts with the character **p**, the genus has **i** as the second character, and species has **u** as the second character.

3. The species whose family as well as genus starts with the character **t**.

This activity will help you get familiar with using simple wildcards that match directories.

Follow these steps to complete this activity:

1. Navigate to the **data** folder.

2. Use the **tree** command with a wildcard for each of the three conditions to get the count of species.

You should get the following answers: 83 species, 26 species, and 19 species.

> **Note**
>
> The solution for this activity can be found on page 273.

Summary

We have introduced a lot of material in this first chapter, which is probably quite novel to anyone approaching the command line for the first time. Even in this brief exploration, we can start to see how seemingly complicated filesystem tasks can be completed with minimal effort.

In the coming chapter, we will add to our toolbox of useful shell programs that process text data. In later chapters, we will learn about the mechanisms to tie these commands together, such as piping and redirection, to perform complex data-processing tasks. We will also learn about regular expressions and shell expansion constructs that let us manipulate textual data in powerful ways.

Command-Line Building Blocks

Learning Objectives

By the end of the chapter, you will be able to:

- Use redirection to control command input and output
- Construct pipelines between commands
- Use commands for text filtering
- Use text transformation commands
- Analyze tabular data using data-processing commands

This chapter introduces you to the two main composing mechanisms of command lines: redirection and piping. You will also expand your vocabulary of commands to be able to perform a wide variety of data-processing tasks.

Introduction

So far, we have learned the basics of how to work with the filesystem with the shell. We also looked at some shell mechanisms such as wildcards and completion that simplify life in the command line. In this chapter, we will examine the building blocks that are used to perform data-processing tasks on the shell.

The Unix approach is to favor small, single-purpose utilities with very well-defined interfaces. Redirection and pipes let us connect these small commands and files together so that we can compose them like the elements of an electronic circuit to perform complex tasks. This concept of joining together small units into a more complex mechanism is a very powerful technique.

Most data that we typically work with is textual in nature, so we will study the most useful text-oriented commands in this chapter, along with various practical examples of their usage.

Redirection

Redirection is a method of connecting files to a command. This mechanism is used to capture the output of a command or to feed input to it.

> **Note**
>
> During this section, we will introduce a few commands briefly, in order to illustrate some concepts. The commands are only used as examples, and their usage does not have any connection to the main topics being covered here. The detailed descriptions of all the features and uses of those commands will be covered in the topic on text-processing commands.

Input and Output Streams

Every command that is run has a channel for data input, termed **standard input** (`stdin`), data output, termed **standard output** (`stdout`) and **standard error** (`stderr`). A command reads data from `stdin` and writes its results to `stdout`. If any error occurs, the error messages are written to `stderr`. These channels can also be thought of as streams through which data flows.

By convention, `stdin`, `stdout`, and `stderr` are assigned the numbers 0, 1, and 2, which are called **file descriptors** (**FDs**). We will not go into the technical details of these, but remember the association between these streams and their FD numbers.

When a command is run interactively, the shell attaches the input and output streams to the console input and output, respectively. Note that, by default, both **stdout** and **stderr** go to the console display.

> **Note**
>
> The terms *console*, *terminal*, and *TTY* are often used interchangeably. In essence, they refer to the interface where commands are typed, and output is produced as text. Console or terminal output refers to what the command prints out. Console or terminal input refers to what the user types in.

For instance, when we use **ls** to list an existing and non-existing folder from the dataset we used in the previous chapter, we get the following output:

```
robin ~/Lesson1/data $ ls podocarpaceae/ nonexistent

ls: cannot access 'nonexistent': No such file or directory

podocarpaceae/:

acmopyle      dacrydium      lagarostrobos  margbensonia  parasitaxus
podocarpus    saxegothaea

afrocarpus    falcatifolium  lepidothamnus  microcachrys  pherosphaera
prumnopitys   stachycarpus

dacrycarpus   halocarpus     manoao         nageia        phyllocladus
retrophyllum  sundacarpus
```

Note the error message that appears on the first line of the output. This is due to the **stderr** stream reaching the console, whereas the remaining output is from **stdout**. The outputs from both channels are combined.

Use of Operators for Redirection

We can tell the shell to connect any of the aforementioned streams to a file using the following operators:

- The **>** or greater-than symbol is used to specify *output redirection* to a file, and is used as follows:

  ```
  command >file.txt
  ```

  This instructs the shell to redirect the **stdout** of a command into a file. If the file already exists, its content is overwritten.

- The **>>** symbol is used to specify *output redirection with append*, appending data to a file, as follows:

  ```
  command >>file.txt
  ```

  This instructs the shell to redirect the **stdout** of command into a file. If the file does not exist, it is created, but if the file exists, then it gets appended to, rather than overwritten, unlike the previous case.

- The **<** or less-than symbol is used to specify *input redirection* from a file. The syntax is as follows:

  ```
  command <file.txt
  ```

  This instructs the shell to redirect a file to the **stdin** of the command.

In the preceding syntax, you can prefix the number of an FD before **<**, **>**, or **>>**, which lets us redirect the stream corresponding to that FD. If no FD is specified, the defaults are **stdin** (FD 0) and **stdout** (FD 1) for input and output, respectively. Typically, the FD prefix 2 is used to redirect **stderr**.

> **Note**
>
> To redirect both **stdout** and **stderr** to the same file, the special operator **&>** is used.

When the shell runs one of the preceding commands, it first opens the files to/from which redirection is requested, attaches the streams to the command, and then runs it. Even if a command produces no output, if output redirection is requested, then the file is created (or truncated).

Using Multiple Redirections

Both input and output redirection can be specified for the same command, so a command can be considered as consisting of the following parts (of which the redirections are optional):

- **stdin** redirection
- **stdout** redirection
- **stderr** redirection
- The command itself, along with its options and other arguments

A key insight is that the order in which these parts appear in the command line does not matter. For example, consider the following **sort** commands (the **sort** command reads a file via **stdin**, sorts the lines, and writes it to **stdout**):

```
sort >sorted.txt <data.txt

sort <data.txt >sorted.txt

<data.txt >sorted.txt sort
```

All of these three commands are valid syntax and perform the exact same action, that is, the content of **data.txt** is redirected into the **sort** command and the output of that in turn is written into the **sorted.txt** file.

It is a matter of individual style or preference as to how these redirection elements are ordered. The conventional way of writing it, which is the style encountered most frequently and considered most readable, is in this order:

```
command <input_redirect_file >output_redirect_file
```

A space is sometimes added between the redirection symbol and the filename. For example, we could write the following:

```
sort < data.txt > sorted.txt
```

This is perfectly valid. However, from a conceptual level, it is convenient to think of the symbol and the file as a single command-line element, and to write it as follows:

```
sort <data.txt >sorted.txt
```

This is to emphasize that the filenames **data.txt** and **sorted.txt** are attached to the respective streams, that is, **stdin** and **stdout**. Remember that the symbol is always written first, followed by the filename. The symbol points to the direction of the data flow, which is either from or into the file.

Heredocs and Herestrings

A useful convention that most commands follow is that they accept a command-line argument for the input file, but if the argument is omitted, the input data is read from **stdin** instead. This lets commands easily be used both with redirection (and piping) as well as in a standalone manner. For example, consider the following:

```
less file.txt
```

This **less** command gets the filename **file.txt** passed as an argument, which it then opens and displays. Now, consider the following:

```
less <file.txt
```

For this second case, the shell does not treat **<file.txt** as an argument to be passed to **less**–instead, it is an instruction to the shell to redirect **file.txt** to the **stdin** of **less**. When **less** runs, it sees no arguments passed to it, and therefore, it defaults to reading data from **stdin** to display, rather than opening any file. Since **stdin** was connected to **file.txt**, it achieves the same function as the first command.

When a command reads input from **stdin** and is not redirected, it accepts lines of text typed by the user until the user presses *Ctrl + D*. The shell interprets that keystroke and signals an **end-of-file** (**EOF**) to the program, causing the input stream to stop, and the program exits.

Here documents (also called **heredocs**) is a special form of redirection that lets you feed multiple lines of text to a command in a similar way, but rather than requiring *Ctrl + D* to signal EOF, you can specify an arbitrary string instead. This feature is especially useful in shell scripts, which we will cover in later chapters. A traditional example of using **here documents** is to type a mail directly into the **sendmail** program to compose and send a mail from the command line itself, without using an editor.

The syntax for **heredocs** is as follows:

```
command <<LIMITSTRING
```

Here, **LIMITSTRING** can be any arbitrary string. Upon typing this, the shell prompts for multiple lines of text, until the limit string is typed on its own line, after which the shell runs the command, passing in all the lines that were typed into the command.

Here strings (also called **herestrings**) is yet another form of input redirection. It allows passage of a single string as input to a command, as if it were redirected from a file. The syntax for **herestrings** is as follows:

```
command <<< INPUT
```

Here, **INPUT** is the string to be passed into the program's **stdin**. If the string is quoted, it can extend over multiple lines.

Buffering

Now, let's talk about a concept called **buffering**, which applies to both redirection and piping. A buffer can be considered analogous to a flush tank for data. Water flows in until the tank is full, after which the valve closes, and the flow of water is blocked. When water drains out of the tank, the valve opens to let the water fill the tank again. The following are the buffers connected to the input and output streams.

stdout buffer

Every program has a buffer connected to its `stdout`, and the program writes its output data into this buffer. When the buffer gets full, the program cannot write any more output, and is put to sleep. We say that this program has *blocked on a write*.

The other end of a command's `stdout` buffer could be connected to the following:

- A file, when redirecting output
- The console, when running directly
- Another command, when pipes are used (we will cover pipes in the next section)

In each case, an independent process deals with taking the data out of this buffer and moving it to the other end. When the buffer has enough space for the blocked write to succeed, the program is woken up or unblocked.

stdin buffer

In a symmetric fashion, every program has a buffer connected to its `stdin`, and the program reads data from this buffer. When the buffer is empty, the program cannot read any more input, and is put to sleep. We say that this program has *blocked on a read*.

The other end of a command's `stdin` buffer could be connected to the following:

- A file, when redirecting input
- The input typed by the user, when running directly
- Another command, when pipes are used

Once again, an independent process deals with filling this buffer with data. When the buffer has enough data for the blocked read to succeed, the program is woken up or unblocked.

The main reason to use buffering is for efficiency—moving data in larger chunks across an input or output channel is efficient. A process can quickly read or write an entire chunk of data from/to a buffer, and continue working, rather than getting blocked. This ensures maximum throughput and parallelism.

Flushing

A program can request a **flush** on its output buffer, which makes it sleep until the output buffer gets emptied. Flushing an input buffer works in a different way. It simply causes all the data in the input buffer to get discarded.

A command has a buffer for each of its input as well as output streams. These buffers can operate in three modes:

- **Unbuffered**: A process immediately blocks when reading or writing if the other end of the stream is not writing or reading, respectively. This is equivalent to flushing immediately after every write.

- **Line buffered**: The buffer is flushed whenever a newline character is encountered.

- **Fully buffered**: The buffer is not flushed. The program tries to write as much as possible and blocks when it can't. The size of the buffer can be set to any arbitrary value by the program.

The choice of buffering modes of a command depends on the task that a program does; for example, almost all text files are typically processed line by line. Text-based commands tend to always use line buffering so that a processed line of text is immediately displayed.

Consider a program that reads the error logs of a web server and filters out the lines that refer to a certain error (for example, a failure of authentication). It would typically read an entire line, check if it met the criteria, and if so print the whole line at once. The output would never contain partial lines.

On the other hand, there are some commands that deal with binary data that is not divisible into lines—these use full buffering, so that transfer speed is maximized.

There are a few applications where a completely unbuffered I/O is used. It can be useful in some very narrow situations. For example, some programs draw user interfaces on text screens using ANSI codes. In such cases, the display needs to be updated instantly in order to provide a usable interface, which unbuffered output allows. Another example is the SSH (secure shell) program, which lets a user access a command-line shell on another computer across the internet. Every keystroke the user types is instantaneously sent to the remote end, and the resultant output is sent back. Here, unbuffered I/O is essential for SSH to provide the feeling of interactivity.

> **Note**
>
> By default, the shell sets up the **stderr** of a command to be unbuffered, since error messages need to be displayed or logged immediately. **stdout** is set up to be line buffered when writing to the console, but fully buffered when being redirected to a file.

In the next section, which covers pipes, we will learn how shell pipelines connect multiple processes as a chain, each of which has its own buffers for **stdin** and **stdout**.

Exercise 9: Working with Command Redirection

We will now use input and output redirection with basic commands. After this exercise, you should be able to capture the output of any command to a file, or conversely feed a file into a command that requires input:

1. Open the command-line shell, navigate to the **data** folder from *Chapter 1, Introduction to the Command Line*, and get a listing:

```
robin ~ $ cd Lesson1/data
robin ~/Lesson1/data $ ls -l
total 16
drwxr-xr-x 36 robin robin 4096 Aug 20 14:01 cupressaceae
drwxr-xr-x 15 robin robin 4096 Aug 20 14:01 pinaceae
drwxr-xr-x 23 robin robin 4096 Aug 20 14:01 podocarpaceae
drwxr-xr-x  8 robin robin 4096 Aug 20 14:01 taxaceae
```

2. Redirect the standard output of **ls** into a file called **dir.txt** and use **cat** to view its contents:

```
robin ~/Lesson1/data $ ls -l >dir.txt
robin ~/Lesson1/data $ cat dir.txt
total 16
drwxr-xr-x 36 robin robin 4096 Aug 20 14:01 cupressaceae
-rw-r--r--  1 robin robin    0 Aug 27 17:13 dir.txt
drwxr-xr-x 15 robin robin 4096 Aug 20 14:01 pinaceae
drwxr-xr-x 23 robin robin 4096 Aug 20 14:01 podocarpaceae
drwxr-xr-x  8 robin robin 4096 Aug 20 14:01 taxaceae
```

Note that when we print the contents of **dir.txt**, we can see an entry for **dir.txt** itself, with a size of zero. Yet obviously **dir.txt** is not empty, since we just printed it. This is a little confusing, but the explanation is simple. The shell first creates an empty **dir.txt** file, and then runs **ls**, redirecting its **stdout** to that file. **ls** gets the list of this directory, which at this point includes an empty **dir.txt**, and writes the list into its **stdout**, which in turn ends up as the content of **dir.txt**. Hence the contents of **dir.txt** reflect the state of the directory at the instant when **ls** ran.

3. Next, run **ls** with a bogus directory, as shown in the following code, and observe what happens:

```
robin ~/Lesson1/data $ ls -l nonexistent >dir.txt
ls: cannot access 'nonexistent': No such file or directory
robin ~/Lesson1/data $ ls -l
total 16
drwxr-xr-x 36 robin robin 4096 Aug 20 14:01 cupressaceae
-rw-r--r--  1 robin robin    0 Aug 27 17:19 dir.txt
drwxr-xr-x 15 robin robin 4096 Aug 20 14:01 pinaceae
drwxr-xr-x 23 robin robin 4096 Aug 20 14:01 podocarpaceae
drwxr-xr-x  8 robin robin 4096 Aug 20 14:01 taxaceae
```

From the preceding output, we can observe that the error message arrived on the console, but did not get redirected into the file. This is because we only redirected **stdout** to **dir.txt**. Note that **dir.txt** is empty, because there was no data written to **stdout** by **ls**.

4. Next, use **>** to create a file with the listing of the **pinaceae** folder, and then use **>>** to append the listing of the **taxaceae** folder to it:

    ```
    robin ~/Lesson1/data $ ls -l pinaceae/ >dir.txt
    robin ~/Lesson1/data $ ls -l taxaceae/ >>dir.txt
    robin ~/Lesson1/data $ cat dir.txt
    ```

    You will see the following output displayed on the console:

    ```
    total 52
    drwxr-xr-x  58 robin robin 4096 Sep  5 15:49 abies
    drwxr-xr-x   3 robin robin 4096 Sep  5 15:49 cathaya
    drwxr-xr-x   5 robin robin 4096 Sep  5 15:49 cedrus
    drwxr-xr-x   3 robin robin 4096 Sep  5 15:49 hesperopeuce
    drwxr-xr-x   6 robin robin 4096 Sep  5 15:49 keteleeria
    drwxr-xr-x  24 robin robin 4096 Sep  5 15:49 larix
    drwxr-xr-x   3 robin robin 4096 Sep  5 15:49 nothotsuga
    drwxr-xr-x  50 robin robin 4096 Sep  5 15:49 picea
    drwxr-xr-x 159 robin robin 4096 Sep  5 15:49 pinus
    drwxr-xr-x   3 robin robin 4096 Sep  5 15:49 pseudolarix
    drwxr-xr-x   6 robin robin 4096 Sep  5 15:49 pseudotsuga
    drwxr-xr-x   3 robin robin 4096 Sep  5 15:49 strobus
    drwxr-xr-x  13 robin robin 4096 Sep  5 15:49 tsuga
    total 24
    drwxr-xr-x   8 robin robin 4096 Sep  5 15:49 amentotaxus
    drwxr-xr-x   3 robin robin 4096 Sep  5 15:49 austrotaxus
    drwxr-xr-x  12 robin robin 4096 Sep  5 15:49 cephalotaxus
    drwxr-xr-x   3 robin robin 4096 Sep  5 15:49 pseudotaxus
    drwxr-xr-x  14 robin robin 4096 Sep  5 15:49 taxus
    drwxr-xr-x   9 robin robin 4096 Sep  5 15:49 torreya
    ```

    Figure 2.1: Contents of `dir.txt` after append redirection

5. Now, use **2>** to redirect **stderr** to a file. Try the following command:

    ```
    robin ~/Lesson1/data $ ls -l nonexistent taxaceae 2>dir.txt
    taxaceae/:
    total 24
    drwxr-xr-x   8 robin robin 4096 Aug 20 14:01 amentotaxus
    drwxr-xr-x   3 robin robin 4096 Aug 20 14:01 austrotaxus
    drwxr-xr-x  12 robin robin 4096 Aug 20 14:01 cephalotaxus
    drwxr-xr-x   3 robin robin 4096 Aug 20 14:01 pseudotaxus
    drwxr-xr-x  14 robin robin 4096 Aug 20 14:01 taxus
    drwxr-xr-x   9 robin robin 4096 Aug 20 14:01 torreya

    robin ~/Lesson1/data $ cat dir.txt
    ls: cannot access 'nonexistent': No such file or directory
    ```

    Note that only the error message on **stderr** got redirected into **dir.txt**.

6. You can also redirect **stderr** and **stdout** to separate files, as shown in the following code:

```
robin ~/Lesson1/data $ ls pinaceae nosuchthing >out.txt 2>err.txt
```

Use the **cat** command to view the output of the two files:

```
robin ~/Lesson1/data $ cat out.txt
pinaceae/:
abies
cathaya
cedrus
hesperopeuce
keteleeria
larix
nothotsuga
picea
pinus
pseudolarix
pseudotsuga
strobus
tsuga
robin ~/Lesson1/data $ cat err.txt
ls: cannot access 'nosuchthing': No such file or directory
```

Figure 2.2: Contents of **out.txt** and **err.txt** showing independent redirection of **stdout** and **stderr**

7. Alternatively, you can redirect both **stdout** and **stderr** to the same file. Try the following command:

```
robin ~/Lesson1/data $ ls pinaceae nothing &>dir.txt
```

You will see the following output if you view the contents of **dir.txt** with the **cat** command:

```
robin ~/Lesson1/data $ cat dir.txt
ls: cannot access 'nothing': No such file or directory
pinaceae:
abies
cathaya
cedrus
hesperopeuce
keteleeria
larix
nothotsuga
picea
pinus
pseudolarix
pseudotsuga
strobus
tsuga
```

Figure 2.3: Contents of the file with both stdout and stderr redirected

Note

The error message precedes the output because **ls** attempts to list the directories in lexicographical order. The **nothing** folder was attempted to be listed first, and then **pinaceae**.

8. Now, let's use input redirection with the **cat** command. When passed the **-n** flag, it adds line numbers to each line. Type the following commands:

```
robin ~/Lesson1/data $ cat -n <pinaceae/pinus/sylvestris/data.txt
>numbered.txt
robin ~/Lesson1/data $ less numbered.txt
```

9. Run the **cat** command without any arguments, type out the lines of text, and finally use *Ctrl + D* to end the process:

```
robin ~/Lesson1/data $ cat
Hello
Hello
Bye
Bye
^D
```

10. Run **cat** in a similar fashion, but use a here document syntax, with the limit string **DONE**, as follows:

```
robin ~/Lesson1/data $ cat <<DONE
> This is some text
> Some more text
> OK, enough
> DONE
This is some text
Some more text
OK, enough
```

> **Note**
>
> Observe the difference between steps 9 and 10. In step 9, **cat** processes each line that is typed and prints it back immediately. This is because the TTY (which is connected to the **stdin** of **cat**) waits for the *Enter* key to be pressed before it writes the complete line into the **stdin** of **cat**. Thereupon, **cat** outputs that line, emptying its input buffer, and goes to sleep until the next line arrives. In step 10, the TTY is connected to the shell itself, rather than to the **cat** process. The shell is, in turn, connected to **cat** and does not send any data to it until the limit string is encountered, after which the entire text that was typed goes into **cat** at once.

11. The **bc** command is an interactive calculator. We can use a herestring to make it do a simple calculation. Type the following to get the seventh power of 1234:

```
robin ~/Lesson1/data $ bc <<< 1234^7
4357186184021382204544
```

When run directly, **bc** accepts multiple expressions and prints the result. In this case, the herestring is treated as a file's content by the shell and is passed into **bc** via **stdin** redirection.

12. Finally, delete the temporary files that we created:

```
robin ~/Lesson1/data $ rm *.txt
```

In this exercise, we learned how to redirect the input and output of shell commands to files. Using files as the input and output of commands is essential to performing more complex shell tasks.

Pipes

A **shell pipeline** or simply a **pipeline** refers to a construct where data is pushed from one command to another in an assembly line fashion. It is expressed as a series of commands separated by a **pipe** symbol |. These pipes connect the **stdout** of each command to the **stdin** of the subsequent command. Internally, a pipe is a special memory **FIFO** (first in, first out) buffer provided by the OS.

The basic syntax of a pipeline is as follows:

```
command1 | command2
```

Any number of commands can be linked:

```
command1 | command2 | command3 | command4
```

Pipelines are analogous to assembly lines in a factory. Like an assembly line lets multiple workers simultaneously do one designated job repeatedly, ending up with a finished product, a pipeline lets a series of commands work on a stream of data, each doing one task, eventually leading to the desired output.

Pipelines ensure maximum throughput and optimal usage of computing power. The time taken for a pipeline task in most cases will be close to the time taken by the slowest command in it, and not the sum of the times for all the commands.

> **Note**
>
> While it is not a very common use case, you can pipe both **stdout** and **stderr** of one command into another command's **stdin** using the |& operator.

Exercise 10: Working with Pipes

In this exercise, we will explore the use of pipes to pass data between commands. Some new commands will be introduced briefly, which will be explained in more detail later:

1. Open the command-line shell and navigate to the data folder from the first exercise:

    ```
    robin ~ $ cd Lesson1/data
    robin ~/Lesson1/data $
    ```

2. The simplest use of pipes is to pipe the output of a command to **less**, as follows:

    ```
    robin ~/Lesson1/data $ tree | less
    ```

    You will get the following output:

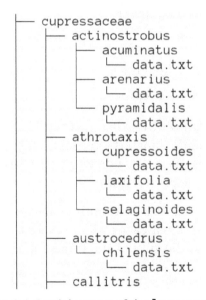

    Figure 2.4: Partial output of the **less** command

3. The **tr** command (which stands for translate) can change the contents of each line based on a rule. Here, we will be converting lowercase text to uppercase text. Type the following command to view the output of **ls** in uppercase:

    ```
    robin ~/Lesson1/data $ ls | tr '[:lower:]' '[:upper:]'
    CUPRESSACEAE
    PINACEAE
    PODOCARPACEAE
    TAXACEAE
    ```

As a general guideline, we should use single quotes for string arguments, unless we have a reason to use other kinds.

4. You can use multiple commands in the same pipeline. Pipe **tree** into **tr** (to convert to uppercase) and then into **less** for viewing, as shown here:

```
robin ~/Lesson1/data $ tree | tr '[:lower:]' '[:upper:]' | less
```

You will get the following output:

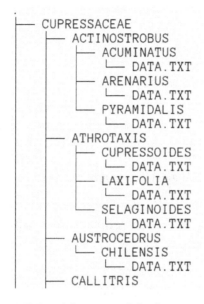

Figure 2.5: Partial output of the less command

5. You can also combine pipes and redirection. Redirect a file into **sort** and pipe its output to **uniq**, and then into **less** for viewing. The **uniq** command removes repeated lines (we will study it in more detail in the next topic):

```
robin ~/Lesson1/data $ cd pinaceae/nothotsuga/longibracteata/
robin ~/Lesson1/data/pinaceae/nothotsuga/longibracteata $ sort <data.txt |
uniq | less
```

The output is as follows:

```
*    *
*  ??
*  ?????
*  ???????
*  ??????????
   * 1.1 Taxonomy
   1. ^ a b Farjon, A., Christian, T. & Zhang, D 2013. Nothots
tember 2015.
   * 1 Description
   * 2 Conservation
   * 3 References
   * 4 Further reading
   * 5 External links
6-8 months after pollination.
   * Abies
   * About Wikipedia
and from Keteleeria by the shorter leaves and smaller cones.
   * Arboretum de Villardebelle - photo of cones
are flat, needle-like, 1.2-4 cm (0.5-1.6 in) long and 1-2 mm
```

Figure 2.6: Partial output of the less command

6. Create a similar pipeline by first using **tr** to convert text from the **data.txt** file to uppercase before sorting, and then redirect the output to the **test.txt** file. View the file with **less** and delete it afterward. Type the following commands:

```
robin ~/Lesson1/data/pinaceae/nothotsuga/longibracteata $ tr '[:lower:]'
'[:upper:]' <data.txt | sort | uniq >test.txt
robin ~/Lesson1/data/pinaceae/nothotsuga/longibracteata $ less test.txt
robin ~/Lesson1/data/pinaceae/nothotsuga/longibracteata $ rm test.txt
```

You will get the following output:

```
*    *
*  ??
*  ?????
*  ???????
*  ??????????
   *  1.1 TAXONOMY
1. ^ A B FARJON, A., CHRISTIAN, T. & ZHANG, D 2013. NOTHOTS
TEMBER 2015.
   *  1 DESCRIPTION
   *  2 CONSERVATION
   *  3 REFERENCES
   *  4 FURTHER READING
   *  5 EXTERNAL LINKS
6-8 MONTHS AFTER POLLINATION.
   *  ABIES
   *  ABOUT WIKIPEDIA
AND FROM KETELEERIA BY THE SHORTER LEAVES AND SMALLER CONES.
   *  ARBORETUM DE VILLARDEBELLE - PHOTO OF CONES
ARE FLAT, NEEDLE-LIKE, 1.2-4 CM (0.5-1.6 IN) LONG AND 1-2 MM
```

Figure 2.7: Partial output of the **less** command

7. Navigate back to the data folder, then run **ls** with the **-R** flag (recursive list) and provide the current directory, as well as a non-existent directory, as arguments to make it generate a listing as well as an error message. The **|&** operator pipes both **stdout** and **stderr** into **less**:

```
robin ~/Lesson1/data/pinaceae/nothotsuga/longibracteata $ cd -
/home/robin/Lesson1/data
robin ~/Lesson1/data $ ls -R . nosuchthing |& less
```

Both the listing and the error message are visible in **less**. This would not be the case when using **|** rather than **|&**.

In this exercise, we have looked at how to build shell pipelines to stream data through multiple commands. Pipes are probably the single most important feature of shells and must be understood thoroughly. So far, we have studied the following:

- Input and output streams

- Redirecting them to and from files

- Buffering

- Use of pipes for connecting a series of commands

- Combining both redirection and pipes

Redirection and piping are essentially like performing plumbing with data instead of water. One major difference is that this command pipelining does not have multiple branches in the flow, unlike plumbing. After a little practice, using pipes becomes second nature to a shell user. The fact that shell commands often work in parallel means that some data-processing tasks can be done faster with the shell than with specialized GUI tools. This topic prepares us for the next one, where we will learn a number of text-processing commands, and how to combine them for various tasks.

Text-Processing Commands

In the previous sections, we learned about the two main composing mechanisms of command lines: redirection and piping. In this topic, we will expand our vocabulary of commands that, when combined, let us do a wide variety of data-processing tasks.

We focus on text-processing because it applies to a wide range of real-life data, and will be useful to professionals in any field. A huge amount of data on the internet is in textual form, and text happens to be the easiest way to share data in a portable way as simple columnar **CSV** (**comma-separated values**) or **TSV** (**tab-separated values**) files. Once you learn these commands, you do not have to rely on the knowledge of any specific software GUI tool, and you can run complex tasks on the shell itself. In many cases, running a quick shell pipeline is much faster than setting up the data in a more complex GUI tool. In a later chapter, you will learn how to save your commands as a sort of automatic recipe, with shell scripts, which can be reused whenever you need, and shared with others too.

> **Note**
>
> Some of the commands we will learn now are quite complex and versatile. In fact, there are entire books devoted to them. In this book, we will only look at some of the most commonly used commands' features.

Shell Input Concepts

Before moving on to the commands, let's get familiar with some nuances of how the shell command line works when we need to input text.

Escaping

Often, we need to enter strings that contain special characters in the command line:

- Characters that mean something to the shell, such as * ? & < > | " ' ( ) { } [ ] ! $

- Characters that are not printable, such as spaces, tabs, newlines, and so on

If we were to use these characters directly, the shell would interpret them, causing undesirable behavior since each of these has a special meaning to the shell. To handle this, we use a mechanism called **escaping** (which is also used in most programming languages). Escaping involves prefixing with an **escape character**, which allows us to *escape* to a different context, where the meaning of a symbol is no longer interpreted but treated as a literal character.

On the command line, the backslash \ serves as the escape character. You need to simply prefix a backslash to enter a special character literally as part of a string. For example, consider the following command:

```
echo * *
```

Since the asterisk is a special character (a wildcard symbol), instead of printing two asterisks, the command will print all the names of all the files and directories in the current directory twice. To print the asterisk character literally, you need to write the following:

```
echo \* \*
```

The two asterisks have now been *escaped*, and will not be interpreted by the shell. They are printed literally, but the backslashes are not printed. This escaping with a backslash works for any character.

Escaping works with spaces, too. For example, the following code will pass the entire filename **My little pony.txt** to **cat**:

```
cat My\ little\ pony.txt
```

It should now be obvious that you can create filenames and paths that contain special characters, but in general, this is best avoided. The unintended consequences of special characters in filenames can be quite perplexing.

Quoting

The shell provides another means of typing a string with special characters. Simply enclose it with single quotes (**strong quoting**) or double quotes (**weak quoting**). For example, look at the following commands:

```
ls "one two"
ls 'one two'
ls one two
```

In the preceding commands, the first two pass a single argument to **ls**, whereas the third passes two arguments. The basic use of single and double quotes is as follows:

• Single quotes tell the shell to consider everything within them literally, and not interpret anything, not even escaping. This means that a single quote itself cannot be embedded within a single quoted string. The string starts at the opening quote character and goes on until the closing quote. Any backslashes within are printed literally. Look at the example below:

```
echo 'This is a backslash \'
This is a backslash \
```

• Double quotes, on the other hand, allow escape sequences within so that you can embed a double quote within a double-quoted string. For example, look at thr following command and its output:

```
echo "This \" was escaped"
This " was escaped
```

Within double quotes, the shell treats everything as literal, except backslashes (escaping), exclamation marks (history expansion), dollars (shell expansion), or the backtick (command substitution). We will deal with the latter three special symbols and their effects in later chapters.

Yet another quoting mechanism provided by Bash is called **dollar-single-quotes**, which are described in the following section.

Escape Sequences

Escape sequences are a generalized way of inserting any character into a string. Normally, we can only type the symbols available on the keyboard, but escape sequences allow us to insert any possible character. These escape sequences only work in strings with dollar-single-quotes. These strings are expressed by prefixing a dollar symbol before a single-quoted string. , for example, as shown below:

```
$'Hello'
```

Within such strings, the same rules as those for single quotes apply, except that escape sequences are expanded by the shell.

> **Note**
>
> When using escape sequences in arguments, if we use strings with dollar-single-quotes, the shell inserts the corresponding symbols before passing the argument to the command. However, some commands can understand escape sequences themselves. In such cases, we may notice that escape sequences are used within single-quoted strings. In these cases, the command itself expands them internally.

Escape sequences originated in the C programming language, and the Bash shell uses the same convention. An escape sequence consists of a backslash followed by a character or a special code. Now, let's look at the list of escape sequences and their meaning, classified into two categories:

The first category is literal characters:

- \" produces a double-quote
- \' produces a single-quote
- \\ produces a backslash
- \NNN produces the ASCII character whose value is the octal value NNN (one to three octal digits)
- \xHH produces the ASCII character whose value is the hexadecimal value HH (one or two hex digits)
- \uXXXX interprets XXXX as a hexadecimal number and prints the corresponding Unicode character in the range U+0000 to U+FFFF
- \UXXXXXXXX interprets XXXXXXXX as a hexadecimal number and prints the corresponding Unicode character in the range U+10000 onward

When the **ASCII code** was initially standardized, it consisted of seven-bit numbers, which represent 128 symbols: 32 control codes, 26 English alphabets, 10 digits, and several symbols. Later, ASCII was extended to eight bits (one byte), which added another 128 characters and was the common standard for decades until the necessity for non-English text ushered in Unicode. Unicode has several thousand symbols defined by a 32-bit or 16-bit number to represent all the characters of almost all written languages of the world.

The second category of escape sequences are ASCII control characters:

In the original ASCII code, the symbols 0 to 31 (which are not printable characters) were control codes that were sent to a mechanical TTY. Traditionally, TTY terminals were like electric typewriters. To wrap around at the end of a line, the carriage had to return to the right (the home position) and the platen had to rotate to advance the paper to the next line. These operations are called **carriage return** and **line feed** with the mnemonics CR and LF, respectively. Similarly, *tab*, *form feed*, *vertical tab*, and so on referred to instructions to move the TTY's carriage and platen.

The following escape codes produce these control characters:

- **\a** produces a terminal alert or bell. The system makes an audible beep when this character is printed to the console.

- **\b** produces a backspace.

- **\e** produces an ASCII 27 character. This is called an **ESCAPE** character, but it has no relation to the term *escape* that we are discussing here in the context of Bash.

- **\f** produces a form feed.

- **\n** produces a newline or linefeed.

- **\r** produces a carriage return.

- **\t** produces a horizontal tab.

- **\v** produces a vertical tab.

The effect of printing these control characters to a console has a similar effect to what it would have on a mechanical TTY with a roll of paper—even the bell character, which activated an actual physical bell or beeper, is still emulated today on a modern shell console window.

An important practical detail to learn in this context is the difference between the DOS/Windows family operating systems and UNIX-based operating systems when they deal with line endings in text files. Traditionally, UNIX always used only the *LF* character (ASCII 10) to represent the end of a line. If an *LF* is printed to a console on UNIX-like operating systems, the cursor moves to the start of the next line. In the DOS/Windows world, however, the end of a line is represented by two characters, *CR LF*. This means that when a text file is created on one OS family and opened or processed on the other, they may fail to display or process correctly, since the definition of what represents a line ending differs. These conventions came into being due to complex historical events, but we are forever stuck with them.

Interestingly, the original Apple macOS used the convention of using only CR, but thankfully, modern MacOS and iOS are derived from FreeBSD Unix, so we don't have to deal with this third variety of line ending. The consequence of this is that our commands and scripts based on UNIX lineage may go haywire if they encounter text files created on the Windows OS family. If we need our scripts to work with data from all sources, we must take care of that explicitly.

For a file that originated on a Windows system, we must replace the sequence \r\n (CR LF) with the sequence \n (LF) before processing it with commands that work on a line-by-line basis. We may also have to do the inverse before we transfer that file back to a Windows system. Most editors, web browsers, and other tools that deal with text files are smart enough to allow for the display or editing of both kinds of files properly.

Another application of escape sequences is to send special characters to the console, called **ANSI codes**, which can change the text color, move the cursor to arbitrary locations, and so on. ANSI codes are an extension of the TTY-based control codes for early video-based displays called virtual terminals. They were typically CRT screens that showed 80 columns and 25 lines of text. They are expressed as an ASCII 27 (ESCAPE) or \e, followed by several characters describing the action to be performed.

These ANSI codes work just the same even today and are useful for producing colorized text or crude graphical elements on the console, such as progress bars. Commands such as **ls** produce their colored output by the same mechanism by simply printing out the right ANSI codes.

We will not cover the details of ANSI codes and their usage, as it is beyond the scope of this book.

Multiline Input

The final feature of shell input we will discuss is multiline commands and multiline strings. When entering an extremely long command line, for readability's sake, we might like to split it into multiple lines. We can achieve this by typing a single backslash at any time and pressing the *Enter* key. Instead of executing the command, the shell prompts for the continuation of the command on the next line. Look at the example below:

```
robin ~ $ echo this is a very long command, let me extend \
> to the next line and then \
> once again
this is a very long command, let me extend to the next line and then once
again
```

The backslash must be the last character of the line for this to work, and a command can be divided into as many lines as desired, with the line breaks having no effect on the command.

In a similar fashion, we can enter a literal multiline string containing newlines, simply by using quotes. Although they appear like multiline commands, multiline strings do not ignore the newlines that are typed. The rules for single and double quoted strings described earlier apply for multiline strings as well. For example:

```
robin ~ $ echo 'First line
> Second line
> Last line'
First line
Second line
Last line
```

Filtering Commands

Commands of this category operate by reading the input line by line, transforming it, and (optionally) producing an output line for each input line. They can be considered analogous to a filtering process.

Concatenate Files: cat

The **cat** command is primarily meant for concatenating files and for viewing small files, but it can also perform some useful line-oriented transformations on the input data. We have used **cat** before, but there are some options it provides that are quite useful. The long and short versions of some of these options are as follows:

- **-n, --number**: Numbers output lines. The numbers are padded with spaces and followed by a tab.
- **-b, --number-nonblank**: Numbers nonempty output lines, and overrides **-n**.
- **-s, --squeeze-blank**: Removes repeated empty output lines.
- **-E, --show-ends**: Displays **$** at the end of each line.
- **-T, --show-tabs**: Displays tab characters as **^I**.

Among the preceding options, the numbering options are particularly useful.

Translate: tr

The **tr** command works like a translator, reading the input stream and producing a *translated* output according to the rules specified in the arguments. The basic syntax is as follows:

```
tr SET1 SET2
```

This translates characters from SET1 into corresponding ones from SET2.

> **Note**
>
> The **tr** command always works only on its standard input and does not take an argument for an input file.

There are three basic uses of **tr** that can be selected with a command-line flag:

- No flag: Replaces any character that belongs to one set with the corresponding ones from another set.
- **-d** or **--delete**: Removes all characters that belong to a given set.
- **-s** or **--squeeze-repeats**: Elides repeated occurrences of any character that belongs to a given set, leaving only one occurrence.
- **-c**: Uses the complement of the first set.

The character sets passed to **tr** can be passed in various ways:

- With a list of characters written as a string, such as **abcde**
- As a range such as **a-z** or **0-9**
- As multiple ranges such as **a-zA-Z**
- As one of the following special **character classes** that consist of an expression in square brackets (only the most common are listed here):

(a) **[:alnum:]** for all letters and digits

(b) **[:alpha:]** for all letters

(c) **[:blank:]** for all horizontal whitespaces

(d) **[:cntrl:]** for all control characters

(e) **[:digit:]** for all digits

(f) **[:graph:]** for all printable characters, not including space

(g) **[:lower:]** for all lowercase letters

(h) **[:print:]** for all printable characters, including space

(i) **[:punct:]** for all punctuation characters

(j) **[:space:]** for all horizontal or vertical whitespaces

(k) **[:upper:]** for all uppercase letters

(l) **[:xdigit:]** for all hexadecimal digits

> **Note**
>
> Character classes are used in many commands, so it's useful to remember the common ones.

Stream Editor: sed

The **sed** command is a very comprehensive tool that can transform text in various ways. It could be considered a mini programming language in itself. However, we will restrict ourselves to using it for the most common function: search and replace.

sed reads from **stdin** and writes transformed output to **stdout** based on the rules passed to it as an argument. In its basic form for *replacing text* in the stream, the syntax that's used is shown here:

```
sed 'pattern'
```

Here, **pattern** is a string such as **s/day/night/FLAGS**, which consists of several parts. In the preceding code, for example:

- **s** is the operation that **sed** is to perform. **s** stands for *substitute*.

- **/** is the delimiter which indicates that everything after this until the next delimiter is to be treated as one string.

- **day** is the string that **sed** searches for.

- **/** again is a delimiter, indicating the end of the search string.

- **night** is the string that **sed** should replace the search string with.

- **/** is again a delimiter, indicating the end of the replacement string.

- **FLAGS** is an optional list of characters that modify how the search and replace is done. The most common characters are as follows:

  (a) **g** stands for global, which tells **sed** to replace all matches of the search string (the default behavior is to replace only the first).

  (b) **i** stands for case-insensitive, which tells **sed** to ignore case when matching.

  (c) A number, **N**, specifies that the Nth match alone should be replaced. Combining the **g** flag with this specifies that all matches including and after the Nth one are to be replaced.

The delimiter is not mandated to be the **/** character. Any character can be used, as long as the same one is used at all three locations. Thus, all the following patterns are equivalent:

```
's#day#night#'
's1day1night1'
's:day:night:'
's day night '
'sAdayAnightA'
```

Multiple patterns can be combined in a pattern by separating them with a semicolon. For instance, the following pattern tells **sed** to replace **day** with **night** and **long** with **short**:

```
's/day/night/ ; s/long/short/'
```

Character classes can be used for the search string, but they need to be enclosed in an extra pair of square brackets. The reason for this will be apparent when we learn **regular expressions** in a later chapter.

The following pattern tells **sed** to replace all alphanumeric characters with an asterisk symbol:

```
's/[[:alnum:]]/*/g'
```

Cut Columns: cut

The **cut** command interprets each line of its input as a series of fields and prints out a subset of those fields based on the specified flags. The effect of this is to select a certain set of columns from a file containing columnar data.

The following is a partial list of the flags that can be used with **cut**:

- **-d DELIM, --delimiter=DELIM**: Uses **DELIM** as the field delimiter (the default is the TAB character).

- **-b LIST, --bytes=LIST**: Selects only specified bytes.

- **-f LIST, --fields=LIST**: Selects only the fields specified by **LIST** and prints any line that contains no delimiter character, unless the **-s** option is specified.

- **-s, --only-delimited**: Does not print lines not containing delimiters.

- **--complement**: Complements the set of selected bytes, characters, or fields.

- **--output-delimiter=DELIM**: When printing the output, **DELIM** is used as the field delimiter. By default, it uses the input delimiter.

Here, the syntax of **LIST** is a comma-separated list of one or more of the following expressions (**M** and **N** are numbers):

- **N**: The Nth element is selected

- **M-N**: Elements starting from the Mth up to Nth inclusive are selected

- **M-**: Elements starting from the Mth up to the last element are selected

- **-N**: Elements from the beginning up to the Nth inclusive are selected

Let's look at an example of using **cut**. The sample data for this chapter has a file called **pinaceae.csv**, which contains a list of tree species with comma-separated fields. This file has data separated by commas, with some values that are empty, and looks like this (only a few lines are shown):

```
ID,Family,Genus,Species,Infraspecific epithet,Source id,IPNI id,Date
kew-2609691,Pinaceae,Abies,alba,,381621,,1759
kew-2609703,Pinaceae,Abies,amabilis,,381632,325658-2,1839
kew-2609719,Pinaceae,Abies,balsamea,,381647,1084057-2,1768
kew-2609725,Pinaceae,Abies,balsamea,phanerolepis,381653,50917432-1,1909
kew-2609730,Pinaceae,Abies,beshanzuensis,,381658,676549-1,1976
kew-2609736,Pinaceae,Abies,borisii-regis,,381664,676550-1,1925
kew-2609740,Pinaceae,Abies,bracteata,,381668,,1845
kew-2609753,Pinaceae,Abies,cephalonica,,381681,261486-1,1838
kew-2609761,Pinaceae,Abies,chensiensis,,381689,676557-1,1892
```

Figure 2.8: View of the first few lines of the data from the pinaceae.csv file

Here, **cut** is used to extract data from the third column onward, using the comma character as the delimiter, and display the output with tabs as a delimiter (only a few lines are shown):

```
robin ~/Lesson2 $ cut -s -d',' -f 3- --output-delimiter=$'\t' pinaceae.csv |
less
```

The output is as follows:

```
Genus    Species Infraspecific epithet    Source id        IPNI id Date
Abies    alba             381621          1759
Abies    amabilis              381632     325658-2         1839
Abies    balsamea              381647     1084057-2        1768
Abies    balsamea     phanerolepis        381653   50917432-1       1909
Abies    beshanzuensis         381658     676549-1         1976
Abies    borisii-regis         381664     676550-1         1925
Abies    bracteata             381668          1845
Abies    cephalonica           381681     261486-1         1838
Abies    chensiensis           381689     676557-1         1892
```

Figure 2.9: Partial output of the cut command

Note the usage of dollar-single-quotes to pass in the tab character to cut as a delimiter.

Paste Columns from Files Together: paste

paste works like the opposite of **cut**. While **cut** can extract one or more columns from a file, **paste** combines files that have columnar data. It does the equivalent of pasting a set of columns of data side by side in the output. The basic syntax of paste is as follows:

```
paste filenames
```

The preceding command instructs the command to read a line from each file specified and produce a line of output that has each of those lines combined, delimited by a tab character. Think of it like pasting files side by side in columns.

The paste command has one option that is commonly used:

- **-d DELIMS, --delimiters=DELIMS**: Uses **DELIMS** as field delimiters (the default is the tab character)

  DELIMS specifies individual delimiters for each field. For example, if it is set to **XYZ**, then X, Y, and Z are used as the delimiters after each column, respectively.

Since **paste** works with multiple input files, typically it is used on its own without pipes, because we can only pipe one stream of data into a command.

A combination of **cut** and **paste** can be used to reorder the columns of a file by first extracting the columns to separate files with **cut**, and then using **paste** to recombine them.

Globally Search a Regular Expression and Print: grep

grep is one of the most useful and versatile tools on UNIX-like systems. The basic purpose of **grep** is to search for a pattern within a file. This command is so widely used that the term **grep** is officially a verb meaning to *search* in the Oxford dictionary.

> **Note**
>
> A complete description of **grep** would be quite overwhelming. In this book, we will instead focus on the smallest useful subset of its features.

The basic syntax of grep is as follows:

```
grep pattern filenames
```

The preceding command instructs the shell to search for the specified pattern within the files listed as arguments. This pattern can be any string or a regular expression. Also, multiple files can be specified as arguments. Omitting the filename argument(s) makes **grep** read from the **stdin**, as with most commands.

The default action of **grep** is to print out the lines that contain the pattern. Here is a list of the most commonly used flags for **grep**:

- **-i, --ignore-case**: Matches lines case-insensitively
- **-v, --invert-match**: Selects non-matching lines
- **-n, --line-number**: For every match, shows the line number in the file as a prefix
- **-c, --count**: Only prints the number of matches per file
- **-w, --word-regexp**: Only matches a pattern if it appears as a complete word
- **-x, --line-regexp**: Only matches a pattern if it appears as a complete line
- **--color, --colour**: Displays results in color on the terminal (no effect will be observed if the output is not to a TTY console)
- **-L, --files-without-match**: Only shows the names of files that do not have a match
- **-l, --files-with-matches**: Only shows the names of files that have a match
- **-m NUM, --max-count=NUM**: Stops after **NUM** matching lines
- **-A NUM, --after-context=NUM**: Prints **NUM** lines that succeed each matching line
- **-B NUM, --before-context=NUM**: Prints **NUM** lines that precede each matching line
- **-C NUM, --context=NUM**: Prints **NUM** lines that precede as well as **NUM** lines that succeed each matching line
- **--group-separator=STRING**: When **-A**, **-B**, or **-C** are used, print the string instead of --- between groups of lines
- **--no-group-separator**: When **-A**, **-B**, or **-C** are in use, do not print a separator between groups of lines
- **-R**: Search all files within a folder recursively

For an example of how grep works, we will use the **man** command (which stands for manual), since it's a handy place to get a bunch of English text as test data. The **man** command outputs the built-in documentation for any command or common terminology. Try the following command:

```
man ascii | grep -n --color 'the'
```

Here, we ask **man** to show the manual page for **ascii**, which includes the ASCII code and some supplementary information. The output of that is piped to **grep**, which searches for the string "the" and prints the matching lines as numbered and colorized:

```
7:          ASCII   is   the   American Standard Code for Information Interchar
10:           The following table contains the 128 ASCII characters.
108:          On older terminals, the underscore code is displayed as a left
109:          the middle.
111:          Uppercase  and lowercase characters differ by just one bit and
114:          The ASCII standard was published by the United States of Ameri
121:          This  page  is  part  of release 4.16 of the Linux man-pages p
```

Figure 2.10: A screenshot displaying the output of the grep command

man uses the system pager (which is **less**) to display the manual, so the keyboard shortcuts are the same as **less**. The output that **man** provides for a command is called a *man page*.

> **Note**
>
> Students are encouraged to read man pages to learn more about any command; however, the material is written in a style more suited for people who are already quite used to the command line, so watch out for unfamiliar or complex material.

Print Unique Lines: uniq

The basic function of the **uniq** command is to remove duplicate lines in a file. In other words, all the lines in the output are unique. The commonly used options of **uniq** are as follows:

- **-d, --repeated**: Prints the lines that occur more than once, but only prints those lines once.

- **-D**: Prints every occurrence of a line that occurs more than once.

- **-u, --unique**: Only prints unique lines; does not print lines that have any duplicates.

- **-c, --count**: Shows the number of occurrences for each line at the start of the line.
- **-i, --ignore-case**: Compares lines case-insensitively.
- **-f N, --skip-fields=N**: Avoids comparing the first N fields.
- **-s N, --skip-chars=N**: Avoids comparing the first N characters.
- **-w N, --check-chars=N**: Compares only N characters in lines.

As you can see, **uniq** has several modes of operation, apart from the default, and can be used in many ways to analyze data.

> **Note**
>
> Note that **uniq** requires that the input file be sorted for it to work correctly.

Exercise 11: Working with Filtering Commands

In this exercise, we will walk through some text-processing tasks using the commands we learned previously. The test data for this chapter contains three main datasets (available publicly on the internet):

- Records of the percentage of land area that was agricultural, in every country (and region) for 1961-2015, with about 12,000 rows
- Records of the population of every country (and region) for 1961-2015, with about 14,000 rows
- Payroll records of public workers in NYC for the year 2017, with about 560,000 rows

These datasets are large enough to demonstrate how well the shell can deal with big data. It is possible to efficiently process files of many gigabytes on the shell, even on limited hardware such as a small laptop. We will first do some simple tasks with the data from earlier chapters and then try some more complex commands to filter the aforementioned data.

> **Note**
>
> Many commands in this exercise and the ones to follow print many lines of data, but we will only show a few lines here for brevity's sake.

1. Open the command-line shell and navigate to the **data** folder from the first exercise:

```
robin ~ $ cd Lesson1/data/
robin ~/Lesson1/data $
```

2. Use **cat** to number the lines of **ls** output, as follows:

```
robin ~/Lesson1/data $ ls -l | cat -n
  1  total 16
  2  drwxr-xr-x 36 robin robin 4096 Sep  5 15:49 cupressaceae
  3  drwxr-xr-x 15 robin robin 4096 Sep  5 15:49 pinaceae
  4  drwxr-xr-x 23 robin robin 4096 Sep  5 15:49 podocarpaceae
  5  drwxr-xr-x  8 robin robin 4096 Sep  5 15:49 taxaceae
```

3. Use **tr** on the output of **ls** to transform it into uppercase using the range syntax:

```
robin ~/Lesson1/data $ ls | tr 'a-z' 'A-Z'
CUPRESSACEAE
PINACEAE
PODOCARPACEAE
TAXACEAE
```

4. Use **tr** to convert only vowels to their uppercase form:

```
robin ~/Lesson1/data $ ls | tr 'aeiou' 'AEIOU'
cUprEssAcEAE
pInAcEAE
pOdOcArpAcEAE
tAxAcEAE
```

5. Navigate to the folder **~/Lesson2** which contains the test data for this chapter:

```
robin ~/Lesson1/data $ cd
robin ~ $ cd Lesson2
```

6. The **land.csv** file contains the historical records we mentioned previously. View this file with **less** to understand its format:

```
robin ~/Lesson2 $ less land.csv
```

The file is in CSV format. The first line describes the field names, and the remaining lines contain data. Here is what the file looks like:

```
Country Name,Country Code,Year,Value
Arab World,ARB,1961,30.9442924784889
Arab World,ARB,1962,30.9441456790578
Arab World,ARB,1963,30.967119790024
```

7. Use **grep** to select the data for Austria, as follows:

```
robin ~/Lesson2 $ grep -w 'Austria' <land.csv
Austria,AUT,1961,43.0540082344393
Austria,AUT,1962,42.7585371760717
Austria,AUT,1963,42.2596270283362
```

As a general rule, we use the **-w** flag with grep when looking for data that is in columnar form. This ensures that the search term is matched only if it is the entire field, otherwise it may match a substring of a field. It is still possible that this will match something like "Republic Of Austria". In this case, we know that "Austria" is always written as a single word, so it works. To handle such ambiguities, we can use regular expressions (described in the next chapter) to exactly specify the matching logic.

We have used input redirection to **grep** instead of just passing the file as an argument. This is only because we are emphasizing the use of redirection and piping. The command would work exactly the same if we passed **land.csv** as an argument instead of redirecting it.

8. Select the data that is after the year 2000 by using **grep** again to look for the lines with "20". Use the following code (the complete output is not shown):

```
robin ~/Lesson2 $ grep -w 'Austria' <land.csv | grep '20'
Austria,AUT,1971,40.2143376120126
Austria,AUT,1978,38.5178009203197
Austria,AUT,1979,38.0588520222814
Austria,AUT,1981,38.2102203923468
Austria,AUT,1983,36.6420440784694
Austria,AUT,1984,36.7304432065876
Austria,AUT,1992,36.4858319205619
Austria,AUT,2000,35.604262533301
Austria,AUT,2001,35.312424315815
```

9. Note that we still got many lines for years before 2000. This is because some of the values for percentage have the string "20" in them. We can work around this by searching for ",20" instead (only a few lines of output are shown here):

```
robin ~/Lesson2 $ grep -w 'Austria' <land.csv | grep ',20'
Austria,AUT,2000,35.604262533301
Austria,AUT,2001,35.312424315815
Austria,AUT,2002,35.1441026883023
Austria,AUT,2003,34.9386049891015
```

We used this slightly hack-ish approach to filter data by searching for ",20". In this case, it worked because none of the percentage values started with "20". However, that is not true for the data in many other countries, and this would have included rows we did not need.

Ideally, we should use some other method to extract these values. The best general option is to use the **awk** tool. **awk** is a general text-processing language, which is too complex to cover in this brief book. The students are encouraged to learn about that tool, as it is extremely powerful.

We can also use **grep** with a simple regular expression to match four digits starting with "20". This will not be subject to the issue of matching wrong lines (partial output is shown here):

```
robin ~/Lesson2 $ grep -w 'Austria' <land.csv | grep -w '20[[:digit:]]
[[:digit:]]'
Austria,AUT,2000,35.604262533301
Austria,AUT,2001,35.312424315815
Austria,AUT,2002,35.1441026883023
Austria,AUT,2003,34.9386049891015
```

The **-w** flag matches an entire word, and the expression '**20[[:digit:]]**
[[:digit:]]' matches 20, followed by two digits. We use character classes, which were described earlier in this topic. We will learn regular expressions in more detail in the next chapter, but for the remaining examples and activities, use this regular expression to match the years for 2000 onward.

10. Next, use **cut** to get rid of the second column, which has the country code, as follows:

```
robin ~/Lesson2 $ grep -w 'Austria' <land.csv | grep -w '20[[:digit:]]
[[:digit:]]' | cut -d, --complement -f2
Austria,2000,35.604262533301
Austria,2001,35.312424315815
Austria,2002,35.1441026883023
Austria,2003,34.9386049891015
```

We used the **--complement** flag to specify that we want everything except field #2. The input field delimiter was set to the comma character.

11. You can pass the **--output-delimiter** flag to **cut** so that it's more readable. Set the delimiter to the tab character using dollar-single-quotes and an escape sequence:

```
robin ~/Lesson2 $ grep -w 'Austria' <land.csv | grep -w '20[[:digit:]]
[[:digit:]]' | cut -d, --complement -f2 --output-delimiter=$'\t'
Austria  2000     35.604262533301
Austria  2001     35.312424315815
Austria  2002     35.1441026883023
Austria  2003     34.9386049891015
```

> **Note**
>
> When a tab character is printed on the console, it does not print a fixed number of spaces. Instead, it tries to print as many spaces as required to reach the next column that is a multiple of the tab width (usually 8). This means that when you print a file with tabs as delimiters, it can appear to have an arbitrary number of spaces between fields. Even though the number of spaces printed varies, there is only one tab character between the fields.

12. Use **cut** to separate out the year and percentage columns into two files. We have to run it twice. We will first redirect the intermediate results from **grep** to a temporary file, then extract the column with the year, and then with the percentage:

```
robin ~/Lesson2 $ grep -w 'Austria' <land.csv | grep -w '20[[:digit:]]
[[:digit:]]' >austria.txt
robin ~/Lesson2 $ cut -d, -f3 <austria.txt >year.txt
robin ~/Lesson2 $ cut -d, -f4 <austria.txt >percent.txt
```

13. Now, let's join the columns back using **paste**, with percentage first and year second, using a space as a delimiter:

```
robin ~/Lesson2 $ paste -d' ' percent.txt year.txt
```

The output will appear as follows:

```
35.604262533301 2000
35.312424315815 2001
35.1441026883023 2002
34.9386049891015 2003
34.7226931460402 2004
34.5943327682248 2005
34.4308549285541 2006
34.2718399573736 2007
34.0211678655332 2008
33.8467872799051 2009
```

Figure 2.11: A screenshot displaying the data with percentage first and year second

14. Sort the preceding command's output to see the data ordered by percentage:

```
robin ~/Lesson2 $ paste -d' ' percent.txt year.txt | sort -n
```

The output will appear as follows:

```
32.8902245434606 2014
32.913693036556 2013
32.9417253371787 2015
33.1322528284517 2012
33.3971245503325 2011
33.6583061849802 2010
33.8467872799051 2009
34.0211678655332 2008
34.2718399573736 2007
34.4308549285541 2006
```

Figure 2.12: A screenshot displaying the data ordered by percentage

We will examine the **sort** command in detail in the next section.

15. The **payroll.tsv** file has data about public workers in NYC in 2017. View the file and observe that the third and fourth columns contain the last and first names of the workers, respectively. Extract those two columns with **cut**. You can also remove the first line which has the field description "Last Name" and "First Name" with **grep** and finally sort it:

```
robin ~/Lesson2 $ less payroll.tsv
robin ~/Lesson2 $ cut -f3,4 payroll.tsv | grep -v 'First' | sort >names.
tsv
```

> **Note**
>
> **grep** is not quite the right tool for this job because it will end up processing every line of the file looking for the string "First", which is unnecessary work. What we really need is just to skip the first line. This can be done with the **tail** command, which we will learn about later.

16. The **wc** command can be used to count the lines in a file. Let's use it to see how many workers are listed:

```
robin ~/Lesson2 $ wc -l names.tsv
562266 names.tsv
```

17. Let's use **uniq** to see how many distinct names exist:

```
robin ~/Lesson2 $ uniq names.tsv | wc -l
410141
```

18. What about people who do not share their name with anyone? Pass **-u** to **uniq** to get only those names that occur once:

```
robin ~/Lesson2 $ uniq -u names.tsv | wc -l
301172
```

In this exercise, we have learned some commands that work on a line-by-line basis on files. Next, we will examine commands that work on entire files at a time.

Transformation Commands

Commands of this category operate by reading more than one line at a time and producing output. These can be thought of as a complete transformation of contents.

Sort Lines: sort

The **sort** command orders the lines of a file (we have seen this in some exercises before). Here is the list of the commonly used options for sort:

- **-o FILE, --output=FILE**: Writes output to **FILE** rather than to **stdout**.

  Since **sort** reads its entire input into memory before writing anything, this flag can be used to sort a file in place. Always specify this as the first option if it is being used, since some systems mandate it. This flag should not be used with **-m** since merging is a different operation altogether and happens line by line.

- **-b, --ignore-leading-blanks**: Ignores blanks that occur at the start of a line.

- **-f, --ignore-case**: Does a case-insensitive sort.

- **-i, --ignore-nonprinting**: Ignores unprintable characters.

- **-n, --numeric-sort**: Treats numbers as values rather than as strings.

  When compared as strings (*lexicographic ordering*), "00" compares by default as greater than "0". With this flag specified, the text is interpreted as a number, so both of the preceding strings are treated as being equal.

- **-r, --reverse**: Sorts in descending order.

- **-s, --stable**: Uses a stable sort.

  Stable sorts preserve the relative order of lines that compare as equal.

- **-u, --unique**: Removes all but the first line of lines that compare equally.

  This flag can perform the same function as the default behavior of **uniq**, so it makes sense to skip piping into **uniq** separately in such cases.

- **-m, --merge**: Merges sorted files.

  Merging uses an efficient algorithm to take the data from already sorted files and merge it into a combined sorted output. Do not use the **-o** flag if using this. The merge flag can save a lot of time in certain cases, such as when adding data to an already existing large sorted file and maintaining its sorted property.

- **-t SEP, --field-separator=SEP**: Treats **SEP** as the field delimiter (useful with **-k**).

- **-k KEYDEF, --key=KEYDEF**: Uses the given field as the sort key.

  KEYDEF is a string consisting of two column numbers separated by commas, for example, **3,5**. This instructs sort to use columns 3, 4, and 5 for sorting. Either field number can have an optional period followed by a second number, specifying the character position from where to consider the field. For example, **-k3.2,3.4** uses the second to fourth characters of the third field in the file. This option can be specified multiple times to specify the secondary key and so on. The second number is optional and, if omitted, defaults to the last column index.

> **Note**
>
> Sorting is an operation that requires the entire file content to be processed before it can output anything. This means that a **sort** command inside a pipeline essentially prevents any further steps in the pipeline from happening until the sort is finished.
>
> Hence, we should be careful about the performance implications of using **sort** and other commands that work on complete files rather than line by line. Usually, the rule of thumb is to save the sorted data to a file if the amount of data is large. Repeatedly sorting a large file in each individual command will be slow. Instead, we can reuse the sorted data.

Remember that the **sort** command works on lexicographic ordering, according to the ASCII code (use the **man ascii** command to view it). This has consequences about how punctuation, whitespace, and other special characters affect the ordering. In most cases, however, the data we process is only text and numbers, so this should not be a frequent problem.

Now, let's look at an example where we can use the **sort** command. Say we receive huge daily event log files from different data centers, say **denver.txt**, **dallas.txt**, and **chicago.txt**. We need to maintain a complete sorted log of the entire year's history too, for example, in a file called **2018-log.txt**.

One method would be to concatenate everything and sort it (remember that **2018-log. txt** already exists and contains a huge amount of sorted data):

```
cat denver.txt dallas.txt chicago.txt >>2018-log.txt

sort -o 2018-log.txt 2018-log.txt
```

This would end up re-sorting most of the data that was already sorted in **2018-log.txt** and would be very inefficient.

Instead, we can first sort the three new files and merge them. We need to use a temporary file for this since we cannot use the **-o** option to merge the file in-place:

```
sort -o denver.txt denver.txt

sort -o dallas.txt dallas.txt

sort -o chicago.txt chicago.txt

sort -m denver.txt dallas.txt chicago.txt 2018-log.txt >>2018-log-tmp.txt
```

Once we have the results in the temporary file, we can move the new file onto the old one, overwriting it:

```
mv 2018-log-tmp.txt 2018-log.txt
```

Unlike sorting, merging sorted files is a very efficient operation, taking very little memory or disk space.

Print Lines at the End of a File: tail

The **tail** command prints the specified number of lines at the end of a file. In other words, it shows the tail end of a file. The useful options for tail are as follows:

- **-n N, --lines=N**: Outputs the last N lines

  If N is prefixed with a + symbol, then the console shows all lines from the Nth line onward. If this argument is not specified, it defaults to 10.

- **-q, --quiet, --silent**: Does not show the filenames when multiple input files are specified

- **-f, --follow**: After showing the tail of the file, the command repeatedly checks for new data and shows any new lines that have been added to the file

The most common use of **tail** other than its default invocation is to follow logfiles. For example, an administrator could view a website's error log that is being continuously updated and that has new lines being appended to it intermittently with a command like the following:

```
tail -f /var/log/httpd/error_log
```

When run this way, **tail** shows the last 10 lines, but the program does not exit. Instead, it waits for more lines of data to arrive and prints them too, as they arrive. This lets a system administrator have a quick view of what happened recently in the log.

The other convenient use of **tail** is to skip over a given number of lines in a file. Recall step 16 of the previous exercise, where we used **grep** to skip the first line of a file. We could have used **tail** instead.

Print Lines at the Head of a File: head

The **head** command works like the inverse of **tail**. It prints a certain number of lines from the head (start) of the file. The useful options for **head** are as follows:

- **-n N, --lines=N**: Outputs the first N lines

  If N is prefixed with a - symbol, then the console shows all except the last N lines. If this argument is not specified, it defaults to 10.

- **-q**, **--quiet**, **--silent**: Does not show the filenames when multiple input files are specified

The **head** command is commonly used to sample the content of a large file. In the previous exercise, we examined the payroll file to observe how the data was structured with **less**. Instead, we could have used **head** to just dump a few lines to the screen.

Combining **head** and **tail** in a pipeline can be useful to extract any contiguous range of lines from a file. For example, look at the following code:

```
tail -n+100 data.txt | head -n45
```

This command would print the lines 100 to 144 from the file.

Join Columns of Files: join

join does a complex data merging operation on two files. The nearest thing that describes it is the working of a database query that joins two tables. If you are familiar with databases, you would know how a join works. However, the best way to describe join is with an example.

Let's assume we have two files specifying the ages of people and the countries to which they belong. The first file is as follows:

```
Alice    25
Charlie  34
```

The second file is as follows:

```
Alice France
Charlie Spain
```

The result of applying **join** on these files is as follows:

```
Alice 25 France
Charlie 34 Spain
```

join requires the input files to be sorted to work. The command provides a plethora of options of which a small subset is described here:

- **-i, --ignore-case**: Compares fields case-insensitively
- **-1 N**: Uses the Nth field of file 1 to join
- **-2 N**: Uses the Nth field of file 2 to join
- **-j N**: Uses the Nth field in both files to join
- **-e EMPTY**: When an input field is missing, this option replaces it with the string specified in **EMPTY** instead
- **-a N**: Apart from paired lines, it prints any lines from file N that do not have a pair in the other file
- **-v N**: Prints any lines from file N that do not pair but does not print the normal output
- **-t CHAR**: Uses **CHAR** as input and output field separator
- **-o FORMAT**: Prints the field's values as per the specified **FORMAT**

FORMAT consists of one or more field specifiers separated by commas. Each field specifier can be either 0, or a number **M.N** where **M** is the file number and **N** is the field number. 0 represents the join field. For example, **1.3,0,2.2** means "Third field of file 1, **join** field, and second field of file 2". **FORMAT** can also be **auto**, in which case **join** prints out all the joined fields.

- **--check-order**: Checks if input files are sorted.

- **--nocheck-order**: Does not check if input files are sorted.

- **--header**: Treats the first line in each file as a header and prints them directly.

join works by reading a line from each file and checking if the values of the join columns match. If they match, it prints the combined fields. By default, it uses the first field to join.

With the **-e** and **-a** flags specified, it can perform an *outer join* in database terminology. For example, look at the following snippet:

```
robin ~ $ cat a.txt
Name      Age
Alice     25
Charlie   34
robin ~ $ cat b.txt
Name    Country
Alice   France
Bob     Spain
robin ~ $ join --header -o auto -e 'N/A' -a2 -a1 a.txt b.txt
Name Age Country
Alice 25 France
Bob N/A Spain
Charlie 34 N/A
```

There was no data about Charlie's country and Bob's age, but a row was output for everyone containing all the data that was available, and N/A where it was not. The **-a1** flag tells **join** to include rows from file 1 that do not have a row in file 2. This brings in a row for Charlie. The **-a2** flag tells **join** to include rows from file 2 that do not have a row in file 1. This brings in a row for Bob. The **-e** flag tells **join** to add a placeholder, N/A, for missing values. The **-o** auto flag is necessary for this outer join operation to work as shown; it ensures that all the columns from both files are included in every row in the output.

In the default mode of operation (without **-a**) we get an *inner join*, which would have skipped any rows for which there is no corresponding match in both files, as shown here:

```
robin ~ $ join --header a.txt b.txt
Name Age Country
Alice 25 France
```

In the preceding output, note that only Alice's row was printed, since data about her exists in both files, but not any of the others.

The combination of **join**, **sort**, and **uniq** can be used to perform all the mathematical set operations on two files, such as disjunction, intersection, and so on. **join** can also be (mis)used to reorder columns of a file by joining a file with itself if it has a column with all distinct values (line numbers, for example).

Output Files in Reverse: tac

tac is used to reverse a file line by line. This is especially useful for quickly reversing the order of already sorted files without re-sorting them. Since **tac** needs to be able to reach the end of the input stream and move backward to print in reverse, **tac** will stall a pipeline until it gets all the piped data input, just like **sort**. However, if **tac** is provided an actual file as input, it can directly seek to the end of the file and start working backward.

The common options for **tac** are as follows:

- **-s SEP, --separator=SEP**: Uses SEP as the separator to define the chunks to be reversed. If this flag is not specified, the newline character is assumed to be a separator.

- **-r, --regex**: Treats the separator string as a regular expression.

The most common use of **tac** is to reverse the lines of a file. Reversing a file's words or characters can also be done by using the **-s** and **-r** flags, but this use case is rare.

Get the Word Count: wc

The **wc** command can count the lines, words, characters, or bytes in a file. It can also tell the number of characters in the widest line of a file.

The common flags for **wc** are as follows:

- **-l, --lines**: Shows the newline count (number of lines)

- **-w, --words**: Shows the word count

- **-m, --chars**: Shows the character count

- **-c, --bytes**: Shows the byte count (this may differ from the character count for Unicode input)

- **-L, --max-line-length**: Shows the length of the longest line

Exercise 12: Working with Transformation Commands

In this exercise, we will continue where we left off from the previous exercises. We will do some more data extraction from the geographical datasets, and then work with the payroll data:

1. View a few lines of the **population.csv** file with **head**:

   ```
   robin ~/Lesson2 $ head -n5 population.csv
   Country Name,Country Code,Year,Value
   Arab World,ARB,1960,92490932
   Arab World,ARB,1961,95044497
   Arab World,ARB,1962,97682294
   Arab World,ARB,1963,100411076
   ```

   This has a similar format to the **land.csv** file we used earlier.

2. Let's use **join** to merge these two datasets together so that we can see the population and land area of each country by year. **join** can only use one column when matching two lines, but here we must join on two columns. To work around this, we need to transform the data so that the two columns we need are physically conjoined. So, first, let's extract columns 1, 3, and 4 into separate files with **cut**:

```
robin ~/Lesson2 $ cut -f1 -d, population.csv >p1.txt
robin ~/Lesson2 $ cut -f3 -d, population.csv >p3.txt
robin ~/Lesson2 $ cut -f4 -d, population.csv >p4.txt
```

Note that we type three commands that are almost the same. In a future chapter, we will learn how to do these kinds of repetitive operations with less effort.

3. Next, let's paste them back together with two different delimiters, the forward slash and tab:

```
robin ~/Lesson2 $ paste -d$'/\t' p1.txt p3.txt p4.txt >p134.txt
robin ~/Lesson2 $ head -n5 p134.txt
Country Name/Year       Value
Arab World/1960 92490932
Arab World/1961 95044497
Arab World/1962 97682294
Arab World/1963 100411076
```

4. Repeat the same steps for the **land.csv** file:

```
robin ~/Lesson2 $ cut -f1 -d, land.csv >l1.txt
robin ~/Lesson2 $ cut -f3 -d, land.csv >l3.txt
robin ~/Lesson2 $ cut -f4 -d, land.csv >l4.txt
robin ~/Lesson2 $ paste -d$'/\t' l1.txt l3.txt l4.txt >l134.txt
robin ~/Lesson2 $ head -n5 l134.txt
Country Name/Year       Value
Arab World/1961 30.9442924784889
Arab World/1962 30.9441456790578
Arab World/1963 30.967119790024
Arab World/1964 30.9765883533295
```

5. Now, we have two files, where the country and year have been combined into a single field that can be used as the join key. Let's sort these files into place in preparation for **join**, but cut off the first line that contains the header using **tail** with **+N:**

```
robin ~/Lesson2 $ tail -n+2 l134.txt | sort >land.txt
robin ~/Lesson2 $ tail -n+2 p134.txt | sort >pop.txt
```

6. Now, let's join these two tables to get the population and agricultural land percentage matched on each country per year. Use **-o**, **-e**, and **-a** to get an outer join on the data since the data is not complete (rows are missing for some combination of countries and years). Also, tell **join** to ensure that the files are ordered. This helps us catch errors if we forgot to sort:

```
robin ~/Lesson2 $ join -t$'\t' --check-order -o auto -e 'UNKNOWN' -a1 -a2
land.txt pop.txt | less
```

Values where the data is not present are set to `'UNKNOWN'`.

The output will look as follows:

```
Afghanistan/1960     UNKNOWN 8996351
Afghanistan/1961     57.7459179609717          9166764
Afghanistan/1962     57.8378212786815          9345868
Afghanistan/1963     57.914407376773 9533954
Afghanistan/1964     58.0109058603682          9731361
Afghanistan/1965     58.0139693042919          9938414
Afghanistan/1966     58.0721747388414          10152331
Afghanistan/1967     58.1732683883222          10372630
Afghanistan/1968     58.174800110284 10604346
Afghanistan/1969     58.1993076616733          10854428
```

Figure 2.13: A screenshot displaying the matched data

7. Let's move on to the payroll data again. Recall that we had extracted the names of all the workers to **names.tsv** earlier. Let's find out the most common names in the payroll. Use **uniq** to count each name, and sort in reverse with numeric sort and view the first 10 lines of the result with **head**:

```
robin ~/Lesson2 $ <names.tsv uniq -c | sort -n -r | head
    253
     69 RODRIGUEZ        MARIA
     59 XXXX      XXXX
     54 RODRIGUEZ        JOSE
     49 RODRIGUEZ        CARMEN
     43 RIVERA   MARIA
     42 GONZALEZ         MARIA
     40 GONZALEZ         JOSE
     38 SMITH    MICHAEL
     37 RIVERA   JOSE
```

We can see the names sorted by most frequent to least frequent (note that 253 names are blank, and 59 names in the records are invalid "XXXX XXXX").

8. Let's save the results of the frequency of names to a file using the following command:

```
robin ~/Lesson2 $ <names.tsv uniq -c | sort -n -r >namecounts.txt
```

9. Find all people who have the word "SMITH" in their last name with the **-w** flag to avoid names like "PSMITH". We assume that no other field could contain "SMITH":

```
robin ~/Lesson2 $ grep -w 'SMITH' namecounts.txt | less
```

We can see the results in decreasing order of frequency. Here are the first few lines you will see:

```
     38 SMITH    MICHAEL
     29 SMITH    ROBERT
     23 SMITH    JAMES
     22 SMITH    MICHELLE
     20 SMITH    CHRISTOPHER
     19 SMITH    JENNIFER
     18 SMITH    WILLIAM
```

10. Now, use **tac** to view the data in the reverse order, and use **head** to see the first five lines. These are some of the rarest names with "SMITH" in them:

```
robin ~/Lesson2 $ grep -w 'SMITH' namecounts.txt | tac | head -n5
      1 ADGERSON-SMITH  KAILEN
      1 ALLYN SMITH     LISA
      1 ANDERSON-SMITH  FELICIA
      1 BAILEY-SMITH    LAUREN
      1 BANUCCI-SMITH   KATHERINE
```

With this exercise, we have learned how to use commands that work for transforming column-based text files in various ways. With some ingenuity, we can mold our text data in any way we please.

Activity 6: Processing Tabular Data – Reordering Columns

In the previous exercises, we used **cut** to extract individual columns and then **paste** to create a file with a subset of the columns in the original data, which is analogous to the *SELECT* operation in databases. Using **cut** and **paste** for this is quite cumbersome, but there is a way to use **join** for this purpose, with a little ingenuity.

In this activity, you will be working with the **land.csv** file, which contains historical data of agricultural land percentage for hundreds of countries. The data is divided into four columns by commas: Country Name, Country Code, Year, and Value. From the high-level instructions provided here, and the concepts learned in this chapter, create two new files that have the data laid out as follows:

- Year, Value, and Country Code, that is, columns 3, 4, and 2
- Value, Year, and Country Name, that is, columns 4, 3, and 1

In this activity, you need to convert a high-level description of a task with hints into actual command pipelines. Refer to the options for the commands and test out your commands carefully, viewing the intermediate results to ensure you are on the right track.

Now, perform the following operations (remember that you can use **less** or **head** to verify a command's output, before writing to a file):

1. Use **sort** to create a sorted version of **land.csv** called **sorted.txt**, and use **tail** to skip the first line, which has the header.

2. Create a numbered version of this sorted file called **numbered.txt** using **cat**.

3. View this file and verify that it has five columns. The first column should have a tab after it, but the rest should be delimited by commas. Use **cat** with the right options to let you distinguish between spaces and tabs.

4. Convert the commas in **numbered.txt** into tabs and create a file called **tabbed.txt**. Use **tr**, and remember the correct use of escape sequences.

5. View **tabbed.txt** to make sure you have a file with five columns separated by tabs. Again, use **cat** with the right options to let you distinguish between spaces and tabs.

6. Use **join** to outer join **tabbed.txt** with itself and extract the columns Year, Value, and Country Code (3, 4, and 2) into a file called **342.txt**. Refer to the options that let you perform an outer join, and the one that lets you select the output columns.

> **Note**
>
> Remember that the columns 3, 4, and 2 in the original file are not at the same position in the numbered file.

7. Repeat step 6. This time, extract columns Value, Year, and Country Name (4, 3, and 1) as **431.txt**.

> **Note**
>
> Again, remember that the columns 4, 3, and 1 in the original file are not at the same position in the numbered file.

Verify that **342.txt** has data of the columns Year, Value, and Country Code. You should get the following output:

```
1961  57.7459179609717 AFG
1962  57.8378212786815 AFG
1963  57.914407376773 AFG
1964  58.0109058603682 AFG
1965  58.0139693042919 AFG
1966  58.0721747388414 AFG
1967  58.1732683883222 AFG
1968  58.174800110284 AFG
1969  58.1993076616733 AFG
1970  58.2146248812915 AFG
```

Figure 2.14: Output of 342.txt

Verify that **431.txt** has data of the columns Value, Year, and Country Name.

```
57.7459179609717 1961 Afghanistan
57.8378212786815 1962 Afghanistan
57.914407376773 1963 Afghanistan
58.0109058603682 1964 Afghanistan
58.0139693042919 1965 Afghanistan
58.0721747388414 1966 Afghanistan
58.1732683883222 1967 Afghanistan
58.174800110284 1968 Afghanistan
58.1993076616733 1969 Afghanistan
58.2146248812915 1970 Afghanistan
```

Figure 2.15: Output of 431.txt

Note

The solution for this activity can be found on page 274.

Activity 7: Data Analysis

In this activity, you will perform data analysis tasks using command-line operations. Use the **land.csv** and **population.csv** files which contain historical agricultural land percentage and population data for all countries, respectively. Extract the data for the median population for all countries in 1998 and the median value of agricultural land percentage for the country of Australia to answer these questions:

1. How much was the median percentage of agricultural land in Australia, and which was the median year?

2. Which country had the median population in 1998, and how much was it?

> **Note**
>
> A statistical median is defined as the middle value in a sorted sequence; half the values are below the median and half are above.
>
> Assuming a sequence has N values, the index of the median is N/2 rounded to the nearest integer. For example, if N is 10, then the median is 5. If N is 17, then the median is 9 because 17/2 is 8.5 and it rounds to 9.

Perform the following operations (remember to use temporary files to save intermediate results):

1. Extract the data for Australia from the land data file.

2. Sort the data based on the percentage values.

3. Count the number of lines of data.

4. Print out the line that is closest to the middle. You can use the **bc** command with herestrings to do calculations (note that **bc** performs integer division by default with the **/** symbol).

5. Extract the data for 1998 from the population data file.

6. Sort the data based on population values.

7. Repeat steps 3 and 4.

The following are the expected answers to the preceding questions:

1. The median of the agricultural land percentage in Australia for this dataset was 60.72% in 1963.

2. Azerbaijan had the median population of 7,913,000 in 1998.

> **Note**
>
> The solution for this activity can be found on page 274.

In this section, we have explored a fairly large subset of the text-processing commands of the UNIX ecosystem. We also looked at an introductory level of their functionalities, which have been exposed through various options.

There are many more options for these commands and several commands that we have not covered, but what we have learned is enough to do many data-processing tasks without resorting to specialized GUI applications.

What we have learned so far is as follows:

*   How to use filter and transform commands on text files
*   How to construct complex pipelines
*   How to perform database-like operations on columnar text data
*   How to combine small simple commands into complex high-level operations

In future chapters, we will cover more use patterns of these commands and more mechanisms to drive them.

Summary

In this chapter, you have been introduced to several concepts such as input, output, redirection, and pipelines. You have also learned basic text-processing tools, along with both common and uncommon use cases of these tools, to demonstrate their flexibility. At a conceptual level, several techniques related to processing tabular data have been explored.

A large number of details have been covered. If you are being introduced to these for the first time, you should attempt to understand the concepts at an abstract level and not be overwhelmed by details (which you can always refer to when in doubt). To this end, some additional complexities have been avoided in order to focus on the essential concepts. The students can pick up more nuances as they continue to learn and practice in the future, beyond this brief book.

In the next chapter, you will learn about several more concepts related to the shell, including basic regular expressions, shell expansion, and command substitution.

3

Advanced Command-Line Concepts

Learning Objectives

By the end of this chapter, you will be able to:

- Write command lists to combine multiple commands logically

- Manage the parallel execution of tasks using job control commands

- Write and utilize regular expressions to match text patterns

- Use shell expansion and substitution syntax to perform string and arithmetic processing

This chapter explains how to work with command lists and control jobs, how to write regular expressions, and how to use various shell expansion features.

Introduction

In the previous chapter, we learned about the mechanisms for connecting commands and files together using redirection and pipes. In this chapter, we will learn about other ways of composing commands and controlling their execution. Then, we will learn about the basics of regular expressions, which are useful for text processing, and finally, learn about a shell feature called expansion, which has many uses.

Command Lists

Command lists are a mechanism used to execute multiple independent commands at once, either sequentially or concurrently. Sequentially, they can be used to run each command one after another (simple sequential execution) or run each command depending on the success or failure of the previous one (dependent execution). However, before we understand how command lists work, we need to learn the concept of **exit codes**.

When any program or command exits, it returns a number, called the exit code, to the shell. This number is zero if the command completes successfully and non-zero otherwise. Exit codes are also sometimes referred to as **return values**.

Command List Operators

Command lists are formed by stringing together commands with an operator in between, such as the ; operator, & operator, and the && or || operators. Now, let's look at each of these operators in detail.

Semicolon Operator

The ; operator is quite simple and is used to execute a command sequentially after the previous one. A list of commands separated by it are executed one by one, just as if you had typed them out individually. For example:

```
ls ; sort file.txt -o sorted.txt ; uniq sorted.txt
```

Each of these commands runs sequentially. Any error that occurs has no effect on the execution of the remaining commands in the list. The exit code of such an expression is that of the last command in the list.

Ampersand Operator

The & operator is used to execute commands concurrently. When added at the end of a command, it launches the command in the background. For instance, look at the following command:

```
sort file.txt >sorted.txt &
```

The **&** operator tells the shell to execute the **sort** command in the background, and not wait for it to finish. While the command executes in the background, we could keep using the shell and run other commands.

> **Note**
>
> When we launch a background command, the shell prints out two numbers: a **job number** and a **process identifier** (**PID**) number. These can be used to identify background processes for job control, which we will learn about later. However, remember that PIDs are unique across all processes in the entire system, but job numbers are specific to the current instance of the shell.

Once we launch a background command, the shell checks its status each time we enter a new command, and if it is complete, it prints that status before the shell prompt is shown. For instance, look at the following snippet:

```
robin ~ $ sort file.txt >sorted.txt &
[1] 13431
```

Here, the job number is 1 and the PID is 13431 (this PID will vary depending on your system—every new process gets a brand new PID).

Now, let's start another command:

```
robin ~ $ ls
file.txt   sorted.txt
[1]+  Done                    sort file.txt > sorted.txt
```

In this case, after launching **sort** in the background, we ran **ls**, and the shell informed us that *Job #1* was done before the prompt appeared. If the background command had printed anything to its **stdout** or **stderr**, it would have overwritten and intermingled with the shell prompt display and the output of any other command we executed after.

> **Note**
>
> The shell has only one output device, which is the console display. This means that if multiple commands are running simultaneously, their output will get intermingled randomly. This includes the output of both **stdout** and **stderr**. Hence, it almost always makes sense to use output redirection when launching commands in the background.

The **&** operator can also be used with multiple commands, as shown here:

```
sort file.txt >sorted.txt & sort file2.txt >sorted2.txt & sort file3.txt
>sorted3.txt &
```

This makes the shell launch all three **sort** commands concurrently, and then immediately display the prompt. Also, notice that there is an extra trailing **&** symbol at the end. Without this, the shell would have waited for the third command to complete before showing its prompt. **&** should not be considered as a separator between commands, but as a suffix after each to signify background launching. This is similar to using a full stop or exclamation mark in normal text.

Logical Operators && and ||

The logical AND and logical OR operators are used to chain commands sequentially and control the execution of each command based on the exit code of the previous one. For example, look at the following command:

```
grep 'unwanted' file && rm file
```

Here, the **grep** command looks for the string "unwanted" within **file**. If it succeeds, it returns a zero, otherwise it returns a non-zero value. The **&&** operator that follows tells the shell to execute the next command (removing the file) only if the exit code of the previous command is zero. You can interpret **&&** in plain language as the phrase "and if it succeeds, then."

&& can be used to chain multiple dependent commands together, with each command executing only if the previous one succeeded. The commands themselves can be entire pipelines and include redirections, as shown here:

```
grep -q 'useful' file && sort file | uniq >sorted.txt && echo 'File was
useful'
```

Here, the following three commands are being chained:

```
grep -q 'useful' file
```

```
sort file | uniq >sorted.txt
```

```
echo 'File was useful'
```

The second command has two commands in a pipeline. Although each command has its own exit code, the shell considers the entire pipeline's exit code to be that of the rightmost command in it. Hence, the exit code of this entire command is just the exit code of **uniq**.

The purpose of **&&** is to make sure that errors in any command abort the whole chain. When we type in commands manually, one after the other, we can check if any command had an error and stop. The **&&** operator performs a similar function and stops executing further commands as soon as one command returns an error.

The **||** operator works in the same manner, except that a command *must* fail for the next command in the chain to execute. You can interpret **||** in plain language as the phrase "or, if it fails, then."

A chain of commands with **&&** stops at the first command that **fails**, whereas a chain of commands with **||** stops at the first command that **succeeds**.

> **Note**
>
> The two operators are sometimes read as "and then" for **&&** and "or else" for **||**.

Using Multiple Operators

When mixing these various operators together, the **&** is applied last. For example, consider the following example, which uses the **sleep** command. This command simply waits for the number of seconds specified as its argument (it is an easy way to simulate a long-running command):

```
robin ~  $ sleep 5 && echo Done &
 [1] 1678
robin ~  $ Done
echo 'Hello'
Hello
[1]+  Done                 sleep 5 && echo Done
```

Here, the shell treats everything before the trailing **&** as a single unit that is launched in the background. Hence, any combination of commands with **&&**, **||**, or **;** is treated as a single unit as far as the **&** operator is concerned.

Notice what happened to the output of the background command (the input that we typed is in bold): we see the prompt appear immediately–the sleep command is running in the background. After 5 seconds, the **sleep** command exits, after which the **echo** command runs. Since the cursor is on the shell prompt, it prints **Done** at the current cursor position on the screen. It looks as if we typed **Done**, but actually, it is the output of **echo** that overwrote the screen at that point, and the cursor moved to the next line. If we type another command and execute it, the shell shows us the status of the last command before executing the new one.

Therefore, as mentioned earlier, it is always recommended to redirect output streams to files for commands executed in the background to avoid garbled or confusing output. A major branch of computer science itself relates to the problem of making multiple independent and concurrent processes share a common resource (like an output device) without interfering with each other. This mixing up of command output is merely one manifestation of this basic problem. The easiest resolution is to not require a common resource (like the console) and make them independent (by redirecting the output distinct files).

Command Grouping

Commands can be grouped together using curly braces {} or parentheses (). This is useful when **&&** and **||** both appear. Grouped commands are treated as one unit. For example, consider the following:

```
command1 && command2 && command3 || echo "command3 failed"
```

The shell works by looking at each command in the list and processing it based on the return value of the previous command. Hence, if **command2** fails, **command3** is skipped, but the **command3 failed** message is printed. To work around such ambiguities, we can group the commands as follows:

```
command1 && command2 && ( command3 || echo "command3 failed" )
```

Alternatively, we can group the commands like so:

```
command1 && command2 && { command3 || echo "command3 failed" ;}
```

Note the semicolon before the closing brace. It is required, as per the syntax rules. Also, there has to be a space before and after the braces (except if the brace is the last character on the line).

When commands are run grouped within parentheses, a separate instance of the shell is launched to run them, called a **subshell**. When using braces, they are run under the same shell context. There are two main differences between running within the same shell versus running in a subshell:

- Changing the directory within a subshell does not affect the CWD of the main shell that launched it

- Environment variables created inside a subshell are not visible in the parent shell, but the converse is true (environment variables will be covered in a later section)

> **Note**
>
> In general, using **||** and **&&** together without braces or parentheses should be avoided, as it can lead to unexpected behavior.

Exercise 13: Using Command Lists

In this exercise, we will use command lists to time certain commands and search for strings in the payroll file that we used in the previous chapter:

1. Navigate to the **Lesson2** folder:

   ```
   robin ~ $ cd ~/Lesson2
   ```

2. Let's measure the time it takes to sort a large file using the **time** command. This command measures the time taken by any task to complete execution. Just prefix **time** before any command to time it:

   ```
   robin ~/Lesson2 $ time sort payroll.tsv >sorted.txt
   real    0m1.899s
   user    0m7.701s
   sys     0m0.295s
   ```

   We need to consider the time under the **real** label, which measures the actual time spent, in other words, the time we would measure on a stopwatch. This is 1.89 seconds in this case—the value will vary depending on the speed of your computer.

The **user** time is a measure of how much computation was performed. It is similar to how we measure man-hours in the real world. It is the sum total of the time spent by each CPU core on this task. In this case (on a machine with 8 CPU cores), the total work done by all the cores is as much as if only one core had worked for 7.7 seconds. Since the CPU cores work in parallel, that work was actually completed in a much shorter time, namely 1.89 seconds.

Note that the **real** time represents how much time elapsed in the real world. If the process spends a long time waiting for an external event such as user or disk input, or network data, it is possible that the **real** time will exceed the user time.

The last label, **sys** time, is the amount of time the operating system was running for during this task. No matter what program is running, it has to give control to the operating system. For example, if something is written to a disk, a program requests the OS for a disk write. Until it is finished, the program is sleeping, and the OS is doing work on behalf of the program. Usually, we need not concern ourselves with **sys** time unless we notice that it is a very significant fraction of the **real** time.

> **Note**
>
> The time taken to run a command usually reduces if it is run multiple times. This is due to *disk caching*. Any data read from a disk is cached in memory by the OS in case a program requests it again. If the same command is run multiple times, the disk (which is hundreds of times slower than the RAM) doesn't have to be read again, thus speeding up the execution. For accurate timing, you should run a command multiple times and take the average, discarding the times for the first few runs.

3. Next, time a command list that sorts the file twice, once directly and once based on the second column in the file using the commands shown here:

```
robin ~/Lesson2 $ time (sort payroll.tsv > sorted.txt ; sort -k2 payroll.
tsv > sorted2.txt)
real    0m3.753s
user    0m14.793s
sys     0m0.418s
```

Note that it takes about twice as long as the previous command, which makes sense, since it is doing twice as much work. Also, you will notice that we placed the command list within parentheses so that the entire list is timed rather than just the first command.

4. Now, run the two **sort** commands concurrently and time the result, as follows:

```
robin ~/Lesson2 $ time (sort payroll.tsv > sorted.txt & sort -k2 payroll.
tsv > sorted2.txt)
real    0m2.961s
user    0m7.078s
sys     0m0.226s
```

As you can see from the preceding output, the two **sort** commands executed concurrently took slightly lesser time to execute than before.

The entry under the **user** label specifies the cumulative time taken by each CPU core. The quotient of the user time by the real time gives a rough estimate of how many cores were being used.

For the command list in step 3, the ratio is close to 4. This is because **sort** internally uses a parallel algorithm, using as many CPU cores as it thinks is best. In step 4, however, the ratio is closer to 2. Even though the time taken was slightly lower, it looks like only 2 cores were used. The exact reason for this kind of performance metric depends on the way **sort** works internally.

5. Let's try the same commands as before, but using three sorts instead:

```
robin ~/Lesson2 $ time (sort payroll.tsv > sorted.txt ; sort -k2 payroll.
tsv > sorted2.txt ; sort -k3 payroll.tsv > sorted3.txt)
real    0m5.341s
user    0m20.453s
sys     0m0.717s
```

The sequential version has become about 33% slower, since it's doing 33% more work than before:

```
robin ~/Lesson2 $ time (sort payroll.tsv > sorted.txt & sort -k2 payroll.
tsv > sorted2.txt &  sort -k3 payroll.tsv > sorted3.txt)
real    0m2.913s
user    0m6.026s
sys     0m0.218s
```

The concurrent version, on the other hand, took approximately the same time, despite doing 33% more work than before.

6. Use the **&&** operator with **grep** using the **-q** option, which doesn't print anything but just sets the exit code. Use this to search for a string in the **payroll.tsv** file:

```
robin ~/Lesson2 $ grep -q 'WALDO' payroll.tsv && echo 'Found'
Found
```

7. Use the **||** operator in a similar fashion:

```
robin ~/Lesson2 $ grep -q 'PINOCCHIO' payroll.tsv || echo 'Not Found'
Not Found
```

> **Note**
>
> If two commands are launched concurrently, it is not necessary for them to take 50% of the time that they would take if they were performed sequentially. Even though the CPU of your system has multiple cores that run independently, the memory, disk, and some operating system mechanisms cannot be used at the same time by two processes. There is always some serial execution in most programs or tasks, which usually increases the execution time. Very few computing tasks are created so that they can be completely in parallel.
>
> You can refer to Amdahl's law, which explains why this happens.

Job Control

Most of the commands we have tried so far take only a few seconds, at most, to complete, but in the real world, it is not uncommon to have tasks that run for long periods of time, which could be anywhere from minutes to hours or even weeks. In fact, some tasks never exit. They run forever, reading live data and processing it. A task or command that is running either in the foreground (the default) or background (when launched with **&**) is called a **job**. In this topic, we will learn about the mechanisms that are used to control jobs.

Keyboard Shortcuts for Controlling Jobs

Various keyboard shortcuts can be used to control jobs. These shortcuts send a **signal** to a program, which can be of various types and have conventional names. Some of these shortcuts and their respective functionalities are discussed in the following table:

Keyboard Shortcut	Operation	How the command interprets it	Signal sent to the program
Ctrl+C	Requests a command to terminate gracefully	This may not be honored by the command immediately, or at all	Sends a SIGINT (interrupt) signal
Ctrl+	Requests a command to terminate immediately	This may not be honored by the command immediately, or at all	Sends a SIGQUIT signal
Ctrl+Z	Suspends the execution of a program and returns the user to the command line immediately	The command cannot bypass this request	Sends a SIGSTOP (suspend) signal

Figure 3.1: A table showing the shortcuts and their functionalities

Look at the following examples:

```
robin ~ $ sleep 100
^C
robin ~ $ sleep 100
^\Quit (core dumped)
robin ~ $ sleep 100
^Z
[1]+  Stopped                 sleep 100
```

We can think of *Ctrl + C* as a request to the program to shut down in an orderly way and *Ctrl + * as a request to pull the plug immediately. Some commands will perform some book-keeping before terminating with **SIGINT** to ensure that the data they output is in a consistent state.

Commands for Controlling Jobs

Now, let's look at some commands that can be used to control jobs.

fg (foreground) and bg (background)

When a command is suspended with *Ctrl + Z*, we can resume its execution with either of these commands: **fg** or **bg**.

fg resumes the command in the foreground and **bg** resumes it in the background. When a program is resumed with **bg**, the effect is as if we had launched it with **&**. We immediately get back to the shell prompt and the command continues in the background. Resuming with **fg** just continues the program. We will only return to the shell prompt after it finishes its execution.

bg is typically used when a command seems to take too long, and we relegate it to the background. For example:

```
robin ~ $ sleep 100
^Z
[1]+  Stopped                 sleep 100
robin ~ $ bg
[1]+ sleep 100 &
robin ~ $ echo This is in the foreground
This is in the foreground
```

Note that **bg** prints out the job number and command of the job it acts on.

A typical use case of **fg** is to pause a long-running command, run some other commands, and then resume the original one. For example:

```
robin ~ $ sleep 100
^Z
[2]+  Stopped                 sleep 100
robin ~ $ echo This is in the foreground
This is in the foreground
robin ~ $ fg
sleep 100
```

By default, **fg** and **bg** operate on the *last suspended job*, but we can pass an argument with the job number of the process that we wish to resume.

jobs

This command lists all running jobs. For example, consider the following commands and their output:

```
robin ~ $ sleep 100 & sleep 100 & sleep 100 &
[1] 7678
[2] 7679
[3] 7680
```

This launches the **sleep** command thrice in the background (as we discussed before, sleep is an easy way to simulate a long-running command). As seen before, the shell prints out the job numbers and PIDs of each.

We can look at the status of the preceding commands using the **jobs** command:

```
robin ~ $ jobs
[1]    Running            sleep 100 &
[2]-   Running            sleep 100 &
[3]+   Running            sleep 100 &
```

The + and - signs displayed after the job number refer to the last and second last jobs.

> **Note**
>
> When one or more processes are suspended, the shell is in the foreground, so we can use either **fg** or **bg** to resume them. In that case, the default job that **fg** and **bg** apply to is the job associated with the + sign (as per what the **jobs** command shows). Similarly, you can use – with **fg** or **bg** to resume the second last job listed by **jobs**.
>
> When any process is running in the background, once again, we have the shell active, so the **fg** command can be used and the same rules for '+' and '–' apply. Obviously, we cannot use **bg** if any process is in the foreground, because the shell is not available to type a command when a foreground process is running. In this case, we have to first use *Ctrl + Z* to suspend the process and get the shell back, and then use **bg**.

The **jobs** command takes two options:

- **-p**: This option displays only the PIDs of jobs. For the preceding example, the following output is obtained:

```
robin ~ $ jobs -p
7678
7679
7680
```

- **-l**: This option displays the PIDs of jobs, as well as other information, including the full command line which launched the job:

```
robin ~ $ jobs -l
[1]   7678 Running                sleep 100 &
[2]-  7679 Running                sleep 100 &
[3]+  7680 Running                sleep 100 &
```

kill

kill sends a signal to the process with the specified PID. Usually, it is used to terminate a process, but we can send any other signal as well. By default, it sends **SIGTERM**, which requests the process to terminate. Look at the following example:

```
robin ~ $ sleep 100 &
[1] 24288
robin ~ $ kill 24288
robin ~ $ jobs
[1]+  Terminated             sleep 100
```

kill can be used to send any signal, including **SIGSTOP**, which will suspend the process, and **SIGCONT**, which resumes a process in the background (like **bg**). If you have a background process, you can no longer suspend it with *Ctrl* + *Z* because the shell is in the foreground, not the program. In that case, you can use **SIGSTOP**. The following example should make it clearer (bold text is what was typed):

```
robin ~ $ sleep 100
^Z
[1]+  Stopped                 sleep 100
robin ~ $ jobs -l
[1]+ 16961 Stopped                 sleep 100
robin ~ $ kill -s SIGCONT 16961
robin ~ $ jobs -l
[1]+ 16961 Running                 sleep 100 &
robin ~ $ kill -s SIGSTOP 16961
[1]+  Stopped                 sleep 100
```

Here, we started a process, and suspended it with *Ctrl* + *Z*. Then, we used jobs to see the PID and sent **SIGCONT** to resume it in the background (we could have used **bg**, too). At this point, *Ctrl* + *Z* would not work to suspend it, since *Ctrl* + *Z* works only on foreground processes, but we can send **SIGSTOP** instead to get the same effect.

> **Note**
>
> Logically, you can only use **kill** if the command line is in the foreground, and you are able to type the command, meaning that the process you affect has to be in the background. However, you can open multiple shell windows on any operating system, and so you can use **kill** from one shell to affect a job or process inside another shell instance if you know the PID.
>
> Remember that PIDs are unique across the entire set of processes running on a system. In such a case, we can terminate a process, irrespective of whether it was in the foreground.

To end a process, we can use any of the following signals with the **-s** option: **SIGINT**, **SIGTERM**, **SIGQUIT**, or **SIGKILL**. A program can choose to ignore any of these signals except for **SIGKILL**.

Typically, *Ctrl* + C is used to terminate a command with **SIGINT**, and if that doesn't work, the **kill** command is used. Note that *Ctrl* + C cannot be used with a background process. If a program doesn't get terminated with either *Ctrl* + C (**SIGINT**) or even **SIGTERM**, we can use **SIGKILL**, as follows:

```
robin ~ $ sleep 100 &
[1] 23993
robin ~ $ kill -s SIGKILL 23993
robin ~ $ jobs
[1]+  Killed                  sleep 100
```

Every signal also has a number associated with it. Usually, it's easier to remember the name, but it is worth remembering that **SIGTERM** is 15 and **SIGKILL** is 9. When specifying the signal by its number, we type the number itself as an option, for example, **kill -9**. We can use the signal number 9 for **SIGKILL** instead of typing the name:

```
robin ~ $ sleep 100 &
[1] 23996
robin ~ $ kill -9 23996
robin ~ $ jobs
[1]+  Killed                  sleep 100
```

Remember, **SIGKILL** is the last resort when nothing else works. If a suspended process is killed, the process dies as soon as it is resumed:

```
robin ~ $ sleep 100
^Z
[1]+  Stopped                 sleep 100
robin ~ $ jobs -l
[1]+   772 Stopped               sleep 100
robin ~ $ kill 772
robin ~ $ fg
sleep 100
Terminated
```

Regular Expressions

A regular expression, also called a **regex** (plural regexes), is a kind of pattern-matching syntax, similar to wildcards, but much more powerful. A complete description of regexes would fill many chapters, so we will restrict ourselves to a reasonable subset in this chapter.

The most common use case of regexes is with the **grep** and **sed** commands, which we studied in the previous chapter. The basic operation we perform with a regex is to match it against some text:

- **grep** can search for text matching a regex

- **sed** can search and replace the text matching a regex with a specified replacement string

> **Note**
>
> Since the special characters in regex syntax overlap with those that the shell uses, always pass regexes in single quotes to ensure that the shell passes them literally to the command, without interpretation. Commands that accept regexes will handle escape sequences by themselves.

There are two kinds of regexes, that is, basic and extended syntax. The only difference between the two is that basic syntax requires escaping many of the special characters, which is less readable. Hence, we will learn the extended syntax here.

A regex can be separated into a series of **elements**, each followed by an optional **quantifier**. Each element and quantifier is matched against the target text. A regex can also contain **anchoring** symbols and syntax called **backreferences** and **subexpressions**. We will learn more about these in the sections that follow.

We will also look at a few examples to make the concepts that are learned here clearer. We will use **grep** with a herestring and the **--color** and **-E** options. The **-E** specifies extended regex support. Without this, **grep** uses basic regex syntax. For clarity, the matching characters in the output here are shown in bold. On screen, they would appear in color.

Elements

Elements, also referred to as **atoms** formally, are analogous to a noun in natural language. An element refers to a set of characters, any of which can match. These characters can be any of the following:

A Literal Character

A literal character matches just itself. You can match any single character in a regex; however, punctuation and other symbols need to be escaped. Although some symbols strictly do not need escaping, it's simpler to just escape everything unless specifically mentioned not to.

A Period

A single period symbol is used to match any possible character with no restrictions.

Character Sets

To match character sets, enclose them in square brackets. These can be defined in many ways. For instance, look at the following.

- `[aeiou]` matches any of the vowels

- `[a-z]` matches a range, everything from a to z

- `[[:alnum:]]` matches the specified character class (recall character classes from the previous chapter)

Multiple ranges can also be combined as follows:

- `[a-z1-9]` matches everything from a to z or 1 to 9.

- `[^abc]` matches any character but a, b, and c. If the first character after the `[` is a ^ (caret) character, the set is inverted.

- `[^[:alnum:]]` matches any character that is not a member of the `[:alnum:]` character class.

Special Backslash Sequences

- **\s** matches any whitespace character.
- **\S** matches any non-whitespace character.
- **\w** matches a "word character", that is, alphanumeric characters or underscores, the same as `[_[:alnum:]]`.
- **\W** matches a non-word character. This is the inverse of **\w**, and is the same as `[^_[:alnum:]]`.
- **\<** matches the beginning of a word.
- **\>** matches the end of a word.
- **\b** matches the end or beginning of a word.
- **\B** matches the inverse of **\b**, that is, it matches a non-word boundary.

Look at the following example, which is used to match multiple whitespace characters:

```
robin ~ $ grep -E --color 'final\s+frontier' <<< 'Space - the final
frontier'
Space - the final    frontier
```

Here, **\s+** means match one or more whitespace characters.

Let's look at how you can match words at the boundaries of a line. First, try the following command:

```
robin ~ $ grep -E --color 'need' <<< 'unneeded needles need lessons'
unneeded needles need lessons
```

This matches all three places where **need** occurs. Now, let's match only the complete word:

```
robin ~ $ grep -E --color '\<need\>' <<< 'unneeded needles need lessons'
unneeded needles need lessons
```

The same effect can be obtained by using **\b** at both ends:

```
robin ~ $ grep -E --color '\bneed\b' <<< 'unneeded needles need lessons'
unneeded needles need lessons
```

You can use **\B** to match a non-word boundary. In this case, we match if neither end of the search string is at a word boundary:

```
robin ~ $ grep -E --color '\Bneed\B' <<< 'unneeded needles need lessons'
unneeded needles need lessons
```

Parenthesized Expression

Any regex can be wrapped in a pair of parentheses and treated as a single element. Let's match "ba" followed by one or more "na". The "na" is treated as a single element because of the parentheses (we will examine the **+** quantifier in the next section):

```
robin ~ $ grep -E --color 'ba(na)+' <<< 'ba bana banana bananana'
ba bana banana bananana
```

Alternative Regexes

Two regexes separated by the **|** (pipe) symbol will match either of the two. This can be applied to any number of regexes, as shown here:

```
(regex1) | (regex2) | (regex2)
```

For instance, in the following command, **b|f** matches one occurrence of "b" or "f":

```
robin ~ $ grep -E --color '(b|f)right' <<< 'fright wright bright '
fright wright bright
```

Parentheses were required in the preceding code since the **|** operator treats the entire expressions on either side as alternatives. To express the same regex without parentheses, we would have to write **'bright|fright'**.

Quantifiers

A quantifier is like an adjective in natural language. It qualifies an element (typically, describing how many times it can occur). The following are the various quantifiers that can be used:

- **No quantifier**: This quantifier matches the preceding element exactly once. For example, the regex **'abcd'** can be considered as four elements a, b, c, and d, with no quantifiers. This regex matches the literal text "abcd".

- **The ? quantifier**: This quantifier matches the preceding element optionally, that is, zero or one time. For example, the regex **'re?d'** matches "red" and "reed". The second e is optional.

- **The * quantifier**: This quantifier matches the preceding element zero or more times. For example, the regex `'mo*'` matches "m", "mo", "moo", "mooo", and so on.

- **The + quantifier**: This quantifier matches the preceding element one or more times. For example, the regex `'co+'` matches "co", "coo", "cooo", and so on.

- **The {} quantifier**: This quantifier matches the preceding element matched a specified number of times. Within the `{}`, you can specify the number of times to match, as follows:

(a) `{n}`: Matches exactly n times

(b) `{n,}`: Matches n or more times

(c) `{,m}`: Matches at most m times

(d) `{n,m}`: Matches at least n times, but at most m times

For example, the regex `'co{2,3}'` matches only "coo" and "cooo."

Anchoring

Anchors force a regex to match only if the expression occurs at a particular location:

- The ^ anchor symbol matches the start of a line. For instance:

```
robin ~ $ grep -E --color '^hip' <<< 'hip hip hurray'
hip hip hurray
```

This matches only the first "hip", since it's at the start of the line.

- The $ anchor symbol matches the end of a line. For example:

```
robin ~ $ grep -E --color 'ho$' <<< 'ho ho ho'
ho ho ho
```

This matches only the last "ho", since it's at the end of the line.

Subexpressions and Backreferences

Subexpressions allow you to delimit a part of an expression, which can be referred to in the regex later via a backreference:

- The part of a regex that is surrounded in parentheses is called a **subexpression**.

- A backslash followed by a single digit N is called a **backreference** (also called a **backref**), which matches the Nth subexpression.

Let's understand this with an example. Sometimes, we need to match some text and then match the same text again. For instance, consider the following HTML fragments:

```
<DIV> This is a div </DIV>

<P> This is a paragraph </P>
```

We need to match any opening tag, followed by text, followed by the same tag being closed again. It is not possible to specify every tag individually. In fact, HTML allows any string of letters to be considered a tag. To match these kinds of expressions, we can use backreferences and subexpressions.

A subexpression is defined by using parentheses around any part of a regex. Every time a subexpression is matched, the literal text that it matched is remembered, and can be matched again with a backref to it by writing a backslash, followed by a number.

For example, let's match the preceding HTML fragment example incrementally, building up a regex step by step (matches in output are indicated in bold):

First, let's match an opening tag. Remember that < and > should not be escaped, as they indicate word boundaries when escaped:

```
robin ~ $ grep --color -E '<([A-Z]+)>' <<< '<DIV> This is a div </DIV>'
<DIV> This is a div </DIV>
```

The part within the parentheses is the first subexpression and can be referred to later as \1. Next, let's match any sequence of spaces and alphabets. This is the tag's contents:

```
robin ~ $ grep --color -E '<([A-Z]+)>[a-zA-Z[:space:]]+' <<< '<DIV> This is
a div </DIV>'
<DIV> This is a div </DIV>
```

Finally, let's match the closing tag using a backref to ensure that the same tagname that opened is used:

```
robin ~ $ grep --color -E '<([A-Z]+)>[a-zA-Z[:space:]]+</\1>' <<< '<DIV>
This is a div </DIV>'
<DIV> This is a div </DIV>
```

The \1 matches the same string that matched within the first set of parentheses. We can use upto 9 subexpressions and refer to them by their number (as per the order of occurrence).

This preceding regex will match any matching opening and closing tag (case sensitively). Remember that if there is no match, **grep** won't print any output:

```
robin ~ $ grep --color -E '<([A-Z]+)>[a-zA-Z[:space:]]+</\1>' <<< '<DIV>
This is a div </P>'
robin ~ $ grep --color -E '<([A-Z]+)>[a-zA-Z[:space:]]+</\1>' <<< '<DIV>
This is a div </DIVE>'
robin ~ $ grep --color -E '<([A-Z]+)>[a-zA-Z[:space:]]+</\1>' <<< '<P> This
is a div </P>'
<P> This is a div </P>
robin ~ $ grep --color -E '<([A-Z]+)>[a-zA-Z[:space:]]+</\1>' <<< '<I> This
is a div </I>'
<I> This is a div </I>
```

If a backref is used, the subexpression and backref to it must be identical, otherwise the regex will be considered a mismatch at the point where the subexpression starts. Therefore, the first two examples show that none of the text matched. This mechanism is also useful for search and replace with **sed**. We can use backrefs in the replacement string to refer to parts of the match.

Constructing regexes should be done very carefully. It is quite easy to write a regex that matches much more or much less text than it was intended to. Just like wildcards, the danger of matching much more is higher, especially if we perform an irreversible operation with the matched text-like replacement.

The regexes we use here are called **POSIX compatible regexes**. A more comprehensive regex standard with many more features, called **Perl compatible regular expressions** (**PCRE**), is also widely used. Most programming languages have regex support built in, or as a library. There are slight variations in the features they support. It is necessary to consider the differences in regex behavior in the environments or programming languages we use.

> **Note**
>
> There are some theoretical limitations to regexes. For example, using regexes to match a complete tag of an XML file is impossible to do correctly. Data Formats such as XML, JSON, and even the source code of many programming languages are often recursive and nested in structure. Regexes cannot deal with a recursive text structure correctly.
>
> Curious students are advised to learn the computer science concepts of formal grammars and parsing in order to understand regexes on a deeper level.

Exercise 14: Using Regular Expressions

In this exercise, we will practice the use of extended regular expressions using **grep** and **sed** by using the dataset that was provided in the first chapter:

1. Navigate to the **data** folder within the **Lesson1** folder:

   ```
   robin ~ $ cd ~/Lesson1/data
   ```

2. Search recursively for all files that contain the words "India" or "China". Search for entire words and display only one match per file (only a few lines are shown in the following output):

   ```
   robin ~/Lesson1/data $ grep -m1 -w -E -R 'India|China' | less
   pinaceae/picea/asperata/data.txt:Immature Picea asperata growing in the
   Jiuzhaigou Valley, Sichuan, China
   pinaceae/picea/aurantiaca/data.txt:endemic to China, where it is only
   known from western Sichuan. Its common name
   pinaceae/picea/spinulosa/data.txt:Himalaya, in India (Sikkim), Nepal and
   Bhutan. It grows at altitudes of
   pinaceae/picea/neoveitchii/data.txt:family. It is found only in China. It
   is threatened by habitat loss.
   ```

```
pinaceae/picea/schrenkiana/data.txt:to the Tian Shan mountains of central
Asia in western China (Xinjiang),
pinaceae/picea/smithiana/data.txt:Afghanistan, northern Pakistan, India to
central Nepal. It grows at altitudes
```

3. Many of these data files specify the typical heights of the trees in this format: 30-50 m. Search all such patterns from these files so that we can mine the height data. We look for patterns that have 2 digits followed by a hyphen, and 2 more digits followed by a space, an "m" and then another space. We will use the **--color** option to highlight these matches (a few lines of the output are shown here with the matches in bold):

```
robin ~/Lesson1/data $ grep -R --color -E '[0-9]{2}-[0-9]{2} m '
pinaceae/picea/asperata/data.txt:It is a medium-sized evergreen tree
growing to 25-40 m tall, and with a trunk
pinaceae/picea/spinulosa/data.txt:It is a large evergreen tree growing to
40-55 m tall (exceptionally to 65 m),
pinaceae/picea/smithiana/data.txt:Picea smithiana is a large evergreen
tree growing to 40-55 m tall
pinaceae/picea/rubens/data.txt:tree that under optimal conditions grows to
18-40 m (59-131 ft) tall with a
pinaceae/picea/obovata/data.txt:It is a medium-sized evergreen tree
growing to 15-35 m tall, and with a trunk
```

Note that we are assuming that no tree is taller than 99 meters.

4. Many websites enforce username and password policies. For example, a username consists of up to 10 characters, starting with a lowercase letter of the alphabet and only containing lowercase alphabets, digits, and underscores. We will now write a regex that can match such usernames: use the **-q** flag of **grep** to not print any output and use **&&** and **||** to print **Valid** or **Invalid** (recall the correct use of brackets in such cases):

```
robin ~/Lesson1/data $ (grep -q -E '^[a-z][a-z0-9_]{,9}$' <<< 'hunter2' &&
echo 'Valid')  || echo 'Invalid'
Valid
robin ~/Lesson1/data $ (grep -q -E '^[a-z][a-z0-9_]{,9}$' <<< 'hunter222'
&& echo 'Valid')  || echo 'Invalid'
Valid
```

The preceding snippets return **Valid** as the output since the input text matches the regex; hence, it follows all the rules we specified.

5. Next, try the following snippets:

    ```
    robin ~/Lesson1/data $ (grep -q -E '^[a-z][a-z0-9_]{,9}$' <<< '2hunter' &&
    echo 'Valid')  || echo 'Invalid'
    Invalid
    robin ~/Lesson1/data $ (grep -q -E '^[a-z][a-z0-9_]{,9}$' <<< 'Hunter22'
    && echo 'Valid')  || echo 'Invalid'
    Invalid
    ```

    The preceding two snippets return **Invalid** as the output since the input text
    either begins with a number or a capital letter.

6. Now, try the following two snippets:

    ```
    robin ~/Lesson1/data $ (grep -q -E '^[a-z][a-z0-9_]{,9}$' <<< 'hunter%2'
    && echo 'Valid')  || echo 'Invalid'
    Invalid
    robin ~/Lesson1/data $ (grep -q -E '^[a-z][a-z0-9_]{,9}$' <<<
    'hunter12345678' && echo 'Valid')  || echo 'Invalid'
    Invalid
    ```

    The preceding two snippets return **Invalid** as the output since one contains
    symbols other than the ones specified in the input and the other contains more
    than 10 characters.

    Notice the use of the anchors ^ and **$** to make sure that the regex matches the
    entire string and not just partially. Alternatively, we could use the **-x** option of
    grep, which will only consider a match if an entire line from start to end matches
    the regex.

7. Phone numbers in North America have the following format: (123) 456-7890. They
    contain 3 digits in parentheses, followed by a space, and then two groups of 3 and
    4 digits separated by a hyphen. Let's create this regex incrementally. First, write a
    regex that matches the 3 digits in parentheses:

    ```
    robin ~/Lesson1/data $ (grep -q -w -E '^\([[:digit:]]{3}\)$' <<< '(123)'
    && echo 'Valid')  || echo 'Invalid'
    Valid
    ```

8. Now, modify the regex to additionally match a space character and then 3 more digits:

```
robin ~/Lesson1/data $ (grep -q -w -E '^\([[:digit:]]{3}\)\ [[:digit:]]
{3}$' <<< '(123) 456' && echo 'Valid')  || echo 'Invalid'
Valid
```

9. Finally, add the last bit. Match a hyphen and 4 more digits:

```
robin ~/Lesson1/data $ (grep -q -w -E '^\([[:digit:]]{3}\)\ [[:digit:]]
{3}-[[:digit:]]{4}$' <<< '(123) 456-7890' && echo 'Valid')  || echo
'Invalid'
Valid
```

10. For the next part of the exercise, navigate to the **Lesson3** folder in the home directory:

```
robin ~/Lesson1/data1 $ cd ~/Lesson3
```

11. A sample file called **markdown.txt** is included in the chapter data. This file contains a small poem in basic markdown. Markdown is a simple text formatting scheme that has many dialects. In markdown, text surrounded by two asterisk symbols becomes bold, and text surrounded by underscores becomes italic. In HTML, bold and italic are specified by surrounding text with **<b>** and **<i>** tags. A closing tag is written as **</tag>**, for example, **<i>** is closed with **</i>**. In the **markdown.txt** file, only individual words are formatted in bold or italic. Use **cat** to view the contents of the file:

```
robin ~/Lesson3 $ cat markdown.txt
A **fly** and a **flea** in a flue,
They were trapped, so they thought "What to _do_?"
"Let us _fly_!" said the **flea**,
"Let us _flee_!" said the **fly**,
So, they _flew_ through a flaw in the _flue_!
```

12. Match the bold text using **grep** first (so that we can ensure we have the right regex):

```
robin ~/Lesson3 $ grep --color -E '\*\*([a-z]+)\*\*' <markdown.txt
A **fly** and a **flea** in a flue,
"Let us _fly_!" said the **flea**,
"Let us _flee_!" said the **fly**,
```

13. Repeat this for the italic text:

```
robin ~/Lesson3 $ grep --color -E '_([a-z]+)_' <markdown.txt
They were trapped, so they thought "What to _do_?"
"Let us _fly_!" said the **flea**,
"Let us _flee_!" said the **fly**,
So, they _flew_ through a flaw in the _flue_!
```

14. Now, compose a **sed** command using backrefs to replace the ** with **** and **** tags:

```
robin ~/Lesson3 $ sed -E -e 's#\*\*([a-z]+)\*\*#<b>\1</b>#g' <markdown.txt
A <b>fly</b> and a <b>flea</b> in a flue,
They were trapped, so they thought "What to _do_?"
"Let us _fly_!" said the <b>flea</b>,
"Let us _flee_!" said the <b>fly</b>,
So, they _flew_ through a flaw in the _flue_!
```

In the preceding snippet, we need to pass the **-E** flag to **sed** to make it accept extended regexes with backreferences. Also, the hash symbol was used as the delimiter for the replacement expression of **sed**. Remember that you can use whatever symbol you want. Now, let's analyze each of the three parts of that expression:

(a) The first part is for matching. **([a-z]+)** matches any word that has two asterisks on either side, and captures the word as a subexpression.

(b) The second part is the replacement string. **\1** replaces the matched string with the bold tag containing a backref to subexpression 1. This means that it uses whatever text was matched in subexpression 1 in the first part.

(c) The final part is the **g** flag, which tells **sed** to perform the substitution globally, and not stop at the first match.

Remember that we should not escape the **<** and **>** symbols, but we must escape *****.

15. **sed** can be passed the **-e** option multiple times. Now, write the entire replacement expression for both bold and italic:

```
robin ~/Lesson3 $ sed -E -e 's#\*\*([a-z]+)\*\*#<b>\1</b>#g' -e 's#_
([a-z]+)_#<i>\1</i>#g' <markdown.txt
A <b>fly</b> and a <b>flea</b> in a flue,
They were trapped, so they thought "What to <i>do</i>?"
"Let us <i>fly</i>!" said the <b>flea</b>,
"Let us <i>flee</i>!" said the <b>fly</b>,
So, they <i>flew</i> through a flaw in the <i>flue</i>!
```

In this exercise, we have practiced using various regex mechanisms. They are often cryptic, but are quite powerful once you understand the nuances. Always construct and test regexes incrementally to avoid errors. The **--color** option of grep is especially useful for seeing what exactly the regex matched when debugging a complicated one.

Activity 8: Word Matching with Regular Expressions

In the last exercise, we learned how to formulate regular expressions to match certain patterns. In this activity, we will practice composing some more regexes to exercise our skills.

The sample data for this chapter contains a file called **words.txt**, which is a word list consisting of one word per line. Your goal is to write regexes that match certain words from this word file. The matching word will be constrained to necessarily have certain characters in certain positions. This is similar to finding possible words to play in a Scrabble game, given a certain rack. You need to write regexes to answer the following questions:

1. Find the number of words that are five letters in length, begin with a consonant, and contain alternating vowels and consonants, for example, river.

2. Find the number of words that are two characters or more, begin with a consonant, and contain alternating consonants and vowels.

3. How many 3 letter words start and end with the same letter?

4. Find the number of words that have two consecutive occurrences of the same vowel. For example, beet and roofing.

5. Find the five letter words that are palindromes.

The **words.txt** file is included in the chapters sample data within the **Lesson3** folder in your home directory. Note that this file may contain words that are not found in an official dictionary. All the words in this file are in lowercase. To answer the preceding questions, follow these steps:

1. Navigate to the sample data folder for this chapter.

2. Use the **grep** command with the word list data, as follows:

    ```
    grep -E pattern words.txt
    ```

    Here, **pattern** represents the regex that matches the requirements for each question. Remember to use the **-c** flag when the count of matches is to be found.

The answers you should get for the preceding questions are as follows:

1. 506

2. 2339

3. 23

4. 1097

5. civic, kayak, level, madam, minim, radar, rotor, and tenet

> **Note**
>
> The solution for this activity can be found on page 276.

Shell Expansion

The basic concept of shell expansion is that the shell substitutes certain expressions that have been typed on the command line with some expanded text. In earlier chapters, we learned to use shell expansion constructs such as wildcards and escape sequences. In this topic, we will learn about several more mechanisms for expansions that the shell provides.

Environment Variables and Variable Expansion

Environment variables in Bash are similar in function to variables in most programming languages; they are names to which values are associated. An environment variable is initialized with the following syntax:

```
VARNAME=VALUE
```

There is no space on either side of the equals symbol, and the value follows the same rules of the shell as those with respect to quoting, escape sequences, and wildcards (and other expansions). The value of an environment variable is expanded with the **$** symbol, as shown here:

```
robin ~ $ ANSWER=42
robin ~ $ echo The answer is "$ANSWER"
The answer is 42
```

Here, the first command initializes the **ANSWER** variable with the value **42**, and the second command prints the value of the variable. We can also use an alternate syntax to expand the value of the variable, as shown here:

```
robin ~ $ echo "${ANSWER}"
42
```

> **Note**
>
> It is always advisable to double-quote variable expansions. Failure to do so may result in unpredictable results if the value inside contains special characters, especially wildcards. In such cases, an unquoted expansion will further undergo wildcard expansion, which may not be what was intended.

For brevity, we can use the **$ANSWER** syntax when just getting a variable's value. But the **${ANSWER}** syntax delimits the variable name, preventing characters after it from being mixed, as shown here:

```
robin ~ $ echo "${ANSWER}S"
42S
robin ~ $ echo "$ANSWERS"
```

Notice that, without braces, the shell tried to expand the **ANSWERS** variable, giving an empty string, whereas with the brace syntax, the extra **S** was delimited from the variable name. A variable that has not been assigned so far is treated as an empty string.

We can extract a substring from a variable, as follows:

```
robin ~ $ NAME=RUMPELSTILTSKIN
robin ~ $ echo I walk on "${NAME:6:6}"
I walk on STILTS
```

The first number within the curly braces specifies the offset, and the second specifies the length. If the first number is omitted, it defaults to 0. If the second number is omitted, it defaults to the maximum possible number within that string. Let's look at a few more examples:

```
robin ~ $ echo Yo Ho Ho and a bottle of "${NAME::3}"
Yo Ho Ho and a bottle of RUM
robin ~ $ echo The earths atmosphere is a thin "${NAME:11}"
The earths atmosphere is a thin SKIN
```

Notice that when we skipped the first number, we had to specify the colon separators anyway, but when we skipped the second, the colon was unnecessary.

The length of a string in an environment variable can be extracted as follows:

```
robin ~ $ NAME='RUMPELSTILTSKIN'
robin ~ $ echo "${#NAME}"
15
```

You can also perform indirection with the **!** symbol. **Indirection** is the process of using the value stored in one variable as a variable name:

```
robin ~ $ STUFF=ANSWER
robin ~ $ ANSWER=42
robin ~ $ echo "${!STUFF}"
42
```

Here, **${!STUFF}** expands to the value of the **ANSWER** variable, whose name is the value of the **STUFF** variable. This is like the concept of a pointer or reference in a programming language.

Variables can also contain arrays or sequences of multiple values, which are initialized by a whitespace-separated list within parentheses, as shown here:

```
robin ~  $ LIST=(1 2 a b c d)
```

We can access elements within an array by specifying the index number within square brackets, as shown here (note that array indexes start at 0):

```
robin ~  $ echo "${LIST[2]}"
a
```

The **@** symbol, when used as an index, returns the entire array:

```
robin ~  $ echo "${LIST[@]}"
1 2 a b c d
```

The same syntax that we used for substrings can also be used for arrays to get a subarray:

```
robin ~  $ echo "${LIST[@]:2:4}"
a b c d
```

We can assign any subarray to a new array variable, as shown here:

```
robin ~ $ LIST2=(${LIST[@]:2:4})
robin ~ $ echo "${LIST2[@]}"
a b c d
```

> **Note**
>
> Although we have used uppercase named variables for illustration purposes, it is advisable to always use lowercase variable names, since the shell has several variables that it uses internally, for example, PATH, HOME, IFS, and so on. Using an uppercase variable name may end up overwriting one of these, resulting in unexpected behavior.

Arithmetic Expansion

The shell can perform simple arithmetic by using **$** with double parentheses. The following is the syntax:

```
$(( expression ))
```

Here, **expression** consists of numbers and/or environment variables that are combined with operators. Let's look at an example:

```
robin ~ $ echo $(( 9 + 10 + 11 + 12 ))
42
```

Variables can be used directly within arithmetic expansions:

```
robin ~ $ echo $(( ANSWER * 2 ))
84
```

The following operations are supported:

Integer Arithmetic

- + for addition, – for subtraction (and negation), * for multiplication, and / for division
- % for remainder/modulus
- ** for exponentiation

Logical or Boolean

These operators treat zero as false and non-zero as true. Similarly, they return 0 for false and 1 for true:

- <, >, <=, and >= for comparing numbers
- == for equality and != for inequality
- && for logical AND and || for logical OR
- ! for negation

Bitwise operators

These work on the individual bits of the binary values of numbers:

- | for OR, & for AND, and ^ for XOR
- << and >> for left and right shift
- ~ for bitwise negation

Compound Assignment Operators

These are similar to the ones in the C language, such as the following:

- +=, -=, *=, /=, and %= for arithmetic
- &=, |=, ^=, <<=, and >>= for bitwise operations

For example:

```
robin ~ $ X=1
robin ~ $ echo $(( X+=1 ))
2
robin ~ $ echo "$X"
2
```

Here, X+=1 means X = X + 1 or "Add 1 to X". All the other compound assignment operators also work similarly.

Increment and Decrement Operators

These are supported in both postfix and prefix forms, just like in the C language:

- ++ is used for increments
- -- is used for decrements

Let's look at the following example:

```
robin ~ $ X=1
robin ~ $ echo $(( ++X ))
2
robin ~ $ echo "$X"
2
```

The prefix form of ++ increments X, and the whole expression evaluates to the new value of X.

Now, observe how the postfix form works:

```
robin ~ $ X=1
robin ~ $ echo $(( X++ ))
1
robin ~ $ echo "$X"
2
```

The postfix form of ++ increments X, and the whole expression evaluates to the **old** value of X. These operators are all the same as what you will find in the C language (for integers) and have the same semantics.

> **Note**
>
> Do not mix multiple instances of the increment and decrement operators (for the same variable) in the same calculation, as it leads to confusing behavior.
>
> Since the operators work on fixed sized signed integers, the behavior on overflow may depend on the hardware of the machine. If your calculation could potentially overflow, keep this in mind. Usually, overflow happens at 2^64 on modern 64-bit systems. It is unlikely that you will calculate such a large number, but it can happen.
>
> If you need much more sophisticated calculation abilities, you can use the **bc** command instead. It is a full-fledged calculator that supports arbitrary precision. Read the man page for **bc** to learn more about it.

Brace Expansion

This mechanism helps us generate multiple strings based on a pattern. The pattern is specified as a sequence of values within curly braces. The shell looks at the values within the braces and replicates the string for each value. It repeats this process for every set of braces in the string. This creates a list of strings based on the sequence or permutations of the elements of multiple sequences. The best way to understand it is to look at some examples.

Here's how you can generate a basic sequence:

```
robin ~ $ echo test{1,2,3}
test1 test2 test3
```

You can also generate range sequences by specifying the range within curly braces, as shown here:

```
robin ~ $ echo test{1..3}
test1 test2 test3
robin ~ $ echo test{3..1}
test3 test2 test1
```

Multiple individual sequences can be generated by using multiple sets of curly braces, one after the other:

```
robin ~ $ echo test/dir{1,2} file{a..c}
test/dir1 test/dir2 filea fileb filec
```

If we have a string with multiple brace ranges, we get all the possible combinations expanded. This is called a **Cartesian product**:

```
robin ~ $ echo test{1,2,3}{a,b,c}
test1a test1b test1c test2a test2b test2c test3a test3b test3c
robin ~ $ echo test/dir{1,2,3}/file{a..c}
test/dir1/filea test/dir1/fileb test/dir1/filec test/dir2/filea test/dir2/fileb
test/dir2/filec test/dir3/filea test/dir3/fileb test/dir3/filec
```

The expressions within the braces can be wildcards:

```
robin ~/Lesson1/data1 $ echo ab{*.jpg,*.png}
abby.jpg abradolf-lincler.jpg abstract_app.png
```

In this case, we can interpret that the brace expansion resulted in `'ab*.jpg ab*.png'`, which then got expanded as wildcards, leading to the files being listed.

Recursive Expansion with eval

We saw how indirection was used previously. We used the result of one variable expansion as the variable name in turn. This worked to one level. Recursive expansion lets us use the results of one expansion as a string to be further expanded. We can do this to any level and with any of the expansion types. The following syntax is used:

```
eval args
```

This expands **args** and executes it as a command.

Let's understand this better with an example. Consider the following commands:

```
robin ~ $ A=1
robin ~ $ B=A
robin ~ $ echo ${A}
1
robin ~ $ echo ${B}
A
robin ~ $ echo ${${B}}
bash: ${${B}}: bad substitution
```

We might have expected that **${${B}}** would get expanded to **${A}**, and in turn to **1**. However, the shell does not expand recursively in this fashion. For this purpose, the **eval** command is provided:

```
eval arg1 arg2 ...
```

This just expands every argument and runs that as a command. With judicious use of escaping, we can make recursive expansion possible. Let's see how we can make the preceding example work:

```
robin ~ $ eval echo \${${B}}
1
```

The way this works is as follows:

- **eval** performs substitution on **echo \${${B}}**
- The first **$** symbol is escaped, so that does not cause any expansion
- **${B}** gets expanded to **A**
- The result is **echo ${A}**
- **eval** executes this as a command, causing it to print 1, which was the result we desired

It can be a little tricky to use **eval**, but it is very useful for using an expanded value within another expansion. The basic rule of thumb for recursive expansion is this: use **echo** to print the string you need to be expanded, then call **eval** on it.

We can use a handy feature of Bash for debugging complex expansions: the **set** command. This command has many uses, but we will examine its use for debugging how the shell works when it expands a command. Let's say we run the following command:

```
set -x
```

The shell writes a trace for each command after it expands the command and before it executes it. The tracing can be turned off with the following command:

```
set +x
```

Let's see how the preceding example plays out with tracing enabled:

```
robin ~ $ A=1
robin ~ $ B=A
robin ~ $ set -x
++ printf '\033]0;%s@%s:%s\007' robin archaic '~'
robin ~ $ eval echo \${${B}}
+ eval echo '${A}'
++ echo 1
1
++ printf '\033]0;%s@%s:%s\007' robin archaic '~'
robin ~ $ set +x
+ set +x
```

Ignore the lines that start with **++ printf**. This is the shell tracing its own behavior, displaying a prompt. To prevent this extraneous output, clear the shell environment variable **PROMPT_COMMAND**, as follows:

```
unset PROMPT_COMMAND
```

The **eval** command's trace was printed by the shell:

- The shell first printed the **eval** command we typed, after performing expansion.

- Since **eval** itself executes the **echo** command, the expansion of that was printed in turn.

- Finally, the output of the **echo** command is seen.

As we can see, using tracing makes it much easier to follow what is happening with complex expansions.

> **Note**
>
> The **eval** command is very powerful. It lets us compose a command as text and execute it. This power also comes with its own caveats: if we compose an incorrect command and **eval** it, it may end up doing things we did not intend. A more serious problem is when executing code provided from an outside source, which may be malicious.
>
> This is a general principle in most software: user input should never be unintentionally interpreted as program code. Security exploits such as SQL injection are a real-world example of this problem.

Command Substitution

This is the most useful shell expansion construct. It expands the output of a command line literally inline. The following syntax is used:

```
$(command)
```

Here, **command** can be an individual command, a command list, or a pipeline. The expanded text can be treated as arguments or assigned to an environment variable. For example:

```
robin ~ $ bc <<< '10^3 + 9^3'
1729
robin ~ $ echo $(bc <<< '12^3 + 1^3')
1729
robin ~ $ HARDY=$(bc <<< '12^3 + 1^3')
robin ~ $ echo $HARDY
1729
```

The first **bc** command shows us the Ramanujan–Hardy number. The sum of 9 cubed and 10 cubed. Note that we used herestring redirection with <<<. In the second command, **bc** is run within the expansion, and its output is expanded as arguments to **echo**. Finally, an expansion was assigned it to a variable and printed with **echo**.

> **Note**
>
> There is an alternative (and practically obsolete) syntax that is used to perform command substitution. It involves just using backquotes around a command, for example, **echo `bc <<< 8^8`**. Students are advised not to use this syntax, but it is often encountered in older shell script books and websites, so we need to be aware of it.

Process Substitution

Process substitution is somewhat related to file redirection, but works in a different way. It is also conceptually distinct from the other types of substitution. Process substitution allows the output of a command to be treated as a file, whose name gets passed as a command-line argument to another command. The basic syntax of process substitution is as follows:

```
command1 <(command2 arg1 arg2) <(command3)
```

For example, consider these commands:

```
cut -f1 -d, land.csv >l1.txt
cut -f3 -d, land.csv >l3.txt
paste -d$'/\t' l3.txt l1.txt > l13.txt
```

We used **cut** to extract the first and third columns from a file and then pasted them into an output file. This approach involved unnecessary complexity:

- We had to make temporary files with unique names
- We had to make sure we typed the filenames exactly in the third command
- We will have to delete the temporary files later

We can instead use process substitution, as follows:

```
paste -d$'/\t' <(cut -f3 -d, land.csv) <(cut -f1 -d, land.csv) >l13.txt
```

The shell interprets the command substitution syntax **<(command)** by running the command, saving the output to a temporary file, and then substituting that filename in place of the expression. The temporary files created by the shell also get deleted automatically. The command within brackets can itself be a pipeline with multiple commands.

The four command composition mechanisms complement each other:

- **Redirection**: Connects files to a command's input/output stream.
- **Pipes**: Connects a command's I/O streams to another command's I/O.
- **Command substitution**: Expands a command's output stream as arguments to another command.
- **Process substitution**: Expands a command's output stream as a file and passes it as an argument to another command.

> **Note**
>
> Throughout this book, we have used the terms "process" and "command" to mean almost the same thing in general. One subtle distinction is that "command" represents what we type to execute a program, while "process" refers to the program that is currently running.
>
> In the context of command and process substitution, however, these names do not quite distinguish between these two operations' modes of operation. You are advised to learn these terms off by heart so that there is no ambiguity when communicating them to others.

Exercise 15: Using Shell Expansions

In this exercise, we will practice the use of shell expansions to perform various string and numeric manipulations, and also try out commands using command and process substitution:

1. First, let's begin with a simple variable expansion, as shown here:

```
robin ~ $ NAME=Robin
robin ~ $ echo Hello $NAME
Hello Robin
```

2. Now, let's try out some arithmetic expressions. Arithmetic expressions can be as complex as you need. Try the following commands:

```
robin ~ $ echo The answer is $((74088 / 42 / 42 + 42 - 42))
The answer is 42
robin ~ $ echo The answer is $((2 * 3 + 4 * 5))
The answer is 26
```

> **Note**
>
> Notice that the precedence of operations follows the convention of DMAS, as you may have learned in school.

3. Use the following commands to generate the Hemachandra/Fibonacci sequence:

```
robin ~ $ A=1 B=1 C=$((A + B)) && echo $A
1
robin ~ $ A=$B B=$C C=$((A + B)) && echo $A
1
robin ~ $ A=$B B=$C C=$((A + B)) && echo $A
2
robin ~ $ A=$B B=$C C=$((A + B)) && echo $A
3
robin ~ $ A=$B B=$C C=$((A + B)) && echo $A
5
robin ~ $ A=$B B=$C C=$((A + B)) && echo $A
8
```

This manual repetition is cumbersome (even if you use shell history to repeat the command). In the next chapter, we will learn how to use loops to perform repeated commands.

Notice that we can assign multiple environment variables as a single command with each assignment separated by whitespace.

4. You can use brace expansions to create an entire tree of directories. First, **cd** to the **Lesson3** folder, then create a temporary folder and **cd** into it:

```
robin ~ $ cd Lesson3
robin ~/Lesson3 $ mkdir test && cd test
```

Test an expansion construct using **echo** to make three directories, a, b, and c, each with the directories 1, 2, and 3 within them:

```
robin ~/Lesson3/test $ echo {a..c}/{1..3}
a/1 a/2 a/3 b/1 b/2 b/3 c/1 c/2 c/3
```

Use **mkdir** with the **-p** flag to actually create the hierarchy and check it with **tree**:

```
robin ~/Lesson3/test $ mkdir -p {a..c}/{1..3}
robin ~/Lesson3/test $ tree
```

The output is shown here:

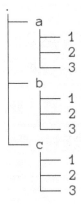

Figure 3.2: A screenshot displaying the output of the tree command

Remember to get back to the parent folder before moving on:

```
robin ~/Lesson3/test $ cd ..
```

5. You can also use quotes when composing brace expansions. Type the following command:

```
robin ~/Lesson3 $ echo The special cards in a deck are
{'ace','king','queen','jack'}{' of spade,',' of diamond,',' of club,',' of
heart,'}
The special cards in a deck are ace of spade, ace of diamond, ace of club,
ace of heart, king of spade, king of diamond, king of club, king of heart,
queen of spade, queen of diamond, queen of club, queen of heart, jack of
spade, jack of diamond, jack of club, jack of heart,
```

6. To try out command substitution, we will calculate the average number of characters per word in our poem. First, run **wc** on the file:

```
robin ~/Lesson3 $ wc markdown.txt
  5  38 203 markdown.txt
```

wc prints the count of lines, words, and characters by default. The values we need are words, 38, and characters, 203. The 5 represents the number of lines, and is not relevant to this problem.

7. Get the output into a variable:

```
robin ~/Lesson3 $ OUTPUT=$(wc markdown.txt)
robin ~/Lesson3 $ echo $OUTPUT
5 38 203 markdown.txt
```

When the shell expands **$OUTPUT** here, since it is not quoted, each word in the output of **wc**, which is **5 38 203 markdown.txt**, gets treated as a separate argument to **echo**. Hence, we see only one space between each word in the output of **echo**. In this case, the result is valid, but as we noted before, it is advisable to use double-quotes around expansions. Suppose we had symbols in the output that were themselves expansions (for example, wildcards). They would have been expanded, leading to unexpected results.

8. Let's assign the variable as an array (we can reuse the same variable to store it). Then, print the entire array's contents with index **@**:

```
robin ~/Lesson3 $ OUTPUT=($OUTPUT)
robin ~/Lesson3 $ echo ${OUTPUT[@]}
5 38 203 markdown.txt
```

Notice that, in the original string, the three values were separated by varying amounts of whitespace. When we assigned that string as an array, the shell treated whitespace as a delimiter to parse the elements. When we print out the array, a space is printed between each element.

9. Assign two variables, index 1 and 2 of the **OUTPUT** array, for the number of words and the number of characters. Remember, the array index starts at 0. Index 0 would have the line count, index 1 would have the word count, and index 2 would have the character count:

```
robin ~/Lesson3 $ WORDS=${OUTPUT[1]}
robin ~/Lesson3 $ CHARS=${OUTPUT[2]}
```

10. Use shell arithmetic to get the average word length:

```
robin ~/Lesson3 $ echo Average chars per word is $((CHARS / WORDS))
Average chars per word is 5
```

Notice that we got an integer as the answer, since Bash performs integer division.

11. Calculate the exact value to 2 decimal places using **bc**:

```
robin ~/Lesson3 $ echo The exact average is $(bc <<< "scale=2; $CHARS /
$WORDS ")
The exact average is 5.34
```

bc uses its own input syntax. Here, we instructed it to use a scale of 2, that is, a precision of 2 decimal places, before performing the division.

12. Use **eval** to perform three levels of indirection:

```
robin ~/Lesson3 $ ANSWER=42
robin ~/Lesson3 $ QUESTION=ANSWER
robin ~/Lesson3 $ WHAT=QUESTION
```

We wish to get 42 by getting the value of the **WHAT** variable, that is, **QUESTION**, then getting the value in that variable, that is, **ANSWER**, and then once again getting the value within that in turn.

13. Print the value of **WHAT** first, using the following command:

```
robin ~/Lesson3 $ echo ${WHAT}
QUESTION
```

14. We got **QUESTION**. Now, we need to convert this into an expression that will evaluate to its value. We do that by surrounding it by braces and prefixing with **$**:

```
robin ~/Lesson3 $ echo \${${WHAT}}
${QUESTION}
```

15. We have printed what we want using **echo**. Now, call **eval** on this:

```
robin ~/Lesson3 $ eval echo \${${WHAT}}
ANSWER
```

16. Once again, we need to convert this into an expression that will expand to its value. Use command substitution to get this output value as a string, wrap it with braces, and prefix it with **$**:

```
robin ~/Lesson3 $ echo $(eval echo \${${WHAT}})
ANSWER
robin ~/Lesson3 $ echo \${$(eval echo \${${WHAT}})}
${ANSWER}
```

17. Now, we have two levels of indirection. Just evaluate the preceding expression with **eval** again to get the correct result that we expected:

```
robin ~/Lesson3 $ eval echo \${$(eval echo \${${WHAT}})}
42
```

This seems complex to look at, but the logic is simple. Use **echo** to construct a command with an expansion and call **eval** on that. Then, repeat this procedure to and fro until all the expansions have been processed.

18. Return to the **Lesson2** folder for the next part of this exercise:

```
robin ~/Lesson3 $ cd ~/Lesson2
```

19. In the last chapter, we looked at an example of merging several log files into an existing sorted file. We can express that cleanly using process substitution.

First, let's make three copies of the payroll data (the fact that we use the same content for all three files does not change the result):

```
robin ~/Lesson2 $ cp payroll.tsv 1.txt ; cp payroll.tsv 2.txt ; cp
payroll.tsv 3.txt
```

20. Make another copy of it and sort it to represent a sorted log file:

```
robin ~/Lesson2 $ sort payroll.tsv >log.txt
```

21. Pass three files to **sort** with the **merge** flag, using process substitution to make the three be sorted themselves:

```
robin ~/Lesson2 $ sort -m log.txt <(sort 1.txt) <(sort 2.txt) <(sort
3.txt) >sortmerge.txt
```

This is a contrived example. The **sort** command itself does the same sort and merge operation internally when multiple files are provided. However, the preceding command would be efficient if we were using some other command inside the substitutions (for example, using **cut** on a sorted column). In such cases, we would avoid creating multiple temporary files and deleting them later.

22. As usual, clean up the huge text files and the temporary directory we generated here:

```
robin ~/Lesson2 $ rm *.txt
robin ~/Lesson2 $ rm -r ../Lesson3/test
```

In this exercise, we learned how to combine shell expansions and other mechanisms we learned before to perform complex tasks ranging from text processing to arithmetic. When we learn shell scripting in the next chapter, we will be able to use Bash as a fairly advanced programming language.

Activity 9: String Processing with eval and Shell Expansion

In the last exercise, we learned how to use various shell expansion constructs. In this activity, you need to perform a simple string-based task using shell expansion and other constructs. Even though the task is simple, it involves some ingenuity to achieve it using only what we have learned so far.

Your goal is simply to take the string "RUMPELSTILTSKIN" and reverse it. Hints are provided, including verification commands, so that you can check whether you are progressing correctly. There are better ways of reversing a string, but the main point of this activity is to practice thinking about how expansion, escaping, and **eval** works. We will only be using the information we have learned so far. You will find using **set -x** useful to debug this rather complex sequence:

1. Start by assigning the preceding string to a variable called NAME.

2. Get the length of the string into a variable called LEN using the variable length expansion construct.

3. Set LEN to LEN-1 so that LEN contains the highest index (0 based) of the input string.

4. Use **echo** to print out a brace expansion that has the range LEN down to 0.

5. Use **eval** on the previous command, and ensure it prints the numbers from LEN down to 0.

6. Edit the command you used in step 4 to print out the substring syntax `${NAME:X:1}`, where **X** here represents a brace expression for the range **LEN** down to 0. Using single quotes to prevent the shell from performing expansion is convenient here.

7. Edit the command in step 6 to escape all the special characters associated with the outer expansion.

8. Run **eval** on the previous command. You should get almost the same output as you did in step 6, the differences being that this command is **eval echo**, but that was just **echo** and **LEN** gets expanded to the string length.

9. Edit the command in step 7 by escaping all the backslashes. The characters associated with the outer expansion should have double backslashes before them.

10. Run **eval** on the previous command. You should get an output with a nested expansion, whose outer expansion characters are escaped.

11. Again, run **eval** on the previous command. You should get `${NAME:N:1}` repeated for every value of N from **LEN** to 0.

12. Run **eval** once more on the previous command. This command starts with **eval eval eval**. The output should be the letters of the name RUMPELSTILTSKIN reversed, but with a space in between each character.

13. Wrap the preceding command in a command substitution and redirect it into **tr** as a herestring. Use the right flags for the **tr** command so that it deletes the spaces in between characters.

The final output you should see after the last command is **NIKSTLITSLEPMUR**. There are three levels of indirection being used here, so think carefully about what we are trying to achieve in each command. Even if you cannot figure out the commands given the preceding guidelines, walk through the solution provided and analyze each step.

> **Note**
>
> The solution for this activity can be found on page 277.

Summary

In this chapter, we have learned about various concepts that let us use the command line in more advanced ways. These advanced features become very useful when writing shell scripts, which let us automate command-line tasks.

The complete set of shell commands and mechanisms is equivalent to a full-fledged programming language. A program written in the shell language is called a shell script. Unlike any other programming language, shell scripts can use or automate any other program that's available on the system to process data.

In the next chapter, we will learn how to write shell scripts so that a complex task can be written out once and repeated whenever necessary.

4

Shell Scripting

Learning Objectives

By the end of this chapter, you will be able to:

- Use looping and conditional constructs in the shell

- Use shell functions

- Perform line-oriented processing using the shell language

- Write shell scripts

- Automate data processing tasks with scripts

This chapter explains advanced scripting features such as conditionals and loops, and also describes how to write shell scripts.

Introduction

In the previous chapters, we learned most of the shell constructs and syntax that are used with the interactive command line. We also built a vocabulary of useful commands and learned how to combine them. In this final chapter, we will learn a few more shell constructs and commands, all of which when combined, will let us use the shell as a generic programming language.

The programs we write for the shell's language are called shell scripts. Any task we perform once can be converted into a shell script that can be repeated later. Scripts can be executed just like any other program in the system, giving us a way to automate our workflows. Since the shell can use any program that's installed on the system, by installing the right command-line utilities, we can automate practically anything we do manually.

Once we have learned this, for the remainder of the chapter, we will create several complex shell scripts that perform a non-trivial task, to cement our understanding of how to use the shell effectively. By the end of this chapter, you should be capable of formulating scripts to solve real-world problems on your own.

Conditionals and Loops

As with any other general-purpose programming language, the shell provides conditional and looping constructs. They are especially useful within shell scripts. We will learn some of the commonly used conditionals and loops in further sections.

> **Note**
>
> Conditionals and loops (along with functions, which we will cover later) make the shell language Turing complete. This is a computer science notion that means that it is equivalent to any general programming language in terms of its capabilities.

Conditional Expressions

As we saw in the previous chapter, every command returns an exit code that is interpreted as true and false for zero and non-zero values, respectively. A **conditional expression** is any shell command evaluating to *true* or *false*. One mechanism that augments this is the [[ ]] construct, which provides a way to test for a condition and return a Boolean. This syntax is as follows:

```
[[ EXPRESSION ]]
```

Here, **EXPRESSION** has a syntax similar to arithmetic expressions with the following operators (as discussed in the subsequent paragraphs). Note that the whitespace after the `[[` and before `]]` is mandatory.

File Operators

These operators return true or false, depending on some property of a file or directory:

- **-e FILE**: Returns true if **FILE** exists either as a file or a directory. For instance, let's create a file called **test** and check whether it exists using this operator:

```
robin ~ $ touch test
robin ~ $ [[ -e test ]] && echo File or directory exists
File or directory exists
```

  We can also use this to check for files that do not exist, as follows:

```
robin ~ $ [[ -e none ]] || echo File or directory missing
File or directory missing
```

- **-f FILE**: Returns true if **FILE** exists. For instance, look at the following snippet:

```
robin ~ $ touch test
robin ~ $ [[ -f test ]] && echo test exists and is a file
test exists and is a file
```

- **-d DIR**: Returns true if the directory **DIR** exists. For instance, look at the following snippet:

```
robin ~ $ mkdir dir
robin ~ $ [[ -d dir ]] && echo Dir exists
Dir exists
robin ~ $ [[ -d dir1 ]] || echo Dir missing
Dir missing
```

String Operators

These operators let us test properties of string literals or strings contained in variables:

- **-z STRING**: Returns true if the string is empty. Look at the following example:

```
robin ~ $ [[ -z '' ]] && echo EMPTY
EMPTY
```

- **-n STRING**: Returns true if the string is not empty (its length is not zero), as shown here:

```
robin ~ $ [[ -n 'SOMETHING' ]] && echo NOT EMPTY
NOT EMPTY
```

- **STRING1 = STRING2** or **STRING1 == STRING2**: Returns true if the two strings are identical. Let's understand this better with an example. In the following snippet, we have defined three variables with strings, as follows:

```
robin ~ $ A=APPLE
robin ~ $ B=HELLO
robin ~ $ C=HELLO
```

We can use the preceding operator to compare any two strings, as shown here:

```
robin ~ $ [[ "$B" = "$C" ]] && echo Same
Same
```

- **STRING1 != STRING2**: Returns true if the strings are not identical. For instance, for the preceding example, the following will be true:

```
robin ~ $ [[ "$A" != "$C" ]] && echo Different
Different
```

- **STRING1 < STRING2**: Returns true if the first string is lexicographically lower. Look at the following example:

```
robin ~ $ [[ "$A" < "$C" ]] && echo Less
Less
```

- **STRING1 > STRING2**: Returns true if the first string is lexicographically higher, as shown in the following example:

```
robin ~ $ [[ "$C" > "$A" ]] && echo Greater
Greater
```

> **Note**
>
> Remember to always use double quotes for string matching. Whether you use a variable or a literal string as either operand, this is recommended since strings can contain spaces, and other characters. We cannot use single quotes since the variables will not expand to their values.

Glob Operators

These operators allow us to test whether a literal string or a string within a variable matches a shell wildcard expression:

- **STRING = PATTERN** or **STRING == PATTERN**: Returns true if the string matches the glob **PATTERN**.

- **STRING != PATTERN**: Returns true if the string does not match the glob **PATTERN**.

Notice that the same operator is used for string and glob matching. These two operations are, however, differentiated based on whether the right-hand side string is quoted. If it is quoted, then it is treated as a string match; otherwise, it is treated as a glob match. Look at the following example:

```
robin ~ $ [[ jpg == 'j?g' ]] || echo Quoted string is not a glob match
Quoted string is not a glob match
```

We used quotes in the right-hand side of the preceding command, and therefore it was interpreted as a string match. To perform glob matching, we need to use the following command:

```
robin ~ $ [[ jpg == j?g ]] && echo Unquoted string is a glob match
Unquoted string is a glob match
```

Variables with glob patterns work the same way. See the following example:

```
robin ~ $ GLOB='j?g'
robin ~ $ [[ jpg == $GLOB ]] && echo Unquoted expansion is also a glob match
Unquoted expansion is also a glob match
```

Note that the quotes on the first line assigning the variable are not part of the string.

If we double quote the preceding variable, though, we would be performing a string match instead. Normally, quotes are a means to automatically escape some special characters, which include wildcard characters. This causes the shell to treat them like any other character, within quoted strings. Recall, however, that any expansion with the $ symbol is still performed within double quotes.

Within the context of the `[[ ]]` syntax, the behavior is slightly different. In such cases, wildcards are never expanded by the shell, regardless of whether or not they are quoted. However, if the right-hand side of an `==` or `!=` expression is not quoted, it is treated as a wildcard pattern to match against the left-hand side. This specific behavior within `[[ ]]` logic applies to both single and double quotes:

```
robin ~ $ [[ jpg == "$GLOB" ]] || echo Double quoted expansion is not a glob
match
Double quoted expansion is not a glob match
```

```
robin ~ $ [[ jpg == 'j?g' ]] || echo Single quoted string is not a glob
match
Single quoted string is not a glob match
```

```
robin ~ $ [[ jpg == j?g ]] && echo Unquoted string is a glob match
Unquoted string is a glob match
```

Numeric Operators

The symbolic operators (that is, the string operators that we saw previously) treat their operands as strings, whereas these operators treat them as numbers. The following numeric operators are commonly used:

- `INT1 -eq INT2`: Returns true if both integers are equal.

- `INT1 -ne INT2`: Returns true if the integers are not equal.

- `INT1 -lt INT2`: Returns true if the first integer is less than the second.

- `INT1 -gt INT2`: Returns true if the first integer is greater than the second.

- `INT1 -le INT2`: Returns true if the first integer is less than or equal to the second.

- `INT1 -ge INT2`: Returns true if the first integer is greater than or equal to the second.

The following example will help illustrate the use of numeric operators:

```
robin ~ $ [[ 100 -gt 20 ]] && echo number compare
number compare
```

If we use quotes for the preceding numbers, the operands will be treated as strings. Remember that strings are ordered lexicographically and, therefore, the following will be true:

```
robin ~ $ [[ "100" < "20" ]] && echo string compare
string compare
```

Regex Operator

This operator allows us to match using regexes.

STRING =~ REGEX: Returns true if the string matches the regex pattern. Regexes should not be quoted. The following examples demonstrate the use of the regex operator for matching strings:

```
robin ~ $ [[ 'abc123' =~ ^[[:alnum:]]*$ ]] && echo matched
matched
robin ~ $ [[ 'abc123' =~ ^[[:alpha:]]*$ ]] || echo no match
no match
```

Within the regex pattern, subexpressions are supported, but backreferences cannot be used. Instead, they are available as special variables after the command has run in the **BASH_REMATCH** internal variable, which is an array of the captured sub expressions, as shown here:

```
robin ~ $ [[ 'rotor' =~ (.)(.).(.)(.) ]] && echo ${BASH_REMATCH[@]}
rotor r o o r
```

The first element of this array contains the entire text matched by the regex, and successive ones contain the subexpressions in order.

Logical Operators

All the other preceding expression types can be combined with logical operators and parentheses:

- **(EXPR)**: Parentheses can be used to group expressions and change the evaluation precedence.
- **! EXPR**: Inverts the result of the expression (logical NOT).
- **EXPR && EXPR**: Returns true if both expressions are true.
- **EXPR || EXPR**: Returns true if either expression is true.

The **&&** and **||** operators use <u>**short-circuit evaluation**</u>, which means that in **EXPR1 &&** **EXPR2**, if **EXPR1** is false, **EXPR2** is not evaluated, and in **EXPR1 || EXPR2**, if **EXPR1** is true, **EXPR2** is not evaluated. This is the same behavior as the command list operators **&&** and **||**. As with the command list versions, here too, parentheses are recommended if **&&** and **||** are mixed. For instance, look at the following snippet:

```
robin ~ $ [[ ! 1 -gt 2 ]] && echo 1 is not greater than 2
1 is not greater than 2
robin ~ $ [[ ( ! 1 -gt 2 ) && ( 3 -gt 2 ) ]] && echo 1 is not greater than 2
and 3 is greater than 2
1 is not greater than 2 and 3 is greater than 2
robin ~ $ [[ ( 2 -lt 1 ) || ( 3 -gt 2 ) ]] && echo 2 is less than 1 or else
3 is greater than 2
2 is less than 1 or else 3 is greater than 2
```

When using conditional expressions, add a space between each token and do not quote the whole expression. Internally, the **[[** works as if it were a command with arguments, and if there is no space between tokens, it does not behave as you would expect. For example, consider the two commands that follow, where we test whether 1 *is not equal* to 1 evaluates to true:

```
robin ~ $ [[ ! ( 1 -eq 1 ) ]] && echo true || echo false
false
robin ~ $ [[ !( 1 -eq 1 ) ]] && echo true || echo false
true
```

The first command evaluated correctly and printed **false**, but the second command gave us the wrong result, because the **!** was adjacent to the bracket.

The following commands also evaluate incorrectly because of the inclusion of quotes around the whole expression:

```
robin ~ $ [[ "! ( 1 -eq 1 )" ]] && echo true || echo false
true
robin ~ $ [[ '! ( 1 -eq 1 )' ]] && echo true || echo false
true
```

The reason is that `[[` treated the whole expression as a single string and it considers any non-blank string as true, as we can see here:

```
robin ~ $ [[ 'anything' ]] && echo true || echo false
true
robin ~ $ [[ '' ]] && echo true || echo false
false
```

Now that we have learn how the `[[ ]]` conditional expression syntax evaluates Boolean expressions, we can progress to conditional statements.

Conditional Statements

We have already learned about a way to perform conditional execution by chaining with **&&** and **||** in a command list. In this section, we'll learn how to express conditionals using the **if** and **case** statements.

The if Statement

The **if** statement can be used to express a conditional with the following syntax:

```
if condition
then
   command1
else
   command2
fi
```

Here, **condition** is any conditional expression or command whose exit code is interpreted as a Boolean (zero, which occurs when a command exits successfully, is treated as true, and a non-zero as false). The two exclusive sets of commands after the **then** and the **else** keywords, **command1** and **command2**, are called **branches** of the **if** statement. These can be one or more commands on multiple lines, including command lists and pipelines. The **else** branch is optional, so the following syntax is also valid (the indentation is only for clarity; the leading spaces before the lines are ignored by the shell):

```
if condition

then

   command

fi
```

if statements can also make multiway branches with the **elif** keyword (which means *else if*):

```
if condition1

then

   command1

elif condition2

then

   command2

elif condition3

then

   command3

fi
```

On the command line, **if** statements are usually typed as a multiline command, as shown here:

```
robin ~ $ if [[ 3 -gt 2 ]]

> then

> echo condition was true

> else

> echo condition was false

> fi

condition was true
```

Notice that the shell lets you continue the command on multiple lines when you press *Enter*, just like with **heredocs**. Although we typed this command on multiple lines, we can also do so on a single line, as follows:

```
robin ~ $ if [[ 3 -gt 2 ]] ; then echo condition was true; else echo
condition was false; fi
condition was true
```

In fact, if you use the up arrow key to retrieve the command from history, the shell itself shows the entire **if** statement on a single line.

> **Note**
>
> In the preceding single line syntax, you will notice that semicolons are needed at certain points. For convenience, though, it usually makes sense to type this on multiple lines, especially in shell scripts.

In the commands we've tried so far, we have always used the exit code of a process directly with **&&** or **||**. We can also retrieve the return code of the last command with the **$?** expansion, as follows:

```
robin ~ $ grep "needle" <<< "haystack"
robin ~ $ echo $?
1
robin ~ $ grep "needle" <<< "needles"
needles
robin ~ $ echo $?
0
```

Recall that zero means true and non-zero means false, so we can use the following:

```
robin ~ $ grep "needle" <<< "needles"
needles
robin ~ $ if [[ $? -eq 0 ]]; then echo found; fi
found
```

We can use the **-q** option to suppress the output of **grep**, since we are only interested in the return value:

```
robin ~ $ grep -q "needle" <<< "needles"
robin ~ $ if [[ $? -eq 0 ]]; then echo found; fi
found
```

We can also use a command directly in the conditional:

```
robin ~ $ if grep -q "needle" <<< "needles"
> then
> echo found
> fi
found
```

> **Note**
>
> Although **if**, **then**, **else**, and **fi** look like shell commands, they are just shell keywords to signify a conditional statement. It is a syntax error to use them outside of this construct.

The case Statement

The **if** statement lets us make a two-way or multiway decision. The **case** statement lets us do a multiway decision based on matching a wildcard. The following syntax is used for **case** statements:

```
case EXPRESSION in

  CASE1)

    command1

    ;;

  CASE2|CASE3)

    command2

    ;;

  CASE4)

    command3

esac
```

In the preceding syntax, **EXPRESSION** is a string or an expansion, and **CASE1**, **CASE2**, and so on are wildcard expressions that are matched against **EXPRESSION** successively. Any number of these blocks can be specified. When any one of them match, the commands under that matching case block up to the ;; are executed and the **case** statement ends. The ;; can be omitted for the final block, since the execution will leave the **case** statement after that anyway.

The case strings are matched using the logic for wildcards, so we can use the ? and * symbols in them. To specify multiple options, the | operator can be used. Usually, the last case is specified as *, which matches any string. Hence, if all other cases failed to match, it will execute the final block. Often, this is referred to as the *default case*. This can be used to handle unexpected values and take a default action. For example:

```
robin ~ $ NUM=10
robin ~ $ case $NUM in
> 1)
> echo One
> ;;
> 2|3|4)
> echo Few
> ;;
> *)
> echo Many
> esac
Many
```

As with the **if** statement, the **case** statement also can be expressed in one line, and that is how it is retained in the shell's history:

```
robin ~ $ NUM=7
robin ~ $ case $NUM in 1) echo One; ;; 2|3|4) echo Few; ;; *) echo Many;
esac
Many
```

Loops

Loops are a mechanism to execute a command repeatedly. Bash provides three types of loops: **for** loops, **while** loops, and **until** loops. We will examine each one in detail in the following sections.

The for Loop

The basic syntax of a **for** loop is shown here:

```
for VAR in SEQUENCE
do
    COMMAND1
    COMMAND2
done
```

The first line specifies a **loop variable** and a sequence of values separated by whitespace. This sequence can involve any shell construct that produces a series of values as a string. For instance, they could be any of the following:

- Literals directly typed, for example, **for i in 1 2 3 4 5**
- An array variable expansion, for example, **for i in ${VALS[@]}**
- A brace expansion, for example, **for n in {1..10}** or **for s in {a,b}{x,y}**
- A filesystem wildcard, for example, **for x in ***

The remaining lines are called the **loop body**. It must start with the **do** keyword and end with the **done** keyword. The loop body can contain any number of lines with individual commands, lists, or pipelines. The **for** loop can be written as a multiline command on the shell, as follows:

```
robin ~ $ for i in 1 2 3
> do
> echo The value is $i
> echo The doubled value is $((i * 2))
> done
The value is 1
The doubled value is 2
The value is 2
```

```
The doubled value is 4
The value is 3
The doubled value is 6
```

It can also be written on one line, as shown here:

```
robin ~ $ for i in 1 2 3 ; do echo The value is $i; echo The doubled value
is $((i * 2)) ; done
```

As with the **if** statement, the shell history for a **for** loop construct is displayed as a single line and semicolons are required at certain places for valid syntax.

The modus operandi of the **for** loop is explained as follows:

1. The first value in the sequence is assigned to the loop variable.

2. The commands within the loop body are executed.

3. If there is another value in the sequence, it is assigned to the loop variable, otherwise Step 5 is executed.

4. Step 2 is executed.

5. The loop is complete.

Within the loop body, the loop variable expands to the current value from the sequence. Every pass through the loop is called an **iteration**.

for loops can also be nested (to any arbitrary depth), as you can see in the following example:

```
robin ~ $ for i in {1..3}
> do
> for j in {1..3}
> do
> echo $j $i
> done
> done
```

The preceding nested loop displays the following output:

```
1 1
2 1
3 1
1 2
2 2
3 2
1 3
2 3
3 3
```

When we use numeric **for** loops, the brace range expansion is limited to only sequential integers. If we need to generate some other arithmetic progression, we can use the **seq** command, the syntax for which is shown here:

```
seq start incr stop
```

This generates the numbers **start**, **start + incr**, **start + incr + incr** ..., all the way up to **stop**. Let's understand this with an example:

```
robin ~ $ seq 1 2 10
1
3
5
7
9
```

Here, we begin with 1 and increment it by 2 each time until we get a value less than or equal to 10. The value for **start**, **incr**, and **stop** can be positive or negative integers or floating-point decimal numbers, as shown in the following snippet:

```
robin ~ $ seq 1 -0.1 0.5
1.0
0.9
0.8
0.7
0.6
0.5
```

We can also use **seq** with a **for** loop using command substitution, as demonstrated here:

```
robin ~ $ for i in $(seq 1 -0.1 0.5)
> do
> echo version-$i
> done
version-1.0
version-0.9
version-0.8
version-0.7
version-0.6
version-0.5
```

The while Loop

The **while** loop has the following syntax:

```
while CONDITION
do
    COMMAND1
    COMMAND2
done
```

Here, **CONDITION** is a conditional expression that is tested on each iteration of the loop. As long as it evaluates to true, the loop body is executed. If the condition was initially false, the body is never executed. As with the **for** loop, the loop body can contain multiple commands, command lists, or pipelines. Here is a practical example:

```
robin ~ $ COUNTER=0
robin ~ $ while [[ $COUNTER -lt 5 ]]
> do
> echo The counter is $COUNTER
> COUNTER=$((COUNTER + 1))
> done
The counter is 0
The counter is 1
The counter is 2
The counter is 3
The counter is 4
```

The same loop can be written as a single line construct too:

```
robin ~ $ while [[ $COUNTER -lt 5 ]]; do echo The counter is $COUNTER;
COUNTER=$((COUNTER + 1)); done
```

As with the other constructs, they are stored in history as a single line.

The until Loop

The syntax for **until** is almost the same as for **while**:

```
until CONDITION
do
    COMMAND1
    COMMAND2
done
```

Unlike a **while** loop, an **until** loop executes its body as long as the **CONDITION** is false. Here's an example:

```
robin ~ $ COUNTER=5
robin ~ $ until [[ $COUNTER -lt 0 ]]
> do
> echo Counter is $COUNTER
```

```
> COUNTER=$((COUNTER-1))
> done
Counter is 5
Counter is 4
Counter is 3
Counter is 2
Counter is 1
Counter is 0
```

As with the other constructs, this one can also be written as a single-line command, as follows:

```
robin ~ $ until [[ $COUNTER -lt 0 ]]; do echo Counter is $COUNTER;
COUNTER=$((COUNTER-1)); done
```

We can use **while** and **until** interchangeably by negating the conditional. For instance, for the preceding example, we can negate the conditional expression used with **until** and use **while** instead, obtaining the same output:

```
robin ~ $ COUNTER=5
robin ~ $ while [[ ! $COUNTER -lt 0 ]]; do echo Counter is $COUNTER;
COUNTER=$((COUNTER-1)); done
Counter is 5
Counter is 4
Counter is 3
Counter is 2
Counter is 1
Counter is 0
```

The choice of whether to use **while** or **until** depends on readability. If you are familiar with Boolean algebra, De Morgan's theorem can sometimes simplify an expression, and in such cases, switching from **while** to **until** or vice versa may result in a more readable conditional expression.

Loop Control

Sometimes, we need a loop to end as soon as some complex condition is fulfilled. At other times, we may want to skip the current iteration of the loop and move on to the next iteration. For these kinds of use cases, the following two keywords are provided:

- **break**: This breaks out of the loop (exits the loop immediately). For instance, take a look at the following snippet, which sums up numbers in a series until the total reaches 50:

```
robin ~ $ SUM=0
robin ~ $ for i in {1..10}
> do
>   SUM=$((SUM + i))
>   if [[ $SUM -gt 50 ]]
>   then
>     echo Done
>     break
>   fi
>   echo Iteration $i: Sum = $SUM
> done
```

Here, we use **break** to print **Done** and break out of the loop as soon as the **if** conditional is true (**SUM** exceeds 50). The following is the output that's obtained:

```
Iteration 1: Sum = 1
Iteration 2: Sum = 3
Iteration 3: Sum = 6
Iteration 4: Sum = 10
Iteration 5: Sum = 15
Iteration 6: Sum = 21
Iteration 7: Sum = 28
Iteration 8: Sum = 36
Iteration 9: Sum = 45
Done
```

- **continue**: This causes the loop to skip the remaining commands in the loop body. Look at the following example:

```
robin ~ $ for i in {1..10}
> do
>  if [[ $i -lt 5 ]]
>  then
>    echo Skipped $i
>    continue
>  fi
>  echo Iteration $i
> done
```

Here, the part of the loop body that is after **continue** is skipped for the first four iterations. Therefore, the following output is obtained:

```
Skipped 1
Skipped 2
Skipped 3
Skipped 4
Iteration 5
Iteration 6
Iteration 7
Iteration 8
Iteration 9
Iteration 10
```

In general, constructs that use **break** and **continue** are considered not very desirable, as they can lead to less readable code (this is true for all programming languages that support them), but they come in handy occasionally. For instance, they are useful when the conditions to exit the loop are too complex to express in the loop's conditional expression.

Generally, tasks of a user that need automation are those that involve repeatedly doing the same thing for different items. In this section, we learned about the constructs that are necessary to let us write entire programs in the shell. A lot of repetitive tasks we did in the exercises in previous chapters could be made much simpler by using loops and conditionals. For instance, in the first chapter, we saw how wildcards let you perform one command on a set of filesystem objects. With loops and conditionals, we can repeatedly perform a complex set of commands on any set of objects that we can name. Using a computer effectively means not having to do the same thing twice manually, and in the context of the command line, the concepts we learned in this topic will help us with that. In the next topic, we will explore shell functions.

Shell Functions

Shell functions are very similar to functions in most programming languages. They allow us to group commands into a unit and provide them with a name. We can later execute the commands in the function by invoking its name, just like any other command. In essence, shell functions let us define our own commands that are indistinguishable from the inbuilt ones.

Function Definition

Functions can be created with this basic syntax:

```
function name()
{
    COMMANDS
}
```

Here, **COMMANDS** may be one or more commands, lists, or pipelines, and represent the **function body**. The braces must be separated from the rest of the syntax with whitespace, typically with newlines. When the function name is typed on the command line as if it were a command, we say that the function has been *invoked* or *called* and the commands in the function body are executed.

> **Note**
>
> The `function` keyword can be omitted when defining a function—it is optional, according to the syntax. You may encounter some shell scripts in the wild where this alternate style is used.

For example, let's create a function called **stuff** that prints some statements, as follows:

```
robin ~ $ function stuff()
> {
> echo Doing something
> echo Doing something more
> echo Done
> }
robin ~ $ stuff
Doing something
Doing something more
Done
```

A redirection can also be added to the function definition after the closing brace, on the same line, as shown here:

```
robin ~ $ function stuff()
> {
> echo Doing something
> echo Doing something more
> echo Done
> } >test.txt
robin ~ $ stuff
robin ~ $ cat test.txt
Doing something
Doing something more
Done
```

Whenever this function is invoked, the output of all its commands will be automatically redirected to **test.txt**.

Function Arguments

While invoking or calling a function, arguments can be passed to it, just like with any shell command, using a syntax called **positional parameters**; these are special expansions that work only with functions. The following is a list of the positional parameters that can be used with functions:

- **$#**: Expands to the number of arguments passed. This can be used to obtain the argument count, as shown here:

```
robin ~ $ function argue()
> {
> echo "I have $# arguments"
> }
robin ~ $ argue "modus ponens" "modus tollens"
I have 2 arguments
```

  In the preceding example, we used **$#** to count the number of arguments passed to the function while calling it, and printed the output.

- **$N or ${N}**: For **N** more than 0, this expands to the Nth argument specified. Braces are mandatory if **N** has more than one digit. Look at the following example:

```
robin ~ $ function greet()
> {
> echo "Greetings, $1!"
> }
robin ~ $ greet "Folks"
Greetings, Folks!
```

  Here, **$1** expands to the first argument of the function **greet**, resulting in the output shown in the preceding code.

- **${*:START:COUNT}**: Expands to the concatenated positional parameters in the range **START** to **COUNT**.

- **${@:START:COUNT}**: Expands to the positional parameters in the range **START** to **COUNT** as individual words.

- **$***: Expands to the entire list of arguments as a single string or word. The arguments are combined with the first character of the IFS (internal field separator) variable as the delimiter (default value is space). For instance, if IFS had a comma as the first character "**$***" expands to a single word "**$1,$2,$3**" and so on. This can be used for argument concatenation, as follows:

```
robin ~ $ function print()
> {
> IFS=,
> echo "$*"
> }
robin ~ $ print 1 2 3 4 hello
1,2,3,4,hello
```

We will discuss the IFS variable in greater detail in a forthcoming section

- **$@**: Expands to the entire list of arguments as separate words. Adding double quotes around it like "**$@**" will result in expansion to a list with each element quoted, that is, "**$@**" expands to separate words "**$1**" "**$2**" "**$3**" and so on. This form is essential if you need to pass the arguments to another command correctly. It will preserve arguments that have spaces in them as a single one. Look at the following example:

```
robin ~ $ function show() { for i in "$@" ; do echo "|$i|"; done; }
robin ~ $ show a b "c d" e
|a|
|b|
|c d|
|e|
```

"**$@**" in this case expands to "**a**" "**b**" "**c d**" "**e**", that is, a single string with multiple quoted arguments. Every token in this is exactly what argument the user passed in.

$@ without quotes, however, behaves differently, as shown here:

```
robin ~ $ function show() { for i in $@ ; do echo "|$i|"; done; }
robin ~ $ show a b "c d" e
|a|
|b|
|c|
|d|
|e|
```

In this case, $@ expanded to $1 $2 $3 and so on when passed to the **for** command; the argument that had a space got split because there were no quotes (remember that quotes never get passed into a command unless escaped). This resulted in "c" and "d" becoming individual arguments. Therefore, in general, unless there is a very specific reason, always use $@ with double quotes rather than any other form.

In the preceding example, if we used quotes with $*, we would get the following output:

```
robin ~ $ function show() { for i in "$*" ; do echo "|$i|"; done; }
robin ~ $ show a b "c d" e
|a b c d e|
```

Notice that $* expanded as one single quoted word with all arguments concatenated, and not multiple ones like $@.

- **$FUNCNAME**: Expands to the name of the currently executing function. It can be used to get the function name, as shown here:

```
robin ~ $ function groot() { echo "I am ${FUNCNAME}!" ; }
robin ~ $ groot
I am groot!
```

> **Note**
>
> Notice that we can define functions on one line, just like any other construct. The semicolon before the closing brace is mandatory, just as with braced command lists.

The shell also provides a command called **shift** to manipulate positional parameters. The syntax is as follows:

```
shift N
```

Here, N is a number (defaults to 1 if unspecified). Conceptually, it "shifts" out the first N arguments from the left, after which the arguments at index 1 onward get the values of arguments N+1 onward. For example, here is a script that adds a specified HTML tag to the given text:

```
robin ~ $ function format()
> {
>    tag=$1
>    echo "<$tag>"
>    shift
>    echo "$@"
>    echo "</$tag>"
> }
```

This takes the first argument as the tag and uses shift to remove it so that $@ expands to the remaining arguments, which are to be the content of the tag. Let's see how this works:

```
robin ~ $ format i Hello
<i>
Hello
</i>
robin ~ $ format b Hello World
<b>
Hello World
</b>
```

This is the most common use case of **shift**: a few arguments are processed individually and shifted out, and the rest are processed as one chunk with $@.

Return Values

Shell commands return an integer exit code, usually to signify an error condition. The general term in computing that's used to refer to a value returned by a function is **return value**. A function returns a value by using the **return** statement. Here is an example of a function that converts Fahrenheit to Centigrade:

```
robin ~ $ function f_to_c()
> {
> f=$1
> f=$(( f - 32 ))
> c=$(( (f * 5) / 9 ))
> return $c
> }
```

A **return** statement can be executed from anywhere within a function and may optionally include the return value. We use **$?** to get the return value of the last function that was run, just like exit codes of commands, as shown here:

```
robin ~ $ f_to_c 100
robin ~ $ echo $?
37
robin ~ $ f_to_c 212
robin ~ $ echo $?
100
```

Unlike general programming languages, the return value of a Bash function is limited to the range 0 to 255 since the mechanism was only intended to pass exit codes (each non-zero exit code represents a particular error condition). Hence, it is typically not possible to use shell functions such as mathematical ones that return numbers. For instance, for the following snippet, our function fails to produce the right answer when the return value exceeds 255:

```
robin ~ $ f_to_c 1000
robin ~ $ echo $?
25
```

The usual workaround is to assign the result to a variable, or directly print it, so that we can capture it via redirection or command substitution:

```
robin ~ $ function f_to_c()
> {
> f=$1
> f=$(( f - 32 ))
> c=$(( (f * 5) / 9 ))
> echo "$c"
> }
```

Now, we can see the right result and store it with command substitution:

```
robin ~ $ f_to_c 1000
537
robin ~ $ temp=$(f_to_c 2000)
robin ~ $ echo $temp
1093
```

Local Variables, Scope, and Recursion

Shell functions provide the notion of scope, which means that within the function body, we can declare variables that are visible to that function alone, called **local variables**. A local variable can be declared using the **local** command, as follows:

```
robin ~ $ function foo()
> {
>     local foovar=200
>     echo $foovar
> }
robin ~ $ foo
200
robin ~ $ echo $foovar
```

As we can see, **foovar** existed only within the **foo** function. After the function exits, it is gone. We would say that **foovar** is within the *scope* of **foo** or that **foovar** is a *local variable* in **foo**.

> **Note**
>
> The variables we have used so far are called **global variables** and are visible to all commands and functions that we invoke from the shell. In general, always declare variables as local unless it needs to be visible to the caller; this prevents subtle errors. It is also a good practice to always initialize all variables you need at the top of a function.

Since functions work just like any other command, we can call functions from within other functions. When a function calls another, the former is termed as the **caller** and the latter as the **callee**. It is possible that a callee itself further invokes another function and so on and so forth in a chain. In such as case, a function may need to look up variables in another function, if the said variable is not defined within its scope. The rules of looking up a variable from within a function follow a system called **dynamic scoping**. When a variable is expanded within a function, its value is looked up with dynamic scoping as follows:

1. If there is a local variable of that name assigned, then that value is used.

2. If not, then the caller of the function is checked, and if there is a local variable of that name assigned, then that value is used.

3. If not, the caller of the caller and that function's caller and so on are checked until the variable is found, or the topmost caller is reached.

4. If the variable is still not found, the global variables for a definition are checked.

An example will make this clearer. Let's create a function called **baz()** that prints three variables:

```
robin ~ $ function baz()
> {
>    echo $var1 $var2 $var3
> }
```

We have not defined any of these variables within **baz()**. Hence, let's define two other functions, **bar()** and **foo()**, that contain these variables' definitions. We will define the third variable globally. For illustration purposes, each variable has, as its value, the name of the scope we defined the variable in:

```
robin ~ $ function bar()
> {
>    local var3='bar'
>    baz
> }
robin ~ $ function foo()
> {
>    local var2='foo'
>    bar
> }
robin ~ $ var1='global'
```

Now, let's see what happens when we call the **foo** function:

```
robin ~ $ foo
global foo bar
```

As we can see, the **baz** function got **var1** from the global scope, **var2** from the scope of **foo**, and **var3** from the scope of **bar**. The chain of calls and variable scopes is as follows:

- Shell calls **foo** (**var1** is defined in the global scope)
- **foo** calls **bar** (**var2** is defined in the scope of **foo**)
- **bar** calls **baz** (**var3** is defined in the scope of **bar**)

We can have a variable named the same in an inner scope as an outer scope. The inner variable hides, or *shadows*, the outer one:

```
robin ~ $ function bar()
> {
>    local var='bar'
>    echo "In bar var is $var"
> }
robin ~ $ function foo()
> {
>    local var='foo'
>    bar
>    echo "In foo var is $var"
> }
```

We get the following output when we call the **foo** function:

```
robin ~ $ foo
In bar var is bar
In foo var is foo
```

Here, the **var** inside the **bar** function (the callee) hid the **var** that was in the scope of **foo** (the caller).

The mechanism of Bash's scoping may seem somewhat complicated to a person encountering it for the first time. Also, it is not very likely that we would need to write functions that make a call chain many levels deep like these examples. Nevertheless, scoping is a concept that is necessary to understand if we use shell functions.

> **Note**
>
> The dynamic scoping mechanism is used by only a few well-known programming languages (Common Lisp and Perl). All other mainstream programming languages use lexical scoping, which is a completely different mechanism. Students who come from a background of other languages such as Java or Swift should be very careful not to confuse the two schemes.

Shell functions also support **recursion**. This means that you can invoke a function from within itself. This is a common idiom in many programming languages. However, the utility of recursion on the shell is quite limited. It introduces unnecessary complexity and performance penalties. The shell was not designed to be a full-scale programming language initially, and although recursion works, there is no real justification to use it in the shell. Every recursive computation can be achieved using loops in a much simpler-to-understand way. We will skip any further discussion of recursion for this reason.

Exercise 16: Using Conditional Statements, Loops, and Functions

In this exercise, we will be writing some functions and conditional constructs. We will not be using any data files, so the CWD where these are practiced are not relevant:

1. We will begin by writing a function called **ucase()** that prints its arguments in uppercase (we can use **tr** for this). Use the following snippet:

   ```
   robin ~/Lesson4 $ function ucase()
   > {
   >    tr "[a-z]" "[A-Z]" <<< "$*"
   > }
   ```

   Try it out by inputting a lowercase string as an argument, as follows:

   ```
   robin ~/Lesson4 $ ucase hello world
   HELLO WORLD
   ```

2. Next, let's write a simple function called **hf()** that generates the Hemachandra/ Fibonacci sequence (a sequence of numbers starting with 0, 1, after which each number is the sum of the previous two). The function will take a number N as an argument and print out the sequence up to element N+2. Let's define the variables in the function first:

   ```
   robin ~/Lesson4 $ function hf()
   > {
   >    local a=0
   >    local b=1
   >    local n=$1
   >    local i=0
   >    echo 0
   >    echo 1
   ```

3. Next, we will use a **while** loop to iterate **n** times. Each time, we calculate the next number of the sequence by adding the last two:

```
>    while [[ $i -lt $n ]]
>    do
>       c=$(( a + b ))
>       echo $c
>       a=$b
>       b=$c
>       i=$(( i + 1 ))
>    done
> }
```

Initially, **a** and **b**, which always represent the last two numbers of the sequence, are assigned the values 0 and 1 at the start of the sequence. During each iteration of the loop, **c**, which is the next number in the sequence, is assigned a value equal to **a+b**. At this point, the last two numbers of the sequence that we know are **b** and **c**, which we transfer to **a** and **b**, respectively, setting up the correct state for the next iteration around the loop. The **i** variable serves as a loop count to keep track of how many times we looped. When it exceeds **n**, the loop exits.

4. Try out this function by passing an arbitrary number as the argument, as follows:

```
robin ~/Lesson4 $ hf 8
0
1
1
2
3
5
8
13
21
34
```

5. Now, we will write a simple function called **greet()** that greets a user, by taking the user's name and the current hour in 24-hour format as an argument. The script will print **Good morning**, **Good afternoon**, **Good evening**, or **Good night**, depending on the following ranges of hours: 5 to 11: Morning, 12 to 15: Afternoon, 16 to 21: Evening, and 22 to 4 (next day): Night.

> **Note**
>
> Note that when we say 5 to 11, we mean the entire time between 0500 and 1059 hours inclusive.

Use conditionals to apply the required logic in the function:

```
robin ~/Lesson4 $ function greet()
> {
>    local timestring='night'
>    [[ $2 -ge 5  && $2 -le 11 ]] && timestring='morning'
>    [[ $2 -ge 12 && $2 -le 15 ]] && timestring='afternoon'
>    [[ $2 -ge 16 && $2 -le 21 ]] && timestring='evening'
>    echo "Good ${timestring}, $1!"
> }
```

6. You can test how this function works by taking times belonging to the different ranges that were mentioned previously:

```
robin ~/Lesson4 $ greet Jack 5
Good morning, Jack!
robin ~/Lesson4 $ greet Jill 12
Good afternoon, Jill!
robin ~/Lesson4 $ greet Tom 16
Good evening, Tom!
robin ~/Lesson4 $ greet Mary 22
Good night, Mary!
```

We avoid handling the "night" case specifically. If none of the other conditions are fulfilled, it must be night. The condition for night is more complex than the others since it involves two ranges of 2200 hours to 2359 hours and 0000 hours to 0400 hours. We avoid needing to write that by using it as the default case.

Shell functions, along with conditional statements, loops, scoped variables, shell arithmetic, and other external tools, give us enough power to write large and complicated programs. In the following section, we will explore how to deal with user and file input in a line-oriented manner using the shell, and then learn how to write shell scripts.

Shell Line Input

In the previous chapters, we learned how to process files line by line using predefined commands such as **cut** or **tr**. However, we are often limited by the fact that one command can do only one operation at a time. The shell provides some facilities to allow processing a file or typed input line by line. Some of these are discussed in the following section.

Line Input Commands

These commands allow us to write scripts that work with input data line by line and process it.

The read Command

The shell provides the **read** command to process input in a line-by-line fashion. This command has two main uses:

- To read input from the user interactively from scripts

- To read input from a file and process it

The **read** command accepts any number of variable names as arguments. When executed, it attempts to read text from its **stdin** and assign the input to the variables. For example, look at the following snippet:

```
robin ~ $ read COLOR THING
red apple
robin ~ $ echo $COLOR $THING
red apple
```

Notice that **read** parsed the line and separated it into fields based on whitespace. The extra whitespace was ignored. Therefore, if we need to enter a space as part of a field value, we can escape it, as follows:

```
robin ~ $ read COLOR THING
dark\ green avocado
robin ~ $ echo $COLOR
dark green
robin ~ $ echo $THING
avocado
```

After reading the second last word, **read** assigns the entire remaining text to the last variable, regardless of whether it is a single word or not, as shown here:

```
robin ~ $ read SUBJECT OBJECT
Jack went up the hill
robin ~ $ echo $SUBJECT
Jack
robin ~ $ echo $OBJECT
went up the hill
```

If no variables are supplied as arguments, the line read is assigned to the **REPLY** variable by default:

```
robin ~ $ read
This is my reply
robin ~ $ echo $REPLY
This is my reply
```

The following options can be passed to **read**:

- **-a** ARR: Assigns the words read to the array variable ARR, starting at index 0. ARR is emptied first. All other arguments that are not options are ignored when this option is used.

- **-d** DELIM: Stops reading the input as soon as the character DELIM is typed (rather than newline). This also means that the command exits as soon as that character is typed. Also, newlines get treated as whitespace.

- **-e**: Uses the readline editing behavior if the **stdin** is an interactive console terminal. By default, **read** uses a very basic editing mode. Specifying this flag allows us to use the same keyboard editing shortcuts as when we type commands in the shell.

- **-i TEXT**: Pre-fills the input with **TEXT** before editing begins. This option only works if **-e** is also specified.

- **-n NUM**: Reads a maximum of **NUM** characters. As soon as **NUM** characters are typed, the command exits.

- **-N NUM**: Reads exactly **NUM** characters. This option ignores **-d**. The command also does not split the input and assigns the entire input to a single variable.

- **-p PROMPT**: Displays **PROMPT** on **stderr**, without printing a newline, before reading input. Only applies if the input is from the console.

- **-r**: Does not handle escape sequences. The backslash is treated like any other character, which is almost always what you need when reading actual files.

- **-s (silent mode)**: Does not show the characters as they are typed if the input is from a console.

- **-t TIMEOUT**: Waits for **TIMEOUT** seconds at most to read the input. If the time limit is exceeded, the command exits and assigns whatever input was available. Timeout can be a floating-point number. The exit code of the command is non-zero if it timed out.

read can be also be used with a loop to process data line by line. Let's understand this with an example:

```
robin ~ $ while read
> do
> echo The line was ${#REPLY} characters long
> done
This is the first line
The line was 22 characters long
This is the next
The line was 16 characters long
```

Since no variable was passed as an argument to **read**, the default variable, **REPLY**, was assigned. The loop ends when we press *Ctrl + D*. Unlike the shell, **read** will not print **^D** to symbolize that the keystroke was pressed.

This example would be very difficult, if not impossible, to write as a pipeline using the **wc** command. We can perform the same action for file input too. Let's try this using the **markdown.txt** file inside the **Lesson3** folder:

```
robin ~/Lesson3 $ while read -r
> do echo ${#REPLY}
> done <markdown.txt
35
50
34
34
45
```

Notice that we redirect the file into the **while** statement itself. The **stdin** of **read** is attached to this file, and at every loop iteration, **read** processes one more line. We use **-r** since we are reading an actual file.

The fundamental difference between using pipelines and **while read** is that in the former, we conceptually run each command on multiple lines of the input, whereas in the latter, we run multiple commands on each line of the input. Pipelines are able to run commands in parallel, whereas this **read** loop is constrained to run each command sequentially.

The readarray Command

The **readarray** command works like **read**, except that it reads multiple lines at a time into an array variable. For example, look at the following snippet (remember that *Ctrl + D* is necessary to end the input):

```
robin ~ $ readarray lines
This is the first line
This is the last line
robin ~ $ echo ${lines[0]}
This is the first line
robin ~ $ echo ${lines[1]}
This is the last line
```

The common options for **readarray** are shown here:

- **-n NUM**: Reads at most **NUM** lines. If **NUM** is 0, all lines are read.

- **-O ORIGIN**: Assigns to array starting at index **ORIGIN**. The default index is 0. If **-O** is not specified, the array is cleared before assigning.

- **-s NUM**: Skips the first **NUM** lines read.

- **-d DELIM**: The first character in **DELIM** is used as the terminator for each line stored in the array rather than the default newline.

- **-t**: Removes a trailing delimiter specified by **-d** (default newline) from each line that's read.

Here is an example of the use of **-t** and **-d**. **readarray** is instructed to remove the trailing period (if any) after each line and assign the output to the **lines** variable:

```
robin ~ $ readarray -t -d'.' lines
First line.
Second line.
No period at the end of this line
robin ~ $ echo ${lines[0]}
First line
robin ~ $ echo ${lines[1]}
Second line
robin ~ $ echo ${lines[2]}
No period at the end of this line
```

The **readarray** command has another alias called **mapfile**; this is merely another name for the same command.

Internal Field Separator

The Bash shell uses an internal variable called **IFS** (short for **Internal Field Separator**). This is used by the shell as the default delimiter whenever it parses input text into fields. There are two main contexts where IFS is used:

- When the shell splits a string into fields with the **read** command

- When we assign a sequence of values to an array variable with parentheses

The IFS is treated as a set of characters, the occurrence of any of which is considered a delimiter between fields. The default IFS is set to the sequence of the space, tab, and newline characters. For instance, look at the following example:

```
robin ~ $ read -a ARR
1 2 3
robin ~ $ for i in ${ARR[@]} ; do echo $i; done
1
2
3
```

In the preceding snippet, the space character is treated as the IFS. However, the IFS can also be assigned to a user-defined value, just like any other environment variable. For instance, we can use the comma as a delimiter and read values into an array variable, as demonstrated here:

```
robin ~ $ IFS=,
robin ~ $ read -a arr
1 is one,2 is two,three is 3
robin ~ $ for i in ${arr[@]} ; do echo "$i" ; done
1 is one
2 is two
three is 3
```

Notice that when the IFS does not include whitespace characters, then the input values can include spaces, without the need for escaping them.

If **IFS** is not set, then the shell behaves as if it were set to the sequence of space, tab, or newline. To clear the **IFS** and restore the default splitting behavior, use the **unset** command. This command can be used to remove any other environment variable as well. Observe the following code. After using **unset** on the **IFS** variable, the shell splits the words on the escaped tab character **\t**, as it would have with the default **IFS**:

```
robin ~ $ IFS=,
robin ~ $ read a b <<< "hello,world"
robin ~ $ echo "$a|$b"
hello|world
robin ~ $ unset IFS
robin ~ $ read a b <<< $'hello\tworld'
robin ~ $ echo "$a|$b"
hello|world
```

The shell input semantics change subtly when we use a whitespace character as a delimiter, as opposed to a non-whitespace character. Consider the following:

```
robin ~ $ IFS=,
robin ~ $ read -a ARR
1,2,,3
robin ~ $ for i in ${ARR[@]} ; do echo \"$i\"; done
"1"
"2"
""
"3"
```

We print quotes before and after the value for clarity. Notice that having two successive commas allows us to define a blank element. Now, let's try the same with IFS set to a space:

```
robin ~ $ IFS="\ "
robin ~ $ read -a arr
1 2 3  4
robin ~ $ for i in ${arr[@]} ; do echo \"$i\"; done
"1"
"2"
"3"
"4"
```

Notice that the two spaces between **3** and **4** were not treated as a blank element (unlike the two consecutive commas in the previous example).

When IFS is set before a **read** command on the same line, it retains its value only for the duration of that command:

```
robin ~ $ IFS=: read -a ARR
1:2:3
robin ~ $ for i in ${ARR[@]} ; do echo \"$i\"; done
"1"
"2"
"3"
robin ~ $ echo \"$IFS\"
" "
```

Here, we set **IFS** to a colon and executed **read** on the same command line. After the command, **IFS** reverted to whatever value it had before (namely a single space character). Usually, we do this so that we need not bother restoring the old value manually.

IFS can also be used with array initialization. Here is an example:

```
robin ~ $ IFS=: arr=(1:2:3)
robin ~ $ for i in ${arr[@]} ; do echo \"$i\"; done
"1"
"2"
"3"
```

However, array initialization has its own quirks when using **IFS**, as you will see in the following code:

```
robin ~ $ IFS=':' arr=(1:2:3 is three:4:5)
robin ~ $ for i in ${arr[@]} ; do echo \"$i\"; done
"1"
"2"
"3"
"is"
"three"
"4"
"5"
```

Notice that it considered both whitespace and colons as delimiters; the only way to avoid that is to use quotes, as follows:

```
robin ~ $ IFS=':' ARR=(1:2:"3 is three":4:5)
robin ~ $ for i in ${ARR[@]} ; do echo \"$i\"; done
"1"
"2"
"3 is three"
"4"
"5"
```

Exercise 17: Using Shell Input Interactively

In this exercise, we will use shell input to write a simple interactive game. The function will choose a random number between 0 and 9 and the user must guess it within five tries:

1. The shell provides a special environment variable called RANDOM that generates a pseudo-random number in the range of 0–32767. Use the following snippet to see how it works:

```
robin ~/Lesson4 $ for i in {1..5}; do echo "$i: $RANDOM"; done
1: 19035
2: 14231
3: 16556
4: 4213
5: 10032
```

2. Next, we will write a function called random_digit() that returns a random number between 0 and 9. We can use the modulus (remainder) operator with 10 to get this, as follows:

```
robin ~/Lesson4 $ function random_digit() { echo $(( $RANDOM % 10 )) ;}
robin ~/Lesson4 $ for i in {1..5}; do random_digit; done
4
9
1
0
5
```

3. Now, we will write a function called read_digit that reads exactly one character from the user with a prompt. Use the following snippet:

```
robin ~/Lesson4 $ function read_digit { guess=''; read -N1 -p "Enter your guess: " guess; echo; }
robin ~/Lesson4 $ read_digit
Enter your guess: 6
```

Note that as soon as you press any key (here, we pressed 6), the read command exits.

4. Now, we can write the complete function, as shown below. First, we tell the user what to do and get a random digit:

```
robin ~/Lesson4 $ function guess_it()
> {
>   echo "I have thought of a random number between 0 and 9 -
 try to guess it in 5 tries"
>   local answer=$(random_digit)
```

With the **count** variable, we will keep track of how many times the user guessed:

```
>   local count=1
```

We loop until 5 tries are done and read a digit from the user:

```
>   while [[ $count -le 5 ]]
>   do
```

If the user pressed a digit key, then we can check if they guessed right. If they guessed right, then the user wins and we exit:

```
>       read_digit
>       if [[ $guess =~ [0-9] ]]
>       then
>         if [[ $guess -eq $answer ]]
>         then
>           echo Correct answer
>           return 0
>         fi
```

If the guess was high or low, give a hint, and increase the **count** variable:

```
>         [[ $guess -lt $answer ]] && echo "Your guess is lower than what I
thought of, try again!"
>         [[ $guess -gt $answer ]] && echo "Your guess is higher than what I
thought of, try again!"
>         count=$(( count + 1 ))
```

If the user had not pressed a digit key, inform them (but we do not treat it as a guess):

```
>      else
>          echo "Please enter a digit!"
>      fi
>    done
```

Once all five iterations complete, the game is over:

```
>    echo "Sorry, you used up 5 guesses!"
>    echo "The number I had thought of was $answer"
> }
```

5. Now, test the game's script, as follows:

```
robin ~/Lesson4 $ guess_it
```

The output for some game interactions are shown in the following screenshot:

```
robin ~/Lesson4 $ guess_it
I have thought of a random number between 0 and 9 - try to guess it in 5 tries
Enter your guess: 7
Your guess is lower than what I thought of, try again!
Enter your guess: 6
Your guess is lower than what I thought of, try again!
Enter your guess: 5
Your guess is lower than what I thought of, try again!
Enter your guess: 4
Your guess is lower than what I thought of, try again!
Enter your guess: 3
Your guess is lower than what I thought of, try again!
Sorry you used up 5 guesses!
The number I had thought of was 8
robin ~/Lesson4 $ guess_it
I have thought of a random number between 0 and 9 - try to guess it in 5 tries
Enter your guess: s
Please enter a digit!
Enter your guess: a
Please enter a digit!
Enter your guess: 7
Your guess is higher than what I thought of, try again!
Enter your guess: 4
Your guess is higher than what I thought of, try again!
Enter your guess: 2
Your guess is lower than what I thought of, try again!
Enter your guess: 3
Correct answer
```

Figure 4.1: Output of example game interactions

Line input provides the final piece that allows Bash to be a general text-processing programming language. With all the constructs we have learned so far, we can start writing shell scripts.

Shell Scripts

Shell scripts are text files that contain shell commands. Such files can be executed as if they were programs. A script can be in any language for which an interpreter exists, for example, Python, PHP, Perl, and so on. Similar to how a Python or Perl interpreter loads a program file and executes it, the Bash shell can load and execute shell scripts. However, before we address shell scripts, we need to visit some concepts about how programs are executed.

Shell Command Categories

We will now learn about the various categories of shell commands and how scripts work like any other command. There are four types of commands that can be invoked by name from the shell. These are listed as follows:

- **Binary Executables**: Also called **executable files** or **binaries**, these contain machine code, and provide most of the functionality of a system, for example, GUI programs such as a web browser, or CLI based programs such as **grep**. The Bash shell itself is an executable. The process of loading and running executables is part of the OS functionality, and not dependent on the shell. Executables that we use primarily from within the shell are called **external commands**.

- **Internal Commands**: While many commands we use on the shell are independent executable files, other commands such as **echo** and **cd** do not have any binary executable behind them. The Bash shell itself performs the action involved. These are called internal commands or **shell built-ins**.

- **Shell Functions**: We examined these in the previous sections. To all intents and purposes, they behave like temporary shell built-ins. They are gone if the shell window is closed.

- **Scripts**: A script is a file containing code written for some programming language. Every script file contains a line explaining which external program is the interpreter that is to be used.

Program Launch Process

A simple description of how an OS launches a program is as follows:

- To launch an executable, the OS is provided with either (a) the absolute path of an executable file or (b) the name of an executable.

- Apart from these, a list of environment variables and their values are passed to it. This is called the **environment block**.

- If it is only a name, the environment variable called PATH is checked. This contains a list of directories called a **search path**. The OS searches for the executable file that is named in each of these directories. If PATH is not specified, some system directories are checked by default. If the file is not found, this process stops here.

- The OS checks whether the file specified is a binary or a script.

- If it is a binary, the machine code from the executable is loaded into memory and executed.

- If it is a script, the interpreter for that script is loaded and the script's absolute file path is passed as its first argument.

- Both binaries and scripts can access the variables in their environment block.

We can examine the PATH variable in the command line (the result will vary depending on the system), as follows:

```
robin ~ $ echo $PATH
/usr/local/sbin:/usr/local/bin:/usr/bin:/usr/lib/jvm/default/bin:/usr/bin/
site_perl
```

This same search path will be passed to the OS when an external command is launched by Bash.

Script Interpreters

For a script to specify the interpreter that it requires, it has to start with a line called a **shebang** or a **hashbang**. It consists of a line beginning with the sequence #!. The remainder of the line contains information about the interpreter to be used. This is usually the full path of the interpreter.

For example, a Python script may have the following shebang:

```
#!/usr/bin/python
```

This means that when the OS launches this script, it will invoke the interpreter **/usr/bin/python** and pass this script's filename to it as an argument. Most scripting languages use the **#** character as a comment, so they ignore this line. The hashbang line syntax with **#!** is only treated specially by the shell if it is the very first line of the script. Any other line starting with a **#** is ignored by Bash as a comment.

For shell scripts, we will use the following shebang line:

```
#!/usr/bin/env bash
```

Usually, the shebang contains a path, but we use this instead. The **env** program locates where Bash is installed on the system and invokes it. We will not go into further details of how **env** works and why the location of Bash may vary on different systems. For the purposes of this book, all the scripts will use this shebang line. Typically, shell scripts use the file extension **.sh**, for example, **script.sh**. In this case, the script is executed as follows:

```
/usr/bin/env bash script.sh
```

Let's look at a simple script called **test.sh** that simply prints out all its arguments:

```
robin ~ $ cat test.sh
#!/usr/bin/env bash


echo $*
```

Note that blank lines are ignored in a script.

For a file to be treated as an executable, it requires a file permission attribute to be set on it. Note that a complete description of file permissions attributes and their uses is beyond the scope of this book. Here, we will just explore how to add this so that our script can execute:

```
robin ~ $ ls -l test.sh
-rw-r--r-- 1 robin robin 29 Oct 27 18:39 test.sh
robin ~ $ chmod u+x test.sh
robin ~ $ ls -l test.sh
-rwxr--r-- 1 robin robin 29 Oct 27 18:39 test.sh
```

Notice the initial attribute string: **-rw-r--r--**. Look at only the three characters at the second index, **rw-**. This represents that the owner of this file (the current user, **robin**) has permissions to read and write this file. The **chmod** command can be used by a file's owner or a system administrator to change permissions. Here, we specify that we want the executable attribute **x** to be added for **u**, the user (the owner of the file). The **chmod** command has more to do with system administration than scripting, so we will not go into further details about it. The final **ls** command shows that we now have **rwx** permissions, so we can read, write, and execute this file.

Now that the file is executable, we can invoke it by specifying its path:

```
robin ~ $ ./test.sh hello from script
hello from script
```

Since it was in the current directory, we specified **./**. If we merely mention the name of the script file, we get an error:

```
robin ~ $ test.sh
bash: test.sh: command not found
```

This error occurs because the current directory is not within the path. When we write scripts that we intend to use repeatedly, we would keep them in a directory and add that directory to the **PATH** variable permanently so that we can run it like any other command.

The shebang-based script execution mechanism has the main advantage that the OS need not maintain a list of file types and associated interpreters. Any program can be used as an interpreter by any user. For example, consider the following:

```
robin ~ $ cat test.cat
#!/usr/bin/env cat
Hello world
robin ~ $ chmod u+x test.cat
robin ~ $ ./test.cat
#!/usr/bin/env cat
Hello world
```

We created a script specifying the **cat** command as the interpreter. The shell invokes **cat** on the script file when it runs.

This particular example is not very useful. We created a file that ends up displaying itself when executed, but it illustrates the flexibility of this mechanism. The shell also allows us to bypass this mechanism entirely and launch scripts directly using the . built-in command, as follows:

```
robin ~ $ ls -l arg.sh
-rw-r--r-- 1 robin robin 9 Oct 28 00:30 arg.sh
robin ~ $ cat arg.sh
echo $@

robin ~ $ ./arg.sh Hello world
bash: ./arg.sh: Permission denied
robin ~ $ . arg.sh Hello world
Hello world
```

We created a file without the shebang line, and did not set the executable permissions. It could not be invoked via the regular method. However, the . command allows us to execute it anyway. This command applies only to Bash scripts, and when executed in this fashion, the commands in the script are run in the current shell rather than as a separate shell process. This command is most useful when you have a script that needs to set environment variables. Normally, scripts are run in a new shell so any variables that they set are not retained when the script exits. However, when launched with ., any variables initialized in the script will be retained after it exits. Bash also provides the **source** command, which is an alias for . and behaves the same.

A function can stop its execution and return its exit code using the **return** statement. Similarly, the **exit** command causes a script to end and pass its exit code to its caller. The **exit** command actually terminates the shell process that is interpreting the script.

> **Note**
>
> Using the **exit** command directly on the Bash command line will cause the shell to terminate, also closing the window itself.

When functions are used in scripts, the function definition must appear before the point of its use.

Practical Case Study 1: Chess Game Extractor

In this section, we will incrementally develop a shell script to perform a data processing task. We have done some data crunching in the previous chapters using pipelines in a limited fashion. Here, we will attempt a more complex task. Depending on your taste, there are a number of editors available to write a script with. You may be familiar with GUI editors such as **SublimeText** or **Notepad++**, but there are several editors that work in the console itself without a GUI. A few are complex and very powerful ones such as **emacs** or **vim**, and some are simple editors such as **gedit** and **nano**. One of these is usually available on most systems. The editor can be launched right from the command line without needing to navigate the GUI Desktop with the mouse or trackpad, by just typing its name like any other command.

Understanding the Problem

The functionality of this script that we want to develop is that it can take a text file containing thousands of chess games in PGN (portable game notation) textual format and extract a desired set of games from it. Generally, the way to go about it would be to create a database, import the data into it, write SQL queries, and so on. Instead, we will simply use the shell to do the job for us with a few lines of code. The advantage of this is that we do not need to do any setup or initialization, and can directly use the script on the PGN file itself.

Before we start writing the script, however, let's examine the format of a PGN file. The file format was designed to be easily readable by humans. A PGN file consists of multiple chess games, each of which looks like this:

```
[Event "World Championship 16th"]
[Site "NLD"]
[Date "1935.11.09"]
[Round "17"]
[White "Alekhine, Alexander A"]
[Black "Euwe, Max"]
[Result "1/2-1/2"]
[ECO "D04d"]
[EventDate "1935.10.03"]

1.d4 d5 2.Nf3 Nf6 3.e3 Bf5 4.Bd3 e6 5.Bxf5 exf5 6.Qd3 Qc8 7.b3 Na6 8.O-O
Be7 9.c4 O-O 10.Nc3 c6 11.Bb2 Ne4 12.Rfc1 Rd8 13.Qe2 Qe6 14.a3 Nc7 15.c5
Re8 16.b4 f4 17.exf4 Nxc3 18.Qxe6 Nxe6 19.Rxc3 Nxf4 20.Rb3 a6 21.g3 Ne6
22.a4 Bf6 23.Rd1 1/2-1/2
```

Figure 4.2: Example of a game in PGN text format

Each game section is followed by a newline and then another game. The game details in square brackets are not always in the same order, and the complete data for many old games is not recorded. The only information that is guaranteed to be present are the names of the players and the result.

Upon observing this file, the first thing to think about is this: what information in this file is relevant to extracting one game from it? If we think a little, it should be obvious that none of the attributes really matter, nor does the data regarding the list of moves in the game. The only salient attributes we need to consider to extract the Nth game from such a file are that a game consists of *several non-blank lines containing attributes, a blank line, another set of non-blank lines containing moves*, followed by *another blank line*. The actual content of the lines is irrelevant for this initial task.

Now, we can describe the logic required to solve this problem. Let N be the number of the game we want to extract:

1. We start with a **count** variable set to 1.

2. Then, we try to read a line of text. If we are unable to do so, we exit the script.

3. If the count is equal to N, then the line we read should be printed.

4. If the line was not blank, we need to go back to step 2 (we are reading through the attribute lines).

5. We read a blank line.

6. If the count is equal to N, the blank line is printed.

7. Next, we read a line of text.

8. If the count is equal to N, the line we read is printed.

9. If the line was not blank, we go back to step 7 (we are reading through the list of moves).

10. We read a blank line.

11. If the count is equal to N, the blank line is printed and we exit the script.

12. The count is incremented.

13. We go back to step 2.

In the following exercises, we will implement the preceding logic incrementally.

Exercise 18: Chess Game Extractor – Parsing a PGN File

In the logic described in the previous section, we have a common pattern repeated twice: read a set of non-blank lines followed by a blank line, and then print them if a certain condition is true. In this exercise, we will implement that common pattern as a script and test it:

1. Open your text editor and add the mandatory hashbang, as shown here:

   ```
   #!/usr/bin/env bash
   ```

2. Next, we need to define a regular expression that can match blank lines (a blank line is a line containing 0 or more whitespace characters). Use the following snippet:

   ```
   regex_blank="^[[:space:]]*$"
   ```

3. Now, use the following **while** loop to read each line of the file, and print the line if the first parameter equals 1. If the line read is a blank line, we need to break out of the loop:

   ```
   while read -r line
   do
     [[ $1 -eq 1 ]] && echo "$line"
     [[ "$line" =~ $regex_blank ]] && break
   done
   ```

The default behavior of the **read** command is to remove any trailing and leading whitespace from the lines. This behavior can be overridden by setting **IFS** to a blank value (this is not the same as unsetting it). This may be significant if you process a file where leading or trailing whitespace has some significance.

Save the file as **pgn_extract1.sh**.

> **Note**
>
> You can find files with the same name along with the code bundle for this book and on GitHub. The script files includes several comments. Any line that starts with **#** is ignored by the shell (and most other scripting languages).
>
> Note that adding comments is a good practice, but the comments should be more about a higher-level meaning than just describing what the code literally does at each point. It is also recommended to use indentation and blank lines to make the code more readable. You are the person most likely to be reading your own code in the future (usually after you have forgotten everything about it), so be kind to your future self and write code neatly and carefully.

4. Let's now move forward to testing our script on the command line. Once again, we should analyze what aspects need to be tested before diving in. The basic test that this script has to pass is the following: keep reading non-blank lines until a blank line is read and print them all if an argument is specified. Clearly, the number of non-blank lines is irrelevant to the test. If it works for 1 line and 2 lines, it has to work for N lines since the **while** loop does the same thing every time. Hence, we can try three test cases, passing 0 or 1 as the first argument for each case. When we pass 1, we expect the script to just print out each line that we type, but when we pass 0, the script should just silently ignore it.

Let's test this by entering a single blank line first. Launch the script with 0 as an argument and just press *Enter* to input a blank line:

```
robin ~/Lesson4 $ ./pgn_extract1.sh 0
```

When 0 is passed, we expect the script to not print anything.

Now, launch the script with 1 as an argument and input a blank line again. Now, the script should just echo the blank line you typed:

```
robin ~/Lesson4 $ ./pgn_extract1.sh 1
```

5. Repeat the same two tests, but this time, instead of just one blank line, type one non-blank line, followed by one blank line. We expect the script to be silent when 0 is passed and just echo what we typed when 1 is passed:

```
robin ~/Lesson4 $ ./pgn_extract1.sh 0
Line 1

robin ~/Lesson4 $ ./pgn_extract1.sh 1
Line 1
Line 1
```

6. Repeat the same thing once more, this time with two non-blank lines followed by one blank line:

```
robin ~/Lesson4 $ ./pgn_extract1.sh 0
Line 1
Line 2

robin ~/Lesson4 $ ./pgn_extract1.sh 1
Line 1
Line 1
Line 2
Line 2
```

The script will never exit unless a blank line is encountered, so that part of the test is implicit. We need not test various types of blank lines because the regex definition is correct by observation: (a) Match start of line, (b) Match 0 or more whitespace characters, and (c) Match end of line.

For this simple case, manual testing is enough, but in general, we should also automate the testing itself. Ideally, we would create three test files, each one testing one of the preceding cases, and write another script to call this one for each input. We would also need to make sure the output was what we expected, typically by creating three files corresponding to the output we expect, and then comparing that with what the script generates as output.

Paradoxically, sometimes, the testing process is more complicated than the code being tested itself. Also, if the test script itself is wrong, we have a "Turtles all the way down" situation where we would need tests for tests, and tests for those tests, and so on ad infinitum. Testing and verification of correctness is an unsolved problem in computer science. There is no recipe to always write correct programs, nor a recipe to detect all incorrect ones. Only a few general rules of thumb exist, which are not specific to any particular flavor of programming:

- Think about the problem before writing code.

- Write code in small modular chunks that can be verified independently.

- Comment your code. Often, the act of describing the intended functionality in plain language will highlight errors in the mind.

- Have your code reviewed by others. Many heads are better than one.

Exercise 19: Chess Game Extractor – Extracting a Desired Game

In this exercise, we will convert the code we wrote into a function and then write a complete script that can extract the Nth game in a file. The value of N is passed as the argument to the script:

1. Our game extraction process involves doing what the code we wrote earlier does, but twice per game, as per our original plan of action. If we ever need to do anything twice, it should be a function. Hence, let's define a function called **read_chunk** containing the same code as in the previous exercise, as shown in the following code. Open your text editor and input the following lines of code:

```
function read_chunk()
{
  while read -r line
  do
     [[ $1 -eq 1 ]] && echo "$line"
     [[ $line =~ $regex_blank ]] && return 0
```

```
    done

    return 1
}
```

Note that we made a small change to the code from the previous exercise. Our original logic requires us to know if this function succeeded in reading the first line or not. Hence, instead of using **break**, we will use a successful return code to indicate that the final blank line was read. Also, if the **while** loop exits, it means that the file has been read fully, and we need to return a non-zero error code, so we have added the line return 1 before the closing brace.

> **Note**
>
> Sometimes, it makes sense to split a larger piece of code into functions, even if those functions are not used more than once. The longer a function, the higher the chance that some bug exists in that code. The rule of thumb is that a function should fit on an 80 x 25 screen.

2. Now, we can move on to implementing the actual game extractor. We start by declaring two variables: **count** represents the number of games we have read so far, and **should_print** is a flag telling us whether the current game being read is the one desired by the user:

```
count=1
should_print=0
```

3. We loop through the lines of the PGN file as long as **count** has not exceeded the argument passed by the user:

```
while [[ $count -le $1 ]]
do
```

4. If the current game is the one requested by the user, set the **should_print** flag to 1:

```
[[ $count -eq $1 ]] && should_print=1
```

5. Read the first chunk of data (the game attributes) passing the **should_print** flag. If it is 1, then this game's data must be printed. If the **read_chunk** function fails, it means that we do not have any more data in the file, and we exit the script. If it succeeds, we need to read through and print the second chunk of the game (the moves list):

```
read_chunk $should_print || exit
read_chunk $should_print
```

6. Finally, we increment the count, and we exit the script if the game that was desired was just printed. We do not have to read any more data, and we are done:

```
count=$(( count + 1 ))
[[ $should_print -eq 1 ]] && exit
done
```

Save the complete script to **pgn_extract2.sh**.

7. We can test our script using a smaller input file, **test.pgn** (provided within the **Lesson4** folder), as follows:

```
robin ~/Lesson4 $ ./pgn_extract2.sh 2 <test.pgn
```

You should see an output similar to the one shown here:

```
[Event "?"]
[Site "Moscow Club Spring"]
[Date "1907.??.??"]
[Round "?"]
[White "Alekhine, Alexander A"]
[Black "Isakov K"]
[Result "1-0"]
[ECO "C44m"]

1.e4 e5 2.Nf3 Nc6 3.c3 d5 4.Qa4 f6 5.Bb5 Ne7 6.exd5 Qxd5 7.0-0 Bd7 8.d4 e4
9.Nfd2 f5 10.Nb3 Ne5 11.Nc5 c6 12.Be2 Bc8 13.Be3 b5 14.Qa5 Nc4 15.Bxc4
Qxc4 16.Nd2 Qd5 17.a4 Ng6 18.f3 Bxc5 19.dxc5 Qd3 20.Bg5 h6 21.Nxe4 hxg5
22.Nd6+ Kd7 23.Rad1 Qe3+ 24.Kh1 Qf4 25.g3 Qxa4 26.Nxb5+ 1-0
```

Figure 4.3: Output of the game extraction code

Since we took the time to think the solution out beforehand and separate the common code into a reusable function, even before testing, we can be quite confident that our code does not have logical errors. Apart from logic errors, a common mistake is typographical errors; these can be avoided by working slowly and carefully and reviewing the code many times before attempting to run it.

Refining Our Script

A fruitful technique when solving problems using programs and scripts is to start with a simple program and make small changes to improve it. This is called **incremental refinement**. By making small changes, we reduce the possibility of errors being introduced, and can reason better about the change in behavior.

We will now incrementally refine our script to add another feature: to display the indexes of the games that ended in fewer than a specified number of moves. Since our script will need to support two separate functionalities, we will use the convention that all shell programs use, namely options:

- **-n N**: Displays the Nth game.

- **-m K**: Displays the indices of games that were won in K moves or less.

Both these options will be mutually exclusive. Whichever is specified first on the command line will determine the function performed.

We will also use the command called **getopts** that is specifically meant to read and extract options and their values from a command line. It has the following syntax:

```
getopts OPTIONLIST VARNAME
```

Here, **OPTIONLIST** is a string containing a list of single characters, each representing a command-line option. For example, **xyz** indicates that we are looking for the options **-x**, **-y**, and **-z**. If an option requires a value, then we specify a colon after the option character. In our case, we have **-m** and **-n**, both of which require a number. Hence, the **OPTIONLIST** we will use is **m:n:**. **VARNAME** is the environment variable into which it stores the option that it detects.

getopts is meant to be called repeatedly. Each time it is called, it tries to recognize one argument. The command-line argument that **getopts** tries to parse is the one whose index is in a variable called **OPTIND**. **OPTIND** starts at 1 by default in every script, and each time **optargs** is successful, **OPTIND** is increased by 1 and the character of that recognized option is stored in **VARNAME**. If there was any value, it is stored in a variable called **OPTARG**.

Thus, the way **getopts** works is as follows:

1. It checks whether the positional parameter at the **OPTIND** index matches one of the flags that's specified.

2. If it matches a specified flag, **VARNAME** is set to the flag and **OPTARG** is set to the value, if any.

3. If it does not match any specified flag, **VARNAME** is set to ? and **OPTARG** is set to that argument's character.

4. **OPTIND** is incremented.

getopts returns a nonzero exit code if **OPTIND** goes past the last positional parameter.

Exercise 20: Chess Game Extractor – Handling Options

Now, we will make our script accept the command-line options -n and -m:

1. Let's begin this exercise by writing a small script that just parses the options we need and prints out our choice. Open your text editor and start with a hashbang line, as usual:

   ```
   #!/usr/bin/env bash
   ```

2. Then, call **getopts**, asking it to recognize either -m or -n:

   ```
   getopts 'm:n:' opt || exit
   ```

   The colons tell it that both these options must be followed by a value. If **getopts** returns a non-zero exit code, then we exit (because one option or the other is mandatory), otherwise the parsed option is in the **opt** variable.

3. Next, use a **case** statement to select the right branch and print what the final script should do given that argument:

   ```
   case $opt in
     m)
       echo Displaying games won in "$OPTARG" moves or less
     ;;

     n)
       echo Displaying game "#$OPTARG"
     ;;

   esac
   ```

Since we only ever accept one of the two options, we need to call **getopts** only once. The **case** statement selects the right branch and we print what the final script should do given that argument. Save the script as `pgn_extract3.sh`.

4. Let's test this script to see if it handles the options correctly. We will test the following conditions:

   (a) **-m** and **-n** individually, with and without a value after it:

   ```
   robin ~/Lesson4 $ ./pgn_extract3.sh -m
   ./pgn_extract3.sh: option requires an argument -- m
   robin ~/Lesson4 $ ./pgn_extract3.sh -m 15
   Displaying games won in 15 moves or less
   robin ~/Lesson4 $ ./pgn_extract3.sh -n
   ./pgn_extract3.sh: option requires an argument -- n
   robin ~/Lesson4 $ ./pgn_extract3.sh -n 30
   Displaying game #30
   ```

   (b) Unrecognized options:

   ```
   robin ~/Lesson4 $ ./pgn_extract3.sh -x
   ./pgn_extract3.sh: illegal option -- x
   ```

   (c) No options:

   ```
   robin ~/Lesson4 $ ./pgn_extract3.sh
   robin ~/Lesson4 $
   ```

   The script, in this case, is expected to just exit without doing anything.

5. By default, **getopts** prints out error messages. We can suppress this by setting the **OPTERR** variable to 0 (it is 1 by default), or by prefixing the option list string with a colon. Edit the script file to add a line:

   ```
   OPTERR=0
   ```

Observe the behavior by repeating the same tests that we carried out previously:

```
robin ~/Lesson4 $ ./pgn_extract3.sh -m
robin ~/Lesson4 $ ./pgn_extract3.sh -m 10
Displaying games won in 10 moves or less
robin ~/Lesson4 $ ./pgn_extract3.sh -n
robin ~/Lesson4 $ ./pgn_extract3.sh -n 10
Displaying game #10
robin ~/Lesson4 $ ./pgn_extract3.sh -x
robin ~/Lesson4 $ ./pgn_extract3.sh
robin ~/Lesson4 $
```

Notice that no error messages are printed by the shell. This mode is useful if we want to handle error conditions ourselves.

6. Now, we will modify the ./pgn_extract3.sh script and add the code we wrote before to handle the -n option. Start by making that into a function called **show_nth_game**. We will use local variables, unlike before, since this is a function:

```
function show_nth_game()
{
  local count=1
  local should_print=0
  while [[ $count -le $1 ]]
  do
     [[ $count -eq $1 ]] && should_print=1
```

The loop remains the same as before. In the earlier code, we used **exit**, but here, we use **break** since we just want to break out of the loop, not exit the whole script:

```
     read_chunk $should_print || break
     read_chunk $should_print

     count=$(( count + 1 ))
     [[ $should_print -eq 1 ]] && break
  done
}
```

7. Then, we can call this function from within the case statement for the **-n** option, as follows:

```
getopts 'm:n:' opt

case $opt in
  m)
    echo Displaying games won in "$OPTARG" moves or less
  ;;

  n)
    echo Displaying Game "#$OPTARG"
    echo
    show_nth_game "$OPTARG"
  ;;
esac
```

Save this modified script as **pgn_extract4.sh**.

8. To test this, we can run the script with **-n** and verify that indeed the correct game is displayed:

```
robin ~/Lesson4 $ ./pgn_extract4.sh -n2 <test.pgn
```

The output should look like this:

```
Displaying Game #2

[Event "?"]
[Site "Moscow Club Spring"]
[Date "1907.??.??"]
[Round "?"]
[White "Alekhine, Alexander A"]
[Black "Isakov K"]
[Result "1-0"]
[ECO "C44m"]

1.e4 e5 2.Nf3 Nc6 3.c3 d5 4.Qa4 f6 5.Bb5 Ne7 6.exd5 Qxd5 7.0-0 Bd7 8.d4 e4
9.Nfd2 f5 10.Nb3 Ne5 11.Nc5 c6 12.Be2 Bc8 13.Be3 b5 14.Qa5 Nc4 15.Bxc4
Qxc4 16.Nd2 Qd5 17.a4 Ng6 18.f3 Bxc5 19.dxc5 Qd3 20.Bg5 h6 21.Nxe4 hxg5
22.Nd6+ Kd7 23.Rad1 Qe3+ 24.Kh1 Qf4 25.g3 Qxa4 26.Nxb5+ 1-0
```

Figure 4.4: Output showing the second game

Adding Features

Now, let's write the functionality for the -m option. As we discussed before, this should allow us to show the index of games that were won in less than a certain number of moves. Let's spend a short time thinking how we can go about it. Note the following observations based on the games.pgn file:

- We need to only consider completed games that have [Result "1-0"] or [Result "0-1"], but not [Result "1/2-1/2"], which represent drawn games.

- The moves list has each move in the format 'N.W B' where N is the move number, and W and B are the moves by the two players.

- The moves list is split into several lines. The split happens after N, W, or B, but never in-between the characters of any of them.

- The last entry in that moves list shows the result 0-1 or 1-0.

The core functionality is to count the moves in the list. We can do this by concatenating all the lines into one string, and then counting the number of . characters in it. This will work as long as the data is in the right format.

The other main task is to only filter games that have a result. We can do that by using a regex to match the '[Result ...]' lines, which show 1-0 or 0-1.

One of the notions when writing programs is to consider future extensibility. In this particular case, we are counting the moves of games which have a result. We can generalize that to process the moves list of a game whose attributes match a given filter. If we implement the script to deal with the general problem, we could easily solve other related problems, such as the following:

- Counting the checks given in games where black won

- Displaying games in a date range where a pawn was promoted

- Displaying games with a certain opening where white won

Keeping this in mind, we will write two functions:

- A function that reads through the initial lines in a game and returns success if one of the attributes matches the specified regex

- A function that reads though the move list and returns all of them concatenated in a string

Exercise 21: Chess Game Extractor – Counting Game Moves

In this exercise, we will implement the functionality we described in the previous section, namely, show games that were won in fewer than a specified number of moves:

1. In the previous section, we described two functions that we needed to write. Let's write the first one, modeled on **read_chunk**, and call it **filter_game**. Open your text editor and write the following code:

   ```
   function filter_game()
   {
       local ret=1
   ```

   ret will be the exit code of this function; this will be zero (success) or non-zero (failure), depending on whether any game attribute matched the regex provided to this function as the first argument. We initially assume that the match fails, so **ret** is set to 1.

2. Read through each line and set **ret** to 0 if it matched the regex:

   ```
   while read -r line
   do
       [[ $line =~ $1 ]] && ret=0
   ```

   For the sake of testing this script, print out the matched line. The remaining loop body is similar to the **read_chunk** function:

   ```
       [[ $line =~ $1 ]] && echo "$line"
       [[ $line =~ $regex_blank ]] && break
   done
   ```

   Before we leave the function, return the exit code, **ret**:

   ```
   return $ret
   }
   ```

3. Now, go back to the command line. We need to construct the regex that will be used to filter the lines, a simple regex with an **|** operator for **0-1** and **1-0**, as shown here:

```
robin ~/Lesson4 $ regex='\[Result "(1-0|0-1)"\]'
robin ~/Lesson4 $ [[ '[Result "1-0"]' =~ $regex ]] && echo matched
matched
robin ~/Lesson4 $ [[ '[Result "0-1"]' =~ $regex ]] && echo matched
matched
robin ~/Lesson4 $ [[ '[Result "1/2-1/2"]' =~ $regex ]] && echo matched
robin ~/Lesson4 $
```

Always test regular expressions on the shell before using them and escape the special characters with care.

4. Now, go back to your script and write a code to test the **filter_game** function. Open the script file and write the following piece of code:

```
for i in {1..30}
do
    filter_game '\[Result "(1-0|0-1)"\]'
    read_chunk 0
done
```

We use **filter_game** to check for games with a win (and print the result), and then we jump over the moves list with **read_chunk**. Therefore, ensure that you add the **read_chunk** function to the script as well. Then, save this script as **pgn_extract5.sh**.

5. Test this script on the command line and verify that it produces the correct output (only a few lines are shown here):

```
robin ~/Lesson4 $ ./pgn_extract5.sh <games.pgn
[Result "0-1"]
[Result "1-0"]
[Result "0-1"]
[Result "0-1"]
```

6. Next, let's add a function called **read_moves** to our script file that fetches the moves list for a game as an array; this function will be almost identical to **read_chunk**, except that it will concatenate all the lines containing the moves into a variable. Remove the **read_chunk** function and write the following lines of code below the **filter_game()** function:

```
function read_moves()
{
  moves=''
```

The **moves** variable is where we will store the entire set of moves that we read in a game. Since we need to use it outside this function, it cannot be a local variable.

7. Just like before, we read each line in turn in a loop. If we encounter a blank line, we can exit successfully, otherwise we just append the next line we read onto **moves**. We add a space when we concatenate, to prevent successive moves' text from getting combined:

```
while read -r line
do
  [[ $line =~ $regex_blank ]] && return 0
  moves="${moves} ${line}"
done
```

If the loop exits, it means there were no more lines in the file left to read, so we return a non-zero (failure) code from the function.

```
  return 1
}
```

8. Since the very first game in the file has a result, we can just call the two methods once to make sure we get the complete moves list as a single line:

```
filter_game '\[Result "(1-0|0-1)"\]'
read_moves
echo "$moves"
```

Save this modified script as **pgn_extract6.sh**.

9. Now, let's test this script:

```
robin ~/Lesson4 $ ./pgn_extract6.sh <games.pgn
```

Testing it produces the following correct result:

```
robin ~/Lesson4 $ ./pgn_extract6.sh <games.pgn
[Result "0-1"]
 1.e4 e5 2.f4 exf4 3.Bc4 d5 4.Bxd5 Qh4+ 5.Kf1 g5 6.Nc3 Ne7 7.d4 Bg7 8.Nf3 Qh5 9
.h4 h6 10.e5 Nbc6 11.Kg1 g4 12.Ne1 Bf5 13.Bxc6+ Nxc6 14.Ne2 Be4 15. Bxf4 Qf5 16
.Qd2 0-0-0 17.Ng3 Qh7 18.Qe2 Nxd4 19.Qc4 Bc6 20.c3 Ne6 21.Qf1 h5 22.Bg5 Bxe5 23
.Bxd8 Bxg3 24.Bf6 Qe4 25.Nd3 Nf4 26.Rh3 Qe3+ 27.Nf2 Nxh3+ 28.gxh3 Bh2+ 29.Kxh2
Qf4+ 30.Kg1 Qg3+ 31.Qg2 Qxg2# 0-1
```

Figure 4.5: Output of concatenated moves list

Note that since the console window is limited in size, the text wraps around, but there is only one continuous line of moves.

10. The next thing to do is count the number of moves in each line from the list and add them together. The easiest way is to count the number of . symbols in each line. We can rely on each move having its number followed by . since we are sure that the file format is always correct. Let's write a function called **count_moves** that does this. The idea is to use **tr** to remove characters other than the '.' and then pass it to **wc** to count the number. There are more efficient ways of doing this, but this is the simplest. Go back to **pgn_extract6.sh** on your text editor and add the following lines of code:

```
function count_moves()
{
    num_moves=$(tr -d -c '.' <<< "$moves" | wc -c)
}
```

The **-d** flag is for deletion and the **-c** '.' flag chooses all characters except the period, giving a string containing as many '.' as there are moves. We then use **wc** **-c** to count these and assign the result to **num_moves** via command substitution.

11. Next, write the code to test this functionality, as follows:

```
for i in {1..3}
do
    filter_game '\[Result "(1-0|0-1)"\]'
    read_moves
    echo "$moves"

    count_moves
    echo "$num_moves" moves in game
    echo
done
```

Save this script as **pgn_extract7.sh**.

12. Now, test the script as follows:

```
robin ~/Lesson4 $ ./pgn_extract7.sh <games.pgn
```

The output for the first three games is shown here:

```
[Result "0-1"]
 1.e4 e5 2.f4 exf4 3.Bc4 d5 4.Bxd5 Qh4+ 5.Kf1 g5 6.Nc3 Ne7 7.d4 Bg7 8.Nf3 Qh5 9.h4 h6 10.e5 Nbc6 11.Kg1 g4 12.Ne1 Bf5 13
.Bxc6+ Nxc6 14.Ne2 Be4 15. Bxf4 Qf5 16.Qd2 0-0-0 17.Ng3 Qh7 18.Qe2 Nxd4 19.Qc4 Bc6 20.c3 Ne6 21.Qf1 h5 22.Bg5 Bxe5 23.Bx
d8 Bxg3 24.Bf6 Qe4 25.Nd3 Nf4 26.Rh3 Qe3+ 27.Nf2 Nxh3+ 28.gxh3 Bh2+ 29.Kxh2 Qf4+ 30.Kg1 Qg3+ 31.Qg2 Qxg2# 0-1
31 moves in game

[Result "1-0"]
 1.e4 e5 2.Nf3 Nc6 3.d4 exd4 4.Nxd4 Nf6 5.Nxc6 bxc6 6.Bd3 d5 7.exd5 cxd5 8. 0-0 Be7 9.Nc3 0-0 10.Bg5 c6 11.Qf3 Ng4 12.Bx
e7 Qxe7 13.Rae1 Qd6 14.Qg3 Qf6 15.h3 Nh6 16.Re5 g6 17.Ne2 Bf5 18.f4 Rfe8 19.Qe3 Rxe5 20. fxe5 Qh4 21.Nd4 Bxd3 22.Rf4 Qe7
23.cxd3 Rc8 24.Rf6 c5 25.Nc6 Qe8 26.e6 Nf5 27.exf7+ Qxf7 28.Rxf5 1-0
28 moves in game

[Result "0-1"]
 1.e4 e5 2.Nf3 d6 3.d4 Nd7 4.Bc4 c6 5.Ng5 Nh6 6.f4 Be7 7.0-0 0-0 8.Nf3 exd4 9.Nxd4 d5 10.exd5 Nb6 11.Be2 Bc5 12.Kh1 Nxd5
 13.Nc3 Re8 14.Nxd5 Qxd5 15. Nb3 Qxd1 16.Bxd1 Bb6 17.Bf3 Bf5 18.c3 Bd3 19.Rd1 Bc2 20.Rf1 Rad8 21.Nd2 Nf5 22.Nb3 Rd6 23.g
3 Bd3 24.Bd2 Bxf1 25.Rxf1 g6 26.Kg2 Rd3 27.Kh3 a5 28.a4 h5 29.g4 hxg4+ 30.Kxg4 Re2 31.Kh3 Rexd2 32.Nxd2 Rxd2 0-1
32 moves in game
```

Figure 4.6: Moves list and count for first three games in games.pgn

We can see that it worked. The **count_moves** function is providing the correct answer.

13. That leaves the final refinement. Instead of printing these games, only print the game index and the moves count for games that finished in the specified number of moves. We will write a function called **show_games_won_in** that will display only those games that were won in a specified number of moves.

There is one problem to take care of though. Our **filter_game** function does not tell us if it failed because the stream had no more data, or because the game had no result. We need to first modify it to distinguish the two circumstances.

We define a variable called **found**, which will contain 1 or 0 depending on whether a game matched or not. Since this value must be read by the caller of the function, it cannot be local. By default, we assume 0:

```
function filter_game()
{
  # Initially assume not found
  found=0
```

14. If the filter matched, only then do we set **found** to 1:

```
while read -r line
do
    [[ $line =~ $1 ]] && found=1
```

15. We return from the function with a zero (success) return code if we read an entire game:

```
    [[ $line =~ $regex_blank ]] && return 0
done
```

16. The loop only ends if the file itself runs out of data, so we return a non-zero (failure) code:

```
    return 1
}
```

17. Now, we can go on to implement the function called **show_games_won_in**. Add the **read_chunk** function to the **pgn_extract7.sh** script and add the preceding function, as shown in the subsequent steps. We declare a local variable called **index** that holds the index of the current game being processed. When a game meets the criteria, we will print this index:

```
function show_games_won_in()
{
  local index=1
```

18. Loop through the games, one by one. Remember that **filter_game** returns non-zero (failure) when the file is exhausted. The found variable is set to 1 if the regex (which describes the games that had a result) matched:

```
while filter_game '\[Result "(1-0|0-1)"\]'
do
```

19. If a game with result was found, we call **read_moves**, which gets the entire move list as one string in the **moves** variable. Then, we call **count_moves**, which sets the **num_moves** variable to the number of moves in the **moves** variable:

```
if [[ $found -eq 1 ]]
then
    read_moves
    count_moves
```

20. If the number of moves was less than or equal to what the user asked for, print out the index of this game as well as the list of moves:

```
    [[ $num_moves -le $1 ]] && echo "Game $index: $num_moves moves" &&
echo "$moves"
```

21. If the game had no result, we just read the list of moves and ignore it:

```
else
    read_chunk 0
fi
```

22. Finally, we increment the game index variable:

```
    index=$(( index + 1 ))
  done
}
show_games_won_in "$1"
```

Save this script as **pgn_extract8.sh**.

23. Test the script, as follows:

```
robin ~/Lesson4 $ ./pgn_extract8.sh 10 <games.pgn
```

You will see the following output:

```
Game 231: 8 moves
 1.d4 d5 2.Nf3 c5 3.Bf4 cxd4 4.Bxb8 Rxb8 5.Qxd4 b6 6.e4 dxe4 7.Qxd8+ Kxd8 8.Ne5 1-0
Game 807: 9 moves
 1.d4 Nf6 2.Nf3 e6 3.c4 d5 4.Nc3 c5 5.cxd5 Nxd5 6.Nxd5 Qxd5 7.e3 Nc6 8.Bb5 cxd4 9.Qxd4 Qxb5 0-1
Game 1342: 9 moves
 1.e4 e5 2.Nc3 Bc5 3.Bc4 Ne7 4.d3 Nbc6 5.Qh5 0-0 6.Bg5 Qe8 7.Nf3 Ng6 8.Nd5 Bb6 9.Nf6+ 1-0
Game 2214: 7 moves
 1.Nf3 Nf6 2.b3 d6 3.g3 e5 4.c4 e4 5.Nh4 d5 6.cxd5 Qxd5 7.Nc3 Qc6 1-0
Game 2296: 9 moves
 1.e4 c6 2.d4 d5 3.Nc3 dxe4 4.Nxe4 Nf6 5.Ng3 e5 6.Nf3 exd4 7.Nxd4 Bc5 8.Be3 Ng4 9.Nxc6 1-0
```

Figure 4.7: Output showing the games won in 10 moves or less

24. Verify that the displayed game indexes actually match the criteria using the earlier version of the script we wrote:

    robin ~/Lesson4 $ ./pgn_extract4.sh -n 2296 <games.pgn

You should get the following output:

```
Displaying Game #2296

[Event "Kecskemet"]
[Site "?"]
[Date "1927.??.??"]
[Round "?"]
[White "Alekhine, Alexander A"]
[Black "Tartakower, Saviely G"]
[Result "1-0"]
[ECO "B15s"]
[EventDate "1927.??.??"]

1.e4 c6 2.d4 d5 3.Nc3 dxe4 4.Nxe4 Nf6 5.Ng3 e5 6.Nf3 exd4 7.Nxd4 Bc5 8.Be3
Ng4 9.Nxc6 1-0
```

Figure 4.8: Output displaying game #2296

25. To complete our script, all we need to do is combine the code in **pgn_extract8.sh** and **pgn_extract4.sh** so that we perform the preceding filtering operation if the **-m** option is specified. Save this to **pgn_extract_final.sh**. Once we do that, we can test both functionalities of the script, as follows:

    robin ~/Lesson4 $ ./pgn_extract_final.sh -m 8 <games.pgn

You should get the following output on using the **-m** option:

```
Displaying games won in 8 moves or less

Game 231: 8 moves
  1.d4 d5 2.Nf3 c5 3.Bf4 cxd4 4.Bxb8 Rxb8 5.Qxd4 b6 6.e4 dxe4 7.Qxd8+ Kxd8 8.Ne5 1-0

Game 2214: 7 moves
  1.Nf3 Nf6 2.b3 d6 3.g3 e5 4.c4 e4 5.Nh4 d5 6.cxd5 Qxd5 7.Nc3 Qc6 1-0
```

Figure 4.9: Output of final script with the -m option

    robin ~/Lesson4 $ ./pgn_extract_final.sh -n 231 <games.pgn

You should get the following output on using the **-n** option:

```
Displaying Game #231

[Event "?"]
[Site "Odessa UKR"]
[Date "1918.??.??"]
[Round "?"]
[White "Alekhine, Alexander A"]
[Black "Kaufman A"]
[Result "1-0"]
[ECO "D02j"]

1.d4 d5 2.Nf3 c5 3.Bf4 cxd4 4.Bxb8 Rxb8 5.Qxd4 b6 6.e4 dxe4 7.Qxd8+ Kxd8
8.Ne5 1-0
```

Figure 4.10: Output of final script with the -n option

With that, we have managed to write our own little command that performs a comprehensive function. It is nowhere near what a tool developed in a sophisticated programming language would be like, but it is quite possible to write something like this in a few hours, and the shell constructs we used are really simple.

There are some obvious limitations to this script:

- It lacks error handling for the input. We are relying on the input file not having any errors, but this is a reasonable expectation in this use case.

- Detecting blank lines with a regex may be slow. We could assume that blank lines are of zero length and detect them faster.

- The command does not provide any information about how to use it. Typically, a command should show a usage screen when run without arguments.

- Processing a text file with read in a loop is often very slow, especially when an external command is invoked within that loop. For example, we invoke **wc** here to count the moves, making it extremely slow. Text manipulation on the shell was never intended to be used for heavy lifting; hence, even operations such as array indexing tend to be much slower than an average programming language.

Every solution to a problem has some compromises based on how far we are willing to go in order to get it optimal. We should consider shell scripting as the "quick and dirty" way of solving problems without requiring too much effort. It is possible to write very powerful and fast shell scripts, but usually, if we hit certain limitations of performance and complexity, it is wiser to switch to a more powerful scripting language such as Python or Perl.

Tips and Tricks

Before we move on to the next case study, we will cover some material that is helpful, but was not covered in previous chapters. They fall into various categories and make some operations much easier. We will briefly describe some of them. Some of the information here will also be needed to solve the problems in Activity 10 in this chapter.

Suppressing Command Output

UNIX-like OSes provide a special file, called **/dev/null**, that can be used as a "black hole" for any data. Any writes to that file silently succeed and the data is discarded. This is useful when you need to suppress the output of commands. For instance, look at the following command:

```
ls >/dev/null
```

This runs **ls** and silently discards its output. Redirecting to **/dev/null** is usually helpful when suppressing error messages from commands that are run in a script.

Arithmetic Expansion

So far, we have used the **$((EXPR))** syntax for arithmetic expressions. However, there are some variations of this that are more convenient. We will look at these in this section.

Using only ((EXPR)) for Mutating Operations

Mutating operations are arithmetic operations that change a value. For example:

- Assignment: **a=1**

- Reassignment: **a=a+1**

- Compound assignment: **a*=b**. Remember that this is equivalent to **a=a*b**

- Post and Pre increment/decrement is **a++** or **--a**

For such expressions, we can leave out the **$** symbol, as shown here:

```
robin ~/Lesson4 $ a=1
robin ~/Lesson4 $ (( a++ ))
robin ~/Lesson4 $ (( a *= 2 ))
robin ~/Lesson4 $ echo $a
4
```

This avoids having to use constructs such as **a=$((a * 2))**.

We can use commas to write many expressions in a single line:

```
robin ~/Lesson4 $ (( a=6, b=2, c=b*a ))
robin ~/Lesson4 $ echo $c
12
```

The Bash shell also provides a command called **let** to perform arithmetic in a more convenient fashion. Look at the following example:

```
robin ~/Lesson4 $ let a=10
robin ~/Lesson4 $ let a++
robin ~/Lesson4 $ echo $a
11
robin ~/Lesson4 $ let b=a*a
robin ~/Lesson4 $ echo $b
121
```

It functions exactly like the **((EXPR))** syntax. The command returns a non-zero exit code (failure) if the expression evaluated to zero and a zero exit code (success) if the expression evaluated to non-zero.

If we need to use multiple expressions with **let** or any character that may cause expansion, quotes are needed:

```
robin ~/Lesson4 $ let "a=6, b=2, c=b*a*a"
robin ~/Lesson4 $ echo $c
72
```

Although this form is easier to type, it is not recommended since it requires quoting to avoid wildcard expansion, whereas **((EXPR))** does not.

Arithmetic Booleans versus Shell Booleans

There is a subtlety in the way the shell treats true and false values that can cause confusion. A command's exit code indicates the error that occurred; hence, a zero exit code signifies *true/success* and a non-zero exit code signifies *false/failure*. This is what is tested by the **if** command. For example:

```
robin ~/Lesson4 $ ls nonexistent &>/dev/null
robin ~/Lesson4 $ echo $?
2
robin ~/Lesson4 $ ls &>/dev/null
robin ~/Lesson4 $ echo $?
0
robin ~/Lesson4 $ if ls nonexistent &>/dev/null; then echo Succeeded; else echo Failed; fi
Failed
robin ~/Lesson4 $ if ls &>/dev/null; then echo Succeeded; else echo Failed; fi
Succeeded
```

Note the use of **&>/dev/null** to make **ls** completely silent. The exit code 2 signifies "File or object not found" error according to the UNIX error codes list.

On the other hand, in most programming languages that originate from C (including the arithmetic expansion syntax), false is zero and true is non-zero:

```
robin ~/Lesson4 $ echo $(( 1 < 2 ))
1
robin ~/Lesson4 $ echo $(( 1 < 0 ))
0
```

In this case, the logic is the opposite of what we saw with the command's exit codes. However, the **if** and other conditional statements will do the right thing if **((EXPR))** or **let** is used:

```
robin ~/Lesson4 $ (( 1 < 2 )) && echo "One is less than Two"
One is less than Two
robin ~/Lesson4 $ (( 2 < 1 )) && echo "Two is less than One"
```

```
robin ~/Lesson4 $
robin ~/Lesson4 $ if (( 1 < 2 )) ; then echo "One is less than Two"; fi
One is less than Two
```

Using ((EXPR)) for arithmetic operations as well as tests can sometimes be preferable to using the [[$VAR1 -op $VAR2]] syntax.

Octal, Hexadecimal, and Other Bases

In the C language, a number that starts with "0x" is treated as a hexadecimal (base 16) number that uses the characters 0-9 and a-f to represent 0 to 15. Numbers that start with a leading "0" are treated as octal (base 8), which uses only the digits 0 to 7.

We can force a number to be interpreted as a particular base by prefixing it with N#, where N is the base. For example:

```
robin ~/Lesson4 $ echo $(( 09 * 09 ))
bash: 09: value too great for base (error token is "09")
robin ~/Lesson4 $ echo $(( 10#09 * 10#09 ))
81
```

In the first case, 09 was treated as an octal number, so 9 is an invalid digit. In the second case, we force base 10 evaluation.

Declaring Typed Variables

We can set the type of a variable to be an integer, read-only, or to be uppercase by default. Integer variables can be initialized using an arithmetic expression (note that the * is not interpreted as a wildcard):

```
robin ~/Lesson4 $ declare -i num
robin ~/Lesson4 $ num=9*8*7
robin ~/Lesson4 $ echo $num
504
```

Uppercase variables always get converted to capitals when expanded:

```
robin ~/Lesson4 $ declare -u name
robin ~/Lesson4 $ name=robin
robin ~/Lesson4 $ echo $name
ROBIN
```

Read-only variables can only be assigned once and cannot be changed or unset:

```
robin ~/Lesson4 $ declare -r C=300000000
robin ~/Lesson4 $ echo $C
300000000
robin ~/Lesson4 $ C=0
bash: C: readonly variable
robin ~/Lesson4 $ unset C
bash: unset: C: cannot unset: readonly variable
```

There are some more aspects of the **declare** command; however, these are not covered in this book.

Numeric for Loops

The **for** loop allows an alternate syntax and semantics very similar to the ones found in C, C++, C#, Java, JavaScript, and other "curly brace" languages:

```
for ((INIT; TEST; INCREMENT))
do
    COMMANDS
done
```

Here, **INIT**, **TEST**, and **INCREMENT** are arithmetic expressions. The **for** loop works as follows:

1. It evaluates **INIT**.

2. It evaluates **TEST** as a Boolean. If it evaluates to non-zero, the commands in the loop body are executed, and if not, the loop is ended immediately.

3. It evaluates **INCREMENT**.

The following is an example of the multiline form of this loop:

```
robin ~/Lesson4 $ for ((x = 0 ; x < 5 ; x++))
> do
>    echo "Counter: $x"
> done
Counter: 0
Counter: 1
Counter: 2
Counter: 3
Counter: 4
```

The single-line form of this loop is shown here:

```
robin ~/Lesson4 $ for ((x = 0 ; x < 5 ; x++)) ; do echo "Counter: $x"; done
Counter: 0
Counter: 1
Counter: 2
Counter: 3
Counter: 4
```

We can initialize and use multiple variables too, as shown here:

```
robin ~/Lesson4 $ for ((x=0,y=5; x < 5; x++, y--)) ; do echo "Counter: $x
$y"; done
Counter: 0 5
Counter: 1 4
Counter: 2 3
Counter: 3 2
Counter: 4 1
```

Remember that these three parts in this construct only accept arithmetic expressions, and the **TEST** expression is true if it evaluates to nonzero (as we discussed previously).

echo

So far, we only used the **echo** command to display simple text strings. However, **echo** has a couple of flags that are useful:

- **-n**: Does not print a newline at the end. For example, look at the following snippet:

    ```
    robin ~/Lesson4 $ echo -n Hello && echo " world"
    Hello world
    ```

- **-e**: Enables backslash escape characters, as shown here:

    ```
    robin ~/Lesson4 $ echo -e "\t\tHello"
                    Hello
    ```

Array Reverse Indexing

The shell provides a way to specify array indices from the end instead of the beginning. The regular way to index arrays is **${arr[@]:IDX:LEN}**, which returns a sub-array of length N from the (zero-based) position **IDX** onwards. We can specify a negative index to get the elements relative to the end. This is very convenient for getting the last element easily without dealing with the length of the array. For example:

```
robin ~/Lesson4 $ arr=(0 1 2 3 4 5 6 7 8 9 10)

robin ~/Lesson4 $ echo ${arr[@]}

0 1 2 3 4 5 6 7 8 9 10

robin ~/Lesson4 $ echo ${arr[@]:1:3}

1 2 3

robin ~/Lesson4 $ echo ${arr[@]: -3: 2}

8 9

robin ~/Lesson4 $ echo ${arr[@]: -5}

6 7 8 9 10
```

If a negative index is used, it is mandatory that the minus sign is preceded by whitespace. Skipping the **LEN** part gets all the elements until the end.

shopt

The **shopt** command changes the way the shell behaves. It can be useful in many situations, especially in scripts. It sets a shell option to on or off. This command takes one or more shell option names as an argument with the following flags:

- **-s OPTNAME**: Enables (sets) each optname.
- **-u OPTNAME**: Disables (unsets) each optname.
- **-q OPTNAME1 OPTNAME2** ...: Queries the list of options and returns a success (zero) exit code if all of them are enabled.

A brief list of shell options for Bash that can be set are as follows:

- **autocd**: If set, typing a directory name changes the CWD to it like the **cd** command.
- **dotglob**: If set, filenames beginning with a . will be matched by wildcards. Usually, such files are not displayed (you can use the **-a** flag of **ls** to list such files).
- **extglob**: If set, extended wildcard expansion is enabled (see the next section).
- **interactive_comments**: If a **#** character appears on a line typed in a command line, everything after that is ignored. This option is enabled by default.
- **nocaseglob**: If set, Bash performs completions for files ignoring case.
- **nocasematch**: If set, Bash performs case-insensitive pattern matching for case statements and **[[** conditional commands.
- **shift_verbose**: If this option is set, the built-in **shift** command will print an error message if there are not enough positional parameters to shift by the number specified number.

There are many more shell options that we will not cover here. The curious students can refer to the man pages for more details.

Extended Wildcards

When the shell's **extglob** option is not set, the following constructs are available:

- The **?** and ***** symbols, which we learned about in the first chapter.
- **[abc]**: matches any of a, b, c
- **[!abc]**: matches anything not a, b, c
- **[a-f]**: matches any of a to f
- **[[:CLASS:]]** syntax for matching character classes

Once **extglob** is enabled, the following constructs become possible:

- **?(PATTERNS)**: Optionally matches **PATTERNS**.
- ***(PATTERNS)**: Matches any one of the expressions in **PATTERNS** any number of times (including zero times).
- **+(PATTERNS)**: Matches any one of the expressions in **PATTERNS** one or more times.
- **@(PATTERNS)**: Matches any one of the expressions in **PATTERNS** exactly once.
- **!(PATTERNS)**: Matches anything except one of the expressions in **PATTERNS**.

Here, **PATTERNS** is a list of wildcard expressions separated by a **|** symbol. For example, **!(*.jpg|*.gif)** matches any file that does not have a **.jpg** or **.gif** extension, and **@(ba*(na)|a+(p)le)** matches "ba," "bana," "banana," "bananana," and so on or "aple," "apple," "apppple," and so on.

They are similar to regexes but have a different syntax, so be careful not to confuse the syntax. For the most part, you will rarely need extended globbing, except for the **!** operator.

man and info Pages

We have mentioned the man (manual) pages before. They contain comprehensive documentation about all the standard commands. New programs that are installed on a system install their own manual pages, too.

To view the help of any command, just run **man** with one argument specifying the item for which you need the manual page. **info** is a more comprehensive help system available with GNU. It has an interactive hyperlink based interface and will automatically show man pages too. The user interface of man is exactly the same as the one in **less**. The best way to learn about these commands is to use **info info** and **man man** to let the two commands themselves describe how you should use them. Note that the shell built-ins do not have their own man pages, but are described under the man pages for Bash and can be accessed with **man bash**. You can also use the **help** command to get usage information for built-in commands individually.

shellcheck

shellcheck is a tool that's available in both online and offline versions to check your scripts for possible errors and bad practices. When developing scripts, use this tool and try to follow all the suggestions it gives to ensure that your scripts do not have potential failure cases.

Activity 10: PGN Game Extractor Enhancement

In the previous exercises, we incrementally developed a shell script to extract chess games from a PGN file. This script has a few shortcomings, though. In this activity, you need to address those shortcomings of the script:

1. Think of a better (and faster) way to count moves, rather than using **wc**.

2. Think of a better way to detect blank lines than using a regex. Assume that the blank lines have no whitespace and are empty.

3. Make the script more readable.

4. Change the script to detect if no arguments are specified and print a simple help text describing what the script can do and what the options are.

5. If there are no games to show for **-m**, show the message **No games**. If the game index passed to **-n** is more than the last game in the file, show **Invalid game index. Maximum is N**, where N represents the count of games in the file.

Follow the steps given here to complete this activity and create five scripts in the files **pgn_extract_act1.sh** to **pgn_extract_act5.sh**:

1. For the first problem, consider starting by splitting the moves list with **IFS='.'** and extracting the last move number from that array.

2. For the second problem, detect blank lines by testing for an empty string.

3. To make the script more readable, use **((EXPR))** based syntax for numerical tests and increments.

4. For the fourth problem, add a default case to the **case** statement that parses the options, and print the command usage help there.

5. For the last problem, maintain a count of games that passed the filter in a variable called **game_count**.

Also measure the time taken for the script at each of the stages. The final script should be at least 3 to 5 times as fast as the initial version for both operations.

> **Note**
>
> The solution for this activity can be found on page 279.

Practical Case Study 2: NYC Yellow Taxi Trip Analysis

In this case study, we will incrementally develop another script to process data. For this example, we will deal with a much larger dataset than the previous one.

> **Note**
>
> The kind of operations we will attempt on the data here are more complex than those in the previous study. In particular, we will process every line of the file individually in complex ways. Sometimes, it is better to use some external tools such as **awk** or even a Python script for this process since the shell has its limits in terms of performance, especially when we do not use pipelines. This example tries more to demonstrate how to program with the shell and does not suggest that the student should always blindly use only the shell.

Understanding the Dataset

The dataset we will use for this is a text file that contains public data about yellow taxi trips in New York City for 2017. We will use a subset of 200,000 lines of that data for this book. The file is in CSV format and contains one line of data for every trip. The following fields are present:

- Pickup time: Lists the pickup dates and times in the format **YYYY-MM-DD HH:MM:SS**. For example, **2017-01-09 11:38:20**.

- Dropoff time: Lists the drop-off time in the same format as for pickup time.

- Passenger count: Lists the number of passengers who took that trip.

- Trip distance in miles: Lists the total distance covered.

- Total fare amount: Lists the total amount charged for the trip.

We will develop scripts that help us extract some statistics about the data involved in the following exercises.

Exercise 22: Taxi Trip Analysis – Extracting Trip Time

As the first task, let's process the CSV file to add another field that contains the time taken by the trip. We need to subtract the time values and convert it into a number of seconds:

1. Let's write the first version of a function called **trip_duration**, which can take the pickup time and dropoff time of a trip as arguments and calculate the number of seconds between the two time values. For convenience, you can type it in an editor first and then paste the whole thing carefully into the command line. First, we will split the dates and times into arrays using a space as the IFS and store the dates in two different variables, **dt_start** and **dt_stop** (which contain the time value as HH:MM:SS), as follows:

```
function trip_duration()
{
  IFS=' '
  local dt_start=( $1 )
  local dt_stop=( $2 )
```

2. Then, we will split the times into hours, minutes, and seconds using the colon as the delimiter and store the resultant values in **t_start** and **t_stop** for **dt_start** and **dt_stop**, respectively, as shown here:

    ```
    IFS=':'
    local t_start=( ${dt_start[1]} )
    local t_stop=( ${dt_stop[1]} )
    ```

3. Next, we will convert the hours and minutes to the absolute seconds and sum all three values, storing the results in the **n_start** and **n_stop** variables:

    ```
    local n_start=$(( t_start[0] * 3600 + t_start[1] * 60 + t_start[2] ))
    local n_stop=$(( t_stop[0] * 3600 + t_stop[1] * 60 + t_stop[2] ))
    ```

4. Finally, we will print the difference between the two input times and close the function:

    ```
    echo $(( n_stop - n_start ))
    }
    ```

5. Now, we will test the preceding function using the following arguments:

    ```
    robin ~/Lesson4 $ trip_duration '2017-10-10 12:00:00' '2017-10-10
    16:00:00'
    14400
    robin ~/Lesson4 $ trip_duration '2017-10-10 12:00:00' '2017-10-10
    13:59:00'
    7140
    robin ~/Lesson4 $ trip_duration '2017-10-10 12:00:00' '2017-10-10
    00:00:00'
    -43200
    ```

6. From the last output in the previous step, you will observe that we have a problem if the stop time is after the start time. This can happen if a trip crosses midnight. If we can assume that no trip ever exceeds 24 hours (which is a given), then we can fix this problem very easily by making the following modification to the last line of the function:

    ```
    echo $(( ((n_stop - n_start) + 86400) % 86400 ))
    ```

We add 86,400 (the number of seconds in a day) and apply modulus with the same value. This will convert negative values to the right answer. You can save the updated version of **trip_duration** as a script file named **taxi1.sh**.

> **Note**
>
> Refer to the **taxi1.sh** to **taxi9.sh** files that are supplied with this code bundle for the set of scripts that were used in this case study.

7. Now, if we test for the last example, we get the right answer:

```
robin ~/Lesson4 $ ./taxi1.sh '2017-10-10 12:00:00' '2017-10-10 00:00:00'
43200
```

8. Next, let's extend this script to read lines of data and print the duration for each trip, as follows. For this, we will use a **while** loop that reads each line, and splits it using the comma as a delimiter. We pass the first two fields to **trip_duration**, which prints the duration of each trip:

```
while read -r line
do
    IFS=','
    fields=( $line )

    trip_duration "${fields[0]}" "${fields[1]}"
done
```

Save this script as **./taxi2.sh**.

9. Test this script for the first five values of the dataset, as follows:

```
robin ~/Lesson4 $ ./taxi2.sh <nyc_taxi.csv | head -n5
737
214
225
323
0
```

You can verify this by looking at the actual values in the dataset, which are shown here:

```
robin ~/Lesson4 $ head -n5 nyc_taxi.csv
2017-01-09 11:13:28,2017-01-09 11:25:45,1,3.30,15.30
2017-01-09 11:32:27,2017-01-09 11:36:01,1,0.90,7.25
2017-01-09 11:38:20,2017-01-09 11:42:05,1,1.10,7.30
2017-01-09 11:52:13,2017-01-09 11:57:36,1,1.10,8.50
2017-01-01 00:00:00,2017-01-01 00:00:00,1,0.02,52.80
```

However, this script has a problem. Look at the example output here (we use **head** just to restrict the number of output lines that are printed):

```
robin ~/Lesson4 $ ./taxi2.sh <nyc_taxi.csv | head -n10
737
214
225
323
0
228
2360
415
./taxi2.sh: line 20: 08: value too great for base (error token is "08")
```

The duration calculation may encounter numbers that start with the digit 0, causing them to be interpreted as octal.

10. Fix that by changing the two lines in the **./taxi2.sh** file that calculate the absolute times, as follows:

```
local n_start=$(( 10#${t_start[0]} * 3600 + 10#${t_start[1]} * 60 +
10#${t_start[2]} ))
local n_stop=$(( 10#${t_stop[0]} * 3600 + 10#${t_stop[1]} * 60 + 10#${t_
stop[2]} ))
```

We added the **10#** prefix so that nothing is treated as octal. We have to use the **${ }** syntax to get the variable name for this to work. Now, the code will produce the right results. Save this script as **taxi3.sh**.

11. Test the fixed code with the first ten instances in the dataset, as follows:

```
robin ~/Lesson4 $ ./taxi3.sh <nyc_taxi.csv | head -n10
737
214
225
323
0
228
2360
415
508
299
```

12. The next step is to add this duration as a column to the data file. Notice that there is an entry with 0 duration. This tells us that the data may have errors. We will filter out any duration that is 2 minutes or less and any that is 3 hours or more using the following snippet of code:

```
while read -r line
do
   IFS=','
   fields=( $line )

   duration=$(trip_duration "${fields[0]}" "${fields[1]}")

   if (( (duration > 120) && (duration < 10800) ))
   then
      echo "${line},${duration}"
   fi
done
```

Save this script as **taxi4.sh**.

13. Try timing this script with 5,000 lines of input (redirect the output to a file) and check the result:

```
robin ~/Lesson4 $ time head -n5000 nyc_taxi.csv | ./taxi4.sh >test.txt
real    0m6.974s
user    0m5.036s
sys     0m2.308s
```

Notice that it takes a very long time to process. This is surprisingly slower than what we saw with pipelines. We want to be able to deal with a million rows of data, and it is impractical if it takes more than a few minutes. Before we move forward, let's try to get this work as fast as possible.

14. The first change to make is to avoid using the command substitution syntax to get the return value of **trip_duration**. Change the last statement of the function, as follows:

```
duration=$(( ((n_stop - n_start) + 86400) % 86400 ))
```

We will also change the invocation in the main code, as follows:

```
trip_duration "${fields[0]}" "${fields[1]}"
```

Save the script as **taxi5.sh**.

15. Now, test how long it takes for the same 5,000 lines on the command line, as follows:

```
robin ~/Lesson4 $ time head -n5000 nyc_taxi.csv | ./taxi5.sh >test.txt
real    0m0.674s
user    0m0.560s
sys     0m0.112s
```

It's much better now—at least a 10x improvement—but we need to process a million lines (and maybe even more). Therefore, let's see if we can do something more.

16. If we observe the data, the time stamps are at the beginning of each line and they are fixed width fields, such as in the following example:

```
2017-01-09 11:13:28,2017-01-09 11:25:45
```

Instead of using word splitting to get the times (the dates are irrelevant) we can just use the array substring syntax to get the two sets of HH, MM, and SS values. The indices are 11, 14, 17 and 31, 34, 37 for the two pairs, respectively. Let's use this logic for our **trip_duration** function (save the changes to a script named **taxi6.sh**):

```
function trip_duration()
{
  # Get the timestamps from the line
  local line="$*"

  hh1=${line:11:2}
  mm1=${line:14:2}
  ss1=${line:17:2}

  hh2=${line:31:2}
  mm2=${line:34:2}
  ss2=${line:37:2}
```

17. The rest of the function remains the same. We convert hours and minutes to absolute seconds and save the summations to the **n_start** and **n_stop** variables. Finally, we print the difference between the time values:

```
n_start=$(( 10#${hh1} * 3600 + 10#${mm1} * 60 + 10#${ss1} ))
n_stop=$(( 10#${hh2} * 3600 + 10#${mm2} * 60 + 10#${ss2} ))

duration=$(( ((n_stop - n_start) + 86400) % 86400 ))
}
```

18. We will run another test to check the performance of our modified script, as follows:

```
robin ~/Lesson4 $ time head -n5000 nyc_taxi.csv | ./taxi6.sh >test.txt
real    0m0.549s
user    0m0.450s
sys     0m0.098s
```

We gained some performance by avoiding local variables. Declaring a local variable has some penalty because it is created and destroyed every time the function is called. The function logic is simpler now and also, in the main code, we no longer need to reset **IFS** within the loop, thus giving a small speedup.

19. Now, let's go ahead and generate the new data that contains this "calculated field" of trip duration:

```
robin ~/Lesson4 $./taxi6.sh <nyc_taxi.csv >nyc_taxi2.csv
robin ~/Lesson4 $ head -n5 nyc_taxi2.csv
2017-01-09 11:13:28,2017-01-09 11:25:45,1,3.30,15.30,737
2017-01-09 11:32:27,2017-01-09 11:36:01,1,0.90,7.25,214
2017-01-09 11:38:20,2017-01-09 11:42:05,1,1.10,7.30,225
2017-01-09 11:52:13,2017-01-09 11:57:36,1,1.10,8.50,323
2017-01-01 00:00:02,2017-01-01 00:03:50,1,0.50,5.30,228
```

20. Let's also see how many invalid rows were eliminated:

```
robin ~/Lesson4 $ wc -l nyc_taxi.csv
200000 nyc_taxi.csv
robin ~/Lesson4 $ wc -l nyc_taxi2.csv
193305 nyc_taxi2.csv
```

Exercise 23: Taxi Trip Analysis – Calculating Average Trip Speed

Now, we can try to run some statistics on the data. For example, we can sum the distances and durations, and then get the average speed:

1. The first problem we face is that the fields for fare and distance have decimal numbers, whereas Bash only performs integer arithmetic. We can get around this problem by noticing that the distances in the data file always have two decimal places of precision.

    We can change the units to a unit of 1/100 of a mile by getting rid of the . symbol. This is a simple string operation wherein we can use a pipeline with **cut** and **tr** to create a temporary file called **test.txt** with just the two columns:

    ```
    robin ~/Lesson4 $ cut -d, -f4,6 < nyc_taxi2.csv | tr -d '.' >test.txt
    ```

    Print the first five instances to verify that the operation works as desired:

    ```
    robin ~/Lesson4 $ head -n5 test.txt
    330,737
    090,214
    110,225
    110,323
    050,228
    ```

2. Now that we can calculate our distance (in units of 100ths of a mile) and time in seconds, let's write a script that can calculate the average speed of a trip. We will merge the previous **cut** command into this script and make the script take the data filename as an argument. The script will expect the input data in the format of **nyc_taxi2.csv**. First, we will create a temporary file to store the data for the fare and distance fields (this will be deleted at the end of the script). Open your text editor and write the following lines of code:

```
temp_file=temp${RANDOM}

# cut the 4th and 6th column - distance and duration, get rid of the
decimal point,
# put the result in the temp file
cut -d, -f4,6 "$1" | tr -d '.' >$temp_file
```

> **Note**
>
> For simplicity, we created a temporary filename based on **$RANDOM**. This is not ideal because, if the file already exists, it gets overwritten. In these examples, we do not care, but ideally, we would use the **mktemp** command, which creates a randomly named file that definitely does not exist on the filesystem.

3. Next, we will read through each line, and sum the distances of each trip as well as the durations. The total distance divided by the total time is the average speed:

```
total_duration=0
total_distance=0
IFS=','

while read distance duration
do
  ((total_duration += 10#${duration}))
  ((total_distance += 10#${distance}))
done <$temp_file
# Redirect the temp file into the loop
```

Notice the use of redirection into the **while** loop.

4. We scale our units from hundredths of a mile to miles and from seconds to hours so that we can print the result in miles per hour:

```
miles=$(bc <<< "scale=2; $total_distance / 100")
hours=$(bc <<< "scale=2; $total_duration / 3600")

echo "$miles miles in $hours hours"
echo "Average speed is:" $(bc <<< "scale=2; $miles / $hours") "miles/hr"
```

5. Finally, we will remove the temporary file we created at the start:

```
# Get rid of the temp file
rm "$temp_file"
```

Save this script as **taxi7.sh**.

6. Now, let's test the script with our dataset:

```
robin ~/Lesson4 $ ./taxi7.sh nyc_taxi2.csv
684290.55 miles in 41841.56 hours
Average speed is: 16.35 miles/hr
```

Exercise 24: Taxi Trip Analysis – Calculating Average Fare

Let's write a simple script to calculate the average fare per trip. We will sum all the fares and divide the number we get by the number of trips:

1. Open your text editor and add the mandatory hashbang:

```
#!/usr/bin/env bash
```

2. We will use **bc** directly on each line. We will first initialize a variable called **total_ fare** and accumulate the fares of each trip into it. We will also maintain a count of the number of trips so that we can get the average:

```
total_fare=0
count=0
IFS=','

while read -a line
do
  fare=${line[4]}
  total_fare=$(bc <<< "scale=2; $fare + $total_fare")
  (( count++ ))
done
```

3. Finally, calculate the average fare and print it:

```
echo -n "Average fare is: "
echo -n $(bc <<< "scale=2; $total_fare / $count")
echo '$'
```

Save this script as **taxi8.sh**.

4. Now, open the command line and time this script on the first 5,000 lines of data:

```
robin ~/Lesson4 $ time head -n5000 nyc_taxi2.csv | ./taxi8.sh
Average fare is: 18.63$

real    0m15.542s
user    0m9.824s
sys     0m6.441s
```

It processed about 300 lines a second, which is very slow. This is an example of where the efficiency of scripting has hit its limits. Launching the **bc** process once every line just to do one calculation is extremely inefficient.

5. Let's try to improve its performance by using a bit of a hack. We can simply get rid of the . character in the fare field, converting dollars to cents:

```
cut -d, -f5 < nyc_taxi2.csv | tr -d '.' >nyc_taxi_fare.csv
```

6. Using this logic, let's write the averaging script. We will use the same temporary file technique as earlier and combine the preceding **cut** command in the script. Add the following code after the hashbang:

```
temp_file=temp${RANDOM}

cut -d, -f5 "$1" | tr -d '.' >$temp_file
```

7. We read each line of the temporary file in turn into the array variable **fare**. Since we removed the decimal point, the file has only one field per line, which is the fare in cents:

```
total_fare=0
count=0
IFS=' '

while read fare
do
```

8. We just accumulate the value in **fare** into **total_fare**, making sure that fare is always interpreted as decimal (base 10):

```
total_fare=$(( 10#${fare} + total_fare ))
(( count++ ))
```

```
done <$temp_file
```

9. Finally, we can print out the answer. We need to divide by 100 since we had converted into cents:

```
echo -n "Average fare is: "
echo -n $(bc <<< "scale=2; ($total_fare / $count) / 100")
echo '$'
```

```
rm "$temp_file"
```

Save the modified script as **taxi9.sh**.

10. Finally, test the script and time it, as shown here:

```
robin ~/Lesson4 $ time ./taxi9.sh nyc_taxi2.csv
Average fare is: 16.57$
real    0m2.654s
user    0m2.282s
sys     0m0.369s
```

This version is extremely fast, processing almost 75,000 lines per second, about 250 times faster than the version with **bc**.

This code uses a roundabout manner of solving a very basic problem. Should we therefore decide that it is quite impractical to attempt such things on the shell? Consider the alternatives we have:

- We could import the CSV into a spreadsheet and quickly calculate the statistics.

- We could import the CSV data into a database and run queries.

- We could write a small program in a general-purpose scripting language to do the calculation.

The disadvantages of each approach are as follows:

- This is a manual process. You would have to click through the UI, type a formula, and so on, as opposed to just typing the script name and filename on the shell. Suppose our file had 10 million rows, or even 100 million rows. The script would still manage to run and complete the job, but opening a huge CSV as a spreadsheet would gobble up massive amounts of memory, even if the application did manage to open it without crashing.

- You would have to learn how to use RDBMS and SQL.

- You would have to learn a programming language and its associated details.

Most of all, even if you did delegate the main processing to something other than the shell, the shell is still the mechanism by which you would automate tasks, for example, scheduling a script that downloads a file and processes it automatically without you having to do anything.

Activity 11: Shell Scripting – NYC Taxi Trip Analysis

In the previous section, we built some scripts to analyze data related to cab trips in NYC. In this activity, you will write new scripts to perform the following tasks. You might have to create temporary files, like we did earlier, to make the processing easier. Use the earlier scripts as a reference and attempt to make the scripts work as fast as possible. Answer the following questions:

1. Calculate the average cab fare per mile.

2. Get the number of trips that happened between 6 AM and 10 AM.

3. Find the most expensive cab ride in terms of $/minute and also print the line number of that trip.

4. Find the speediest cab ride in terms of miles/hour and also print the line number of that trip.

Follow the steps given here to complete this activity and name each script file from `taxi_act1.sh` to `taxi_act4.sh`:

1. For the first problem, extract the fields for distance and fare, and total both of them. Remember that we have to use integer arithmetic, so scale up both values by a factor of 100 before adding them to the respective totals. Finally, divide the total miles by the total fare to get the answer.

2. For the second problem, notice that the time values in HH:MM:SS can be compared correctly with string comparison. We already have written code that extracts the fares, distances, and durations. Reuse that logic and the `nyc_taxi2.csv` file that we generated earlier. You can use a simple conditional expression to increment a count if the pickup time is in the of 6 to 10 AM range.

3. For the third problem, start by creating variables that are holding the maximum fare and the line number of that trip. Assume that the maximum fare is 0. Iterate over each line, calculating the per minute fare, and if the value is higher than the maximum fare we know so far, assign that value and the line number to the respective variables. Remember that we are dealing with integer arithmetic and scale the values to whatever is needed to get a reasonably precise answer.

4. For the fourth problem, the same logic as the previous problem applies; we are just working with different fields in the data.

The following are some general hints for this activity:

- Think carefully about how you scale the numbers when you need to apply division. Our durations are in seconds, fare values are in cents and speed in 100ths of miles per hour when we remove the decimal point from the fields. Scaling the denominator reduces precision and scaling the numerator adds precision.

- Remember that some values start with the digit 0 and will be treated as octal unless you force base 10.

- Do the conversion to the desired units finally using **bc** when printing the result, but do not use **bc** to process every line.

You should get the following answers to the preceding questions:

1. Average fare per mile is 4.68$.

2. Number of trips that started after 6 AM and ended before 10 AM is 16,133.

3. Highest fare per minute is 91.27$.

   Even though the answer seems an impossible fare, that calculation is correct since the recorded input data on that row is incorrect.

4. Highest speed of any trip is 330.48 miles/hour.

   Even though the answer is an impossible 330 mph, that calculation is correct since the input data on that row has some incorrect data.

> **Note**
>
> At times, you may get some hard-to-believe answers. When this happens, check the solution manually by viewing the line and verifying the calculation. Strange answers often point to data that is incorrectly recorded. For the purpose of this activity, we do not care about the incorrect input data, but merely perform the calculations correctly. The solution for this activity can be found on page 280.

Summary

We have covered a large amount of material in this chapter and practiced with real-world examples and longer scripts. You should now have got a fairly comprehensive idea of how to program with the shell and also got a hint of how to go about solving real-world problems with it.

There is a lot more material that is beyond the scope of an introductory book, but we hope that students will investigate and learn more as they gather experience and seek more knowledge.

Shell scripts have been automating a large number of servers for more than 40 years now and the shell, even if a bit rough on the edges and somewhat archaic in its approach, is the workhorse and Swiss-army knife of all system administrators and serious developers.

In this fairly brief book, we have learned quite a bit about how to use the command line, as well as the popular tools associated with it. Just like a workshop can be extended with new tools to build more complex things, this framework of the command line lets us keep extending the scope to which we can automate our tasks. Whichever field you work in, you can find command-line-based tools for that particular domain to make the process painless. Everything from processing video and audio media, extracting content from the web, modifying documents, converting between formats, creating graphs from data, automatically deploying websites, to even controlling your home appliances have their own specific command-line tools.

We hope that the students explore the command line tools available for their specific domain and utilize what they learned in this book to automate tedious tasks, improve their productivity and gain a better understanding of computers in general.

Appendix

About

This section is included to assist the students to perform the activities in the book.
It includes detailed steps that are to be performed by the students to achieve the objectives of
the activities.

Chapter 1: Introduction to the Command Line

Activity 1: Navigating the Filesystem and Viewing Files

1. Use the **cd** command to navigate to the appropriate folder and use **less** to read the relevant information:

    ```
    robin ~ $ cd Lesson1/data
    robin ~/Lesson1/data $ cd pinaceae/cedrus/deodara/
    robin ~/Lesson1/data/pinaceae/cedrus/deodara $ less data.txt
    ```

2. Use the **cd** command to navigate the appropriate folder and view the file with **less**. Use the **/** command to search for the phrase "derives from" and read the rest of the sentence to get the answer:

    ```
    robin ~/Lesson1/data/pinaceae/cedrus/deodara $ cd ../../..
    robin ~/Lesson1/data $ cd pinaceae/abies/pindrow/
    robin ~/Lesson1/data/pinaceae/abies/pindrow $ less data.txt
    ```

3. Navigate to the right folder and run the **tree** command, which reports the number of directories in it. Each directory is a species:

    ```
    robin ~/Lesson1/data/pinaceae/abies/pindrow $ cd ../../..
    robin ~/Lesson1/data $ cd taxaceae/taxus/
    robin ~/Lesson1/data/taxaceae/taxus $ tree
    ```

4. Navigate to the top-level **data** folder and run the **tree** command, which reports the number of files. Each file is associated with one species:

    ```
    robin ~/Lesson1/data/taxaceae/taxus $ cd ../..
    robin ~/Lesson1/data $ tree -d
    ```

Activity 2: Modifying the Filesystem

1. Use the **cd** command to go into the **Lesson1** folder and create a new folder called **activity2**:

    ```
    robin ~/Lesson1/data $ cd ~
    robin ~ $ cd Lesson1/
    robin ~/Lesson1 $ mkdir activity2
    ```

2. Navigate to the folder for the genus specified and view the subfolders which represent each species:

    ```
    robin ~/Lesson1 $ cd data/taxaceae/torreya/
    robin ~/Lesson1/data/taxaceae/torreya $ ls
    californica  fargesii  grandis  jackii  nucifera  parvifolia  taxifolia
    ```

3. Use the **cp** command to copy a data file from one sub-directory of the **data/ taxaceae/torreya** folder into the output folder:

```
robin ~/Lesson1/data/taxaceae/torreya $ cp californica/data.txt ../../../
activity2/
```

4. Use the **mv** command to rename the file as per the species name:

```
robin ~/Lesson1/data/taxaceae/torreya $ mv ../../../activity2/data.txt
../../../activity2/californica.txt
```

5. Repeat steps 3 and 4 for all the species that are requested:

```
robin ~/Lesson1/data/taxaceae/torreya $ cp fargesii/data.txt ../../../
activity2/
robin ~/Lesson1/data/taxaceae/torreya $ mv ../../../activity2/data.txt
../../../activity2/fargesii.txt
robin ~/Lesson1/data/taxaceae/torreya $ cp grandis/data.txt ../../../
activity2/
robin ~/Lesson1/data/taxaceae/torreya $ mv ../../../activity2/data.txt
../../../activity2/grandis.txt
robin ~/Lesson1/data/taxaceae/torreya $ cp jackii/data.txt ../../../
activity2/
robin ~/Lesson1/data/taxaceae/torreya $ mv ../../../activity2/data.txt
../../../activity2/jackii.txt
robin ~/Lesson1/data/taxaceae/torreya $ cp nucifera/data.txt ../../../
activity2/
robin ~/Lesson1/data/taxaceae/torreya $ mv ../../../activity2/data.txt
../../../activity2/nucifera.txt
robin ~/Lesson1/data/taxaceae/torreya $ cp parvifolia/data.txt ../../../
activity2/
robin ~/Lesson1/data/taxaceae/torreya $ mv ../../../activity2/data.txt
../../../activity2/parvifolia.txt
robin ~/Lesson1/data/taxaceae/torreya $ cp taxifolia/data.txt ../../../
activity2/
robin ~/Lesson1/data/taxaceae/torreya $ mv ../../../activity2/data.txt
../../../activity2/taxifolia.txt
```

To view the list of copied files, use the following code:

```
robin ~/Lesson1/data/taxaceae/torreya $ cd ~
robin ~ $ cd Lesson1/activity2/
robin ~/Lesson1/activity2 $ ls -l
```

Activity 3: Command-Line Editing

1. Use the **cd** command to navigate to the data folder used in the first exercise:

   ```
   robin ~/Lesson1 $ cd data
   robin ~/Lesson1/data $
   ```

2. Type a line of the input file manually, for example, **Podocarpaceae Lepidothamnus Intermedius.**

3. Edit the line to get **echo podocarpaceae/lepidothamnus/intermedius/data.txt**.

4. Use as few keystrokes as possible to generate a command that prints out the name of the file associated with that species. A possible sequence of operations to accomplish this is as follows:

   (a) Use *Home* to navigate to the start. (b) Type **echo** followed by a space. (c) Press *Alt* + L to convert the capital letter to lowercase and jump to the next word. (d) Delete the space and type a forward slash. (e) Repeat steps c and d. (f) Press *Alt* + L once again to lowercase and jump to the end. (g) Type **/data.txt** or press *Tab* twice to append the filename and complete the process.

   It is possible to simplify the last step to one keystroke by using the cut and paste feature. We would have to cut **data.txt** once initially and paste it later.

   The commands you should end up with are as follows:

   ```
   robin ~/Lesson1/data $ echo pinaceae/cedrus/deodara/data.txt
   pinaceae/cedrus/deodara/data.txt
   robin ~/Lesson1/data $ echo cupressaceae/thuja/aphylla/data.txt
   cupressaceae/thuja/aphylla/data.txt
   robin ~/Lesson1/data $ echo taxaceae/taxus/baccata/data.txt
   taxaceae/taxus/baccata/data.txt
   robin ~/Lesson1/data $ echo podocarpaceae/podocarpus/alba/data.txt
   podocarpaceae/podocarpus/alba/data.txt
   ```

Activity 4: Using Simple Wildcards

1. Use the **cd** command to navigate to the appropriate folder and **mkdir** to create the three directories:

```
cd ~/Lesson1/data1
mkdir images
mkdir binaries
mkdir misc
```

2. Use the following wildcard-based commands to move the files to the right locations:

```
mv *.jpg *.jpeg *.png *.gif images/
mv *.a *.so *.so.* binaries/
mv *.* misc/
```

3. Use the **tree** command in each folder to get the counts of each type:

```
tree images
tree binaries
tree misc
```

Activity 5: Using Directory Wildcards

1. Navigate to the **data** folder:

```
cd ~/Lesson1/data
```

2. Use the following **tree** commands one by one and read the count of files:

```
tree p*/?a*
tree p*/?i*/?u*
tree t*/t*
```

Chapter 2: Command-Line Building Blocks

Activity 6: Processing Tabular Data – Reordering Columns

1. The following commands are to be used in the given order:

```
robin ~/Lesson2 $ tail -n+2 land.csv | sort >sorted.txt
robin ~/Lesson2 $ cat -n sorted.txt >numbered.txt
robin ~/Lesson2 $ cat -T numbered.txt | head -n3
  1^IAfghanistan,AFG,1961,57.7459179609717
  2^IAfghanistan,AFG,1962,57.8378212786815
  3^IAfghanistan,AFG,1963,57.914407376773
robin ~/Lesson2 $ tr ',' '\t' <numbered.txt >tabbed.txt
robin ~/Lesson2 $ cat -T tabbed.txt | head -n3
  1^IAfghanistan^IAFG^I1961^I57.7459179609717
  2^IAfghanistan^IAFG^I1962^I57.8378212786815
  3^IAfghanistan^IAFG^I1963^I57.914407376773
robin ~/Lesson2 $ join -o1.4,1.5,1.3 tabbed.txt tabbed.txt >342.txt
robin ~/Lesson2 $ join -o1.5,1.4,1.2 tabbed.txt tabbed.txt >431.txt
```

2. To view the expected content in the two output files, use the following commands:

```
robin ~/Lesson2 $ head 342.txt
robin ~/Lesson2 $ head 431.txt
```

Activity 7: Data Analysis

The following command sequence can be used (outputs are shown):

```
robin ~/Lesson2 $ grep 'Australia' land.csv >australia.txt
robin ~/Lesson2 $ sort -o australia.txt -k4 -t, -n australia.txt
robin ~/Lesson2 $ wc -l australia.txt
55 australia.txt
robin ~/Lesson2 $ bc <<< 55/2
27
robin ~/Lesson2 $ tail -n+28 australia.txt | head -n1
Australia,AUS,1963,60.720227015347
robin ~/Lesson2 $ grep -w '1998' population.csv >pop.txt
robin ~/Lesson2 $ sort -o pop.txt -k4 -t, -n pop.txt
robin ~/Lesson2 $ wc -l pop.txt
249 pop.txt
robin ~/Lesson2 $ bc <<< 249/2
124
robin ~/Lesson2 $ head -n125 pop.txt | tail -n1
Azerbaijan,AZE,1998,7913000
```

Chapter 3: Advanced Command-Line Concepts

Activity 8: Word Matching with Regular Expressions

The commands to be used to answer the questions can be found here:

1. The following command can be used to find the number of words that are five letters in length, begin with a consonant, and contain alternating vowels and consonants:

   ```
   grep -c -E '^([^aeiou][aeiou]){2}[^aeiou]$' <words.txt
   506
   ```

2. Use the following command to find the number of words that are two or more characters long, begin with a consonant, and contain alternating consonants and vowels:

   ```
   grep -c -E '^([^aeiou][aeiou])+[^aeiou]?$' <words.txt
   2339
   ```

3. Use the following command to count the three-letter words that start and end with the same letter:

   ```
   grep -c -E '^(.).\1$' <words.txt
   23
   ```

4. The following command can be used to find the number of words that have the same vowel repeating twice consecutively in it:

   ```
   grep -c -E '([aeiou])\1' <words.txt
   1097
   ```

5. The following command looks for five-letter words that are palindromes:

   ```
   grep  -E '^(.)(.).\2\1$' <words.txt
   civic
   kayak
   level
   madam
   minim
   radar
   rotor
   tenet
   ```

Activity 9: String Processing with eval and Shell Expansion

The commands to be used to complete this activity are shown as follows. The outputs of the commands are shown for clarity:

```
NAME=RUMPELSTILTSKIN
LEN=${#NAME}
LEN=$((LEN-1))


echo {$LEN..0}
{14..0}


eval echo {$LEN..0}
14 13 12 11 10 9 8 7 6 5 4 3 2 1 0


echo '${NAME:{$LEN..0}:1}'
${NAME:{$LEN..0}:1}


echo '\$\{NAME:{$LEN..0}\:1\}'
\$\{NAME:{$LEN..0}\:1\}


eval echo '\$\{NAME:{$LEN..0}\:1\}'
${NAME:{14..0}:1}


echo '\\$\\{NAME:{$LEN..0}\\:1\\}'
\\$\\{NAME:{$LEN..0}\\:1\\}


eval echo '\\$\\{NAME:{$LEN..0}\\:1\\}'
\$\{NAME:{14..0}\:1\}
```

```
eval eval echo '\\$\\{NAME:{$LEN..0}\\:1\\}'
```

${NAME:14:1} ${NAME:13:1} ${NAME:12:1} ${NAME:11:1} ${NAME:10:1} ${NAME:9:1}
${NAME:8:1} ${NAME:7:1} ${NAME:6:1} ${NAME:5:1} ${NAME:4:1} ${NAME:3:1}
${NAME:2:1} ${NAME:1:1} ${NAME:0:1}

```
eval eval eval echo '\\$\\{NAME:{$LEN..0}\\:1\\}'
```

N I K S T L I T S L E P M U R

```
tr -d ' ' <<< $(eval eval eval echo '\\$\\{NAME:{$LEN..0}\\:1\\}')
```

NIKSTLITSLEPMUR

Chapter 4: Shell Scripting

Activity 10: PGN Game Extractor Enhancement

The solutions are provided in five script files, **pgn_extract_act1.sh** to **pgn_extract_act5.sh**. Each script contains the changes made in the previous problem steps, so **pgn_extract_act5.sh** has all the issues that were mentioned previously addressed. The following are the possible solutions:

1. The following code can work:

   ```
   function count_moves()
   {
     IFS='.'
     local moves_arr=( $moves )
     local second_last=${moves_arr[@]: -2 : 1}

     IFS=' '
     local second_last_arr=( $second_last )

     num_moves=${second_last_arr[@]: -1 : 1}
   }
   ```

2. Detecting blank lines can be done by testing for an empty string, such as the following:

   ```
   [[ -z $line ]] && return 0
   ```

3. Instead of expressions such as **count=$((count + 1))**, we can write **((count ++))**. We can also change the **[[ ]]** based conditionals, which test numeric variables such as **[[$should_print -eq 1]]**, to arithmetic expressions such as **((should_print == 1))**. Such changes can be done in many places in the script.

4. Add a default case to the case statement that parses the options, and print the command usage help there, as follows (compose a readable multiline help text and use multiple echo statements if necessary):

   ```
   *) echo "Command help text"
   ```

5. Maintain a count of games that passed the filter in a variable called **game_count**, and add something like the following at the end of the **show_games_won_in()** function:

```
(( game_count == 0 )) && echo -e "No games\n"
```

The variable should be initialized to 0 initially and incremented every time a game fulfills the filter criteria.

Activity 11: Shell Scripting – NYC Taxi Trip Analysis

The solutions are provided in the files **taxi_act1.sh** to **taxi_act4.sh**. To check the output, run each script file over the dataset, as follows. The first one has been shown as an example:

```
robin ~/Lesson4 $ ./taxi_act1.sh nyc_taxi2.csv
```

```
Average fare per mile is: 4.68$
```

The script **taxi_act2.sh** needs the input file **nyc_taxi2.sh** passed in via input redirection as follows:

```
./taxi_act2.sh <nyc_taxi2.csv
```

The scripts for each of the files are given as follows:

taxi_act1.sh

```
#!/usr/bin/env bash


# get a temp file name for the fares and the distances
temp_file_fares=temp${RANDOM}
temp_file_dists=temp${RANDOM}


//{…}


rm "$temp_file_fares"
rm "$temp_file_dists"
```

Live link: https://bit.ly/2zX5pAR

taxi_act2.sh

```
#!/usr/bin/env bash

//{…}

IFS=', '
count=0

//{…}

  [[ $start > '06:00:00' && $stop < '10:00:00' ]] && (( count++ ))
done
```

Live link: https://bit.ly/2LhOLQC

taxi_act3.sh

```
#!/usr/bin/env bash
# Calculates the higest taxi fare per minute

# get a temp file name for the fares
temp_file_fares=temp${RANDOM}

//{…}

rm "$temp_file_fares"
```

Live link: https://bit.ly/2SKa2VN

taxi_act4.sh

```bash
#!/usr/bin/env bash

# get a temp file name for the distances
temp_file_dists=temp${RANDOM}

//{…}

rm "$temp_file_dists"
```

Live link: https://bit.ly/2PxfCJb

Index

About

All major keywords used in this book are captured alphabetically in this section. Each one is accompanied by the page number of where they appear.

W

www.ingramcontent.com/pod-product-compliance
Lightning Source LLC
Chambersburg PA
CBHW080625060326
40690CB00021B/4820